FRANCE
1789–1962

Modern History Reference Series

FRANCE
1789–1962

James J. Cooke

DAVID & CHARLES
Newton Abbot
ARCHON BOOKS
Hamden, Connecticut
1975

This edition first published in 1975 in Great Britain by
David & Charles (Holdings) Limited, Newton Abbot, Devon,
in Canada by Douglas David & Charles Limited,
132 Philip Avenue, North Vancouver BC,
and in the United States of America by Archon Books,
an imprint of The Shoe String Press, Inc, Hamden,
Connecticut 06514

ISBN 0 7153 6405 7 (Great Britain)

Library of Congress Cataloging in Publication Data

Cooke, James J.
    Modern history reference series—France, 1789–1962

    1. France—History—1789–   —Dictionaries. I. Title,
DC35.C66   944'.003   74-32356
ISBN 0–208–01510–8

Set in eleven on thirteen point Baskerville
and printed in Great Britain
by Latimer Trend & Company Ltd Plymouth

pour Joséphine, Jacques et Victoire

Introduction

One of the major problems in modern French history is the often confusing changes of governments and the appearance of many politicians, men of letters, and military leaders who very briefly play their role upon the stage and disappear. To the English or American mind this appears to be a kaleidoscopic madness which fails to lend itself to themes and steady interpretations. Certainly, there are basic threads within the history of modern France, but almost as certainly there is a certain Gallic tendency to the scattered. Students and often their professors complain of bewilderment when faced by the sweep of modern French development. It is the primary purpose of this dictionary to bring some order to that tapestry which is in itself most beautiful, but is made up of many threads.

Perhaps unfortunately for those who search for a Germanic thoroughness in French history, most French historians have their particular likes and dislikes which are reflected in their work. The social historian disdains mundane political facts. The political historian turns his back to the colonial period as not being worthy of a political investigator's research efforts. The result has often been an incomplete picture of France. However, a dictionary is, in its own right, not a monograph nor a coherent, chronological study of a period of history in a country. This work does try to bring to the reader and to the student of French history a number of facts and figures on many aspects of France's contemporary development. There is great space devoted to France's colonial expansion period. After Dien Bien Phu and Algeria this is needed. In a world which at least pays lip service to social progress there are words explaining the major and lasting pieces of social legislation which the French Assemblies have enacted. For the political historian there are kings and premiers, and for the *littérateur* there are the authors who have made a definite and concerted contribution to France's social, intellectual, and political progress.

Not everyone will be satisfied with the entries, for invariably the compiler will leave out a favourite deputy or an esoteric event. To these complaints the only plea can be one of space and an author's discretion. Frankly, not every minister of posts and telegraph can have a space if a dictionary of modern French history is to be published in one usable volume.

It would also be impossible to list all of the major sources used in the research for this work. However, certain key volumes need to be cited. The entries on the colonial period and for much of the Third Republic come from my own research in France. This work, done in many archives, first resulted in *New French Imperialism: The Third Republic and Colonial Expansion, 1880–1910* (Newton Abbot, 1973). Many sources, dates and facts came from Pierre Grimal *(et al)*, *Dictionnaire des biographies*, 2 volumes (Paris, 1958) and from William A. Neilson *(et al)*, *Webster's Biographical Dictionary*, 1st edition (Springfield, Mass, 1943). The previous labours of many historians and political scientists helped in the compiling of this book. I relied upon such works as Alf Heggoy, *The African Policies of Gabriel Hanotaux* (Athens, Georgia, 1972), Leo Gershoy, *The French Revolution and Napoleon* (New York, 1944), Philip Williams, *Crisis and Compromise* (New York, 1966), Christopher Andrew, *Théophile Delcassé and the Making of the Entente Cordiale* (New York, 1968), Jacques Chastenet, *La République des républicains 1879–1893* (Paris, 1954) and *La République triomphante 1893–1906* (Paris, 1955).

This list is obviously incomplete, and a full bibliography would, of course, include the works of men like D. W. Brogan, Thomas Iiams, Stanley Hoffman, Albert Mathiez, Gordon Wright, Maurice Reclus, Hubert Deschamps, Nathaniel Greene, Alfred Cobban, Arnold Wolfers, George Lefebvre and many others. Over 250 different monographs and scholarly articles were consulted during the period of preparation.

8

A number of my colleagues assisted in one way or the other in the preparation of this dictionary and deserve a special mention. Professor Jackson Taylor of the University of Mississippi went beyond the call of duty for a scholar in reading and commenting on the draft of the manuscript. His extensive knowledge, gained while working under Professor Leo Gershoy of NYU, contributed greatly to the completion of this book. Other professors and staff members who gave generously of their time to the book were William E. Strickland, Michael deLaval Landon, Joseph Kiger, and the staff of the University of Mississippi library.

Special thanks must be given to Annette Seago and Bobbie Shaw who suffered through three drafts of the work, one of which was written in almost undecipherable script. My wife, who shares my love of France, also shared the labour of research and writing, and for this she must be thanked.

University, Mississippi   James J. Cooke

Abd el Aziz (1881–1943)   Abd el Aziz ruled Morocco as sultan from 1894 to 1908. Pleasure-loving and corrupt, Abd el Aziz was unable to ensure domestic tranquillity, and in 1904 the French government took steps to expand the Algero-Moroccan border at the expense of Morocco. The sultan, after William II's visit to Tangier in 1905, called for a conference to decide the fate of his state. At the Algeciras Conference (qv) France appeared to have the agreement of the western powers to take the region, since it appeared that Aziz could no longer assure internal order. After a rebellion against him in 1908 he was allowed to live in retirement and isolation.

Abdel Kader (1807–1883)   An Algerian Muslim resistance leader, Kader fought against the French takeover of Algeria from 1832 to 1837. Kader, who after a pilgrimage to Mecca received the title of Emir, organised the Algerian tribes against the French occupation. In 1835 he defeated French troops at Mactu, but in 1837 his capital, Mascara, was taken. The Peace of Tafna of 1837 only lasted two years and when fighting broke out again, Kader sought refuge in Morocco. After the battle of Isly in 1844, Kader was handed over to the French and was imprisoned in France until 1860 when he was liberated by Napoléon III. Abdel Kader then served French interests in Algeria and won the Grand Cordon of the Legion of Honour. In 1871 he urged Algerians not to raise the standard of revolt, and until his death in 1883 he lived fairly comfortably as a revered leader.

Action Française   The *Action Française* was a rightist, ultra-patriotic organisation devoted to the maintenance of French glory and prestige in the post-1870 world. Born out of the frustrations following the Franco-Prussian war and the diplomatic isolation imposed on France by Bismarck, the *Action Française* was created, as an organised group, during the Dreyfus affair.

Founded by Charles Maurras (qv) in 1898, it bitterly opposed Dreyfus. First called the *Ligue de la patrie française*, the organisation changed its name to *Action Française* in 1899. By 1908–9, with the organising of the *Camelots du Roi* (qv), the *Action* decided on violence to counteract the left. The *Action Française* ardently supported France's war effort from 1914 to 1918, but after 1925 it began to praise openly Mussolini's Italian Fascist system. Maurras, still the ideologist of the organisation, manifested radical anti-semitism. The *Action Française* was condemned by Pope Pius XI in 1926, and after this moved closer to street violence, openly participating in the riots of 1934. Maurras realised the danger posed by Hitler and tried to mount an anti-German campaign, but since this would mean union with the left, the campaign floundered. During the Vichy period Maurras and the *Action Française* openly supported Marshal Pétain (qv) and his government. From 1941 to 1943 anti-semitism again emerged as a part of the official programme. After the liberation of France, Maurras was tried for treason and imprisoned until 1952; with his passing, the *Action Française* declined as a political force. It was a symbol of the times—a period of reaction against decline and national decay—but, tarnished by its flirtations with anti-semitism and fascism, the movement declined as a representative of French conservative opinion.

Affre, Denis (1793–1848) Affre, a cleric, became archbishop of Paris in 1840. A noted Gallican, he was known for his royalist sympathies. When the revolution of 1848 broke out, the archbishop tried to stop the violence by interposing himself, in June, between General Cavaignac (qv) and the Paris rebels. During the June Days he was taken prisoner and shot. There is some dispute over who executed him.

Algeciras, Conference of In March 1905 William II, emperor of Germany, made an unexpected visit to Tangier harbour in order to challenge French moves to take Morocco and to test the strength of the newly signed Entente Cordiale (qv). His speech there championed the cause of Moroccan independence. The French, under the careful diplomatic leadership of Théophile Delcassé (qv) and the militant imperial urging of Eugène Etienne (qv) and the *Comité du Maroc* (qv), had moved toward annexing Morocco. In 1905 their actions there were confronted by German hostility, resulting in the First Moroccan Crisis (qv). At the insistence of Abd el Aziz (qv), sultan of Morocco, a general conference was convened at Algeciras in Spain to decide the future of Morocco. On 16 January 1906, the conference opened and Spain, Britain, France and Italy acted together against Germany, Austria and Morocco. The United States appeared to favour French claims. By the final act of 7 April 1906, a neutral inspector-generalship was created. In addition, French and Spanish police, acting within the confines of Morocco, were authorised. While an open-door trading policy was in theory established, most observers believed that France was recognised as the predominant power in Morocco, and that an end to the Moroccan question was still to be found.

Algeria   See: Abdel Kader; Etoile Nord Africaine (ENA); Evian Accords; Parti Populaire Algérien (PPA).

Alis, Harry (Hippolyte Percher) (1857–1895)   Hippolyte Percher, better known as Harry Alis, was one of France's most articulate spokesmen for the cause of imperial expansion. Distressed at France's slow response to the scramble for Africa in the 1880s, Alis, who was trained as a journalist and was the editor of the influential *Journal des Débats*, called France to greater colonial efforts. In 1890, along with Eugène Etienne (qv) and other prominent imperialists, he helped found the *Comité de l'Afrique française* (qv) which aimed at popularising the concepts of empire and at countering Britain in Africa. Alis became the first editor of the *Bulletin*, the monthly organ of the French African committee, and while editor he focused attention on French efforts in West Africa and in Morocco. In 1895 Alis delivered some bitter attacks against anti-colonialist deputies, and on 1 March 1895, he was killed by an anti-imperialist representative in a duel. Alis's works include two

13

important books, *A la conquête du Tchad* (Paris, 1891) and *Nos Africains* (Paris, 1894) and many articles supporting colonialism.

Allemane, Jean (1843–1935)   Born to a humble family in Boucou, Haute Garonne on 25 August 1843, Allemane was first sent to jail for participating in a workers' strike in Paris in 1862. As a young member of the Paris Commune (qv) of 1871, Allemane fought against the conservative forces of the Versailles army. In May 1871 he was arrested and was later deported to New Caledonia. Allowed to return to France in 1879, ten years later he helped found the Fraternal Society of the Old Fighters of the Commune. In 1888 he associated himself with Jules Guèsde (qv) and the Workers Party, and by 1900 was known as one of the key leaders of the French socialist movement. Allemane helped found in 1905 the SFIO, *Section Française de l'Internationale Ouvrière* (qv). He became one of the major socialist figures in Paris, and up to 1920 continued to guide the socialist movement. He showed some sympathy with the new French Communist Party (PCF) (qv), even though he disapproved of Marxist ideology. Died at Herblay, Seine et Oise on 6 June 1935.

Alliance Démocratique   The alliance was founded in the late nineteenth century as a loose coalition of centre parties and the bourgeoisie. Basically conservative in outlook, it made short-lived alignments with the moderate radicals. By 1900 the alliance had in its ranks some of France's best-known politicians. Maurice Rouvier (qv), Louis Barthou (qv), Raymond Poincaré (qv), Eugène Etienne (qv), and Charles Jonnart (qv) were members who had a definite impact on French internal, foreign, and colonial policies. The influential newspaper *Le Temps* was closely associated with the *Alliance démocratique* and usually the journal supported its positions on critical issues. At the turn of the century the *Alliance démocratique* tried to remain aloof from the bitter church-state controversy. At times the alliance was attacked as being uncommitted and indifferent to the issue; most of its members tended to write according to their own consciences on clerical matters. But it influenced government by placing members in cabinet and administrative positions, and in 1919 strove to found an anti-socialist coalition. In the 1930s the group weakened considerably as a force in French political life.

Allocations Familiales   An important part of the French social security system, the *allocations familiales*, or family allowances, paid subsidies to all French families with two or more children. A part of the *Code de la famille* approach, the *allocations* were aimed at preserving the family unit and encouraging a higher standard of living with an increasing birthrate. After World War II, the *allocations* were continued and increased as part of France's growing social welfare system. They were, for a time, extended if a rural family sent a child to special classes on modern farming techniques. The Social Charter of 1945 reconfirmed the *allocations* which had existed in France since the Law of 14 July 1913 (qv).

Amiens, Congress of   The political fortunes of organised labour, after the founding of the *Confédération Générale du Travail* (CGT) (qv), were in drastic decline. In 1905 Jean Jaurès (qv) began a movement to unify this sector of French political life. At the Congress of Amiens in 1906 the critical issues of the workers' relationship with the state came to the forefront. It was decided that the socialists in the Chamber would not support anything but a definite socialist government and would remain in constant opposition. This opposition remained in force until Léon Blum's (qv) Popular Front (qv) of 1936. The concept of Syndicalism (qv) was articulated in the Charter of Amiens of 1906. The Charter of Amiens was, for the CGT and socialism, a declaration of war on capitalist France.

Amiens, Peace of   A peace negotiated over a long period, beginning early 1801; a preliminary peace concluded October 1801. The finalised version was signed on 25 March 1802 by England and France. France profited by the treaty since it left her in control of Holland, Belgium and the left bank of the Rhine. Northern Italy was left under basically French domination. Since no precautions were written into the treaty, Bonaparte was left with a fairly free hand on the continent. This raised French prestige and angered British public opinion over what appeared to be excessively generous terms. The Peace of Amiens gave France a period without war, and while this lasted only a year, Napoléon Bonaparte's (qv) popularity reached a point where he requested that he be made Consul for life, a move which the nation approved by a resounding vote in a referendum.

Ancients, Council of In August 1795, a year after the fall of Maximilien de Robespierre (qv), the Thermidorians created a constitution which was basically a conservative document. Legislative powers were granted to a legislative corps made up of the Council of Ancients and the Council of Five Hundred (qv). In theory, annual elections were held to elect men to the Council of Ancients which was made up of 250 men over forty years of age. Interestingly, the Council members had to be married or widowed as a requirement for membership. This provision aimed directly at excluding priests from membership in the Council. They could veto proposals of the Council of Five Hundred or they could accept the proposals, which would then become law. The Council of Ancients also picked the five Directors from lists drawn up by the Five Hundred.

André, Louis Joseph (1838–1913) A brilliant student at the *Ecole Polytechnique*, André became an officer in 1861. In 1870 he saw action as an artillery officer, and after the Franco-Prussian war held various posts; he did not become a general until 1893. In 1900 President of the Council René Waldeck-Rousseau (qv) asked André to take the War Ministry portfolio, although he was not a deputy. Emile Combes (qv), upon assuming the duties of president of the council, requested that André retain his post since André shared Combes's militant views on church–state issues. A reformer, André introduced far-reaching army changes, such as prohibiting the sale of liquor on army posts, encouraging sports, introducing new training techniques and supporting technological improvements in weapons. However, he was accused of spying on officers to record their political views and religious affiliations and because of these charges, although known as an able technician and writer, he was forced to resign in 1904. Owing to his age he retired from active service.

Anglo-French Accords   These accords, signed on 5 August 1890, were an early attempt to regularise British and French imperial actions in Africa. A vague, undefined line was drawn from the town of Saye on the bend of the Niger river to Barruwa on the shores of Lake Chad. Territory north of the line in theory belonged to France, south of the line to England. By 1892–5, both states found the accords unenforceable.

Angoulême, Duc d' (1755–1844)   Louis Antoine de Bourbon, Duc d'Angoulême, was born at Versailles 6 August 1775, son of the Comte d'Artois, the future Charles X (qv), king of France. He followed his father into exile during the revolution, returned to France in 1814, and organised royalist opposition to the return of Napoléon Bonaparte (qv) during the Hundred Days (qv). Louis XVIII (qv) made him commander-in-chief of the French forces in Spain in 1823. When Charles X came to the throne in 1824, Angoulême was proclaimed the dauphin. In the Chamber, from 1824 to 1830, he was prominent in his support of absolutism, and when Charles X fell in 1830, he fled from France. He died at Goritz, Austria, on 3 June 1844.

Apparentement   From 1946 to 1950 the French parliamentary system struggled to find a suitable method for fair representation. In 1950 General Charles de Gaulle (qv) approved of two electoral systems, a majority list system and proportional representation, but both were rejected by the Chamber for political reasons. The Chamber tried again, successfully, in May 1951 to amend the laws of 1946. The law of 1951 kept the same basic constituencies with one exception—the Gironde which was divided—and kept the old method of lists, by party, with a candidate for each seat. The law also contained a new provision for *apparentement*: a device to be applied outside Paris, it meant that parties, with their lists, could form an alliance, or an *apparentement*. The votes for this alliance counted together, as if the voters had cast their ballots for a single list. When a list won an absolute majority, proportional representation was then used to distribute seats within the alliance. The system aided parties who usually controlled the government, and parties such as the communists called it the Ballot of the Thieves. Some democratic politicians continued to argue that it would still mean voters casting ballots for lists rather than for men, and this weakened the whole concept of democracy. *Apparentement* failed, in the long run, to provide stability for the Fourth Republic.

Arago, Dominique Jean-François (1786–1853)   A medical doctor and astronomer, Arago was known as a great scientist and liberal. He first gained recognition as a scientist from 1804 to 1809 when he assisted in a number of geographical measurements of the earth's surface. In 1809 he was elected to the Academy of Science and continued his work as an astronomer. Teaching at the prestigious *Ecole Polytechnique*, Arago won a reputation as a brilliant mathematician. After 1810, however, he turned to a study of physics and optics, and in the 1820s he offered a popular course on astronomy at the Paris Observatory. Arago was also recognised for his liberal political views. He was elected a deputy and joined the opposition against the July Monarchy; he had participated in the overthrow of Charles X (qv) in 1830. From 1830–48 he argued for scientific progress such as the telegraph and electricity. His opposition to government monopolies brought him into direct conflict with the Orléanist administration. In 1848 he served as chief of state, acting as a force for restraint and moderation during the violent June Days. Although he refused to take an oath of loyalty to Napoléon III, he was honoured by the state upon his death.

Arago, Emmanuel (1812–1896)   A lawyer, Arago, who was a son of the noted scientist Dominique Jean-François Arago (qv), was elected deputy in 1848. He was re-elected deputy from Paris in 1869, and later served as an opponent of the Empire. A member of the Government of National Defence and elected senator; a faithful advocate of Thiers's (qv) conservative policies.

Arago, Etienne (1803–1892)   Etienne Arago, who was the brother of Dominique Jean-François Arago (qv), the noted scientist, was a journalist who founded the liberal, anti-Orléanist newspaper *La Réforme*. In 1848 he was elected deputy and served as postal director. Exiled by Napoléon III (qv), he was granted amnesty in 1859. In 1870 he served as mayor of Paris, but resigned in 1871 to return to private life.

Arenberg, Auguste Prince d' (1837–1924)   Of noble origins, d'Arenberg rallied to the Republic in 1870, became a deputy in 1877 and served in the Chamber until 1902. In 1890 he joined in the founding of the *Comité de l'Afrique française* (qv). From 1891 to 1893 he was prominent in the debates over West and Central Africa. After 1893 he maintained his interest in colonial topics, but also became involved in the attempts to reconcile the Catholic church to the state. As president of the French African committee, d'Arenberg was able to guide France's colonial efforts toward calming the bitter feelings with Britain 1898–1904.

Assignats   On 19 December 1789, by two decrees, the National Assembly authorised the issue of assignats, or paper money, based on the value of confiscated church lands. It was hoped this would pay off old debts, arrest any rise in the debt and enable the Assembly to distribute church lands more equally among a land-hungry population. The paper money did not prove popular, and the church, which still held great power, worked against the whole project. After April 1790 the Assembly made the assignats legal paper money, with a value placed at the actual numerical value of the bill plus the amount of accrued interest. In 1790 it was noted that specie was fast disappearing from public circulation, and that the assignats were falling rapidly in value. The social effect of the assignat was what the National Assembly had hoped. The availability of the means to purchase land lessened internal violence which had occurred in 1790, and the number of small peasant landholders increased greatly by 1791; 1½ billion livres of church lands were sold to them. But by 1791 it was clear that the value of assignats was declining. In 1793 a law was passed imposing prison sentences on those who refused to accept them as legal tender. By 1795 the paper currency was almost worthless, and 1796 saw a very real financial crisis in France. The Directory in 1796 had to deal with the declining value of the assignats, and in 1797 the directors decreed that business could be carried on in specie and that the assignats were fully repudiated. This caused distress to only a few, though the problem of debt was not properly handled.

Assimilation A colonial concept, assimilation called for the integration of colonial subjects into the political, cultural and sometimes social mainstream of French life. The assimilationists saw themselves as the conductors of civilisation and of the ideals of 1789 to the empire, and they believed that the *mission civilisatrice* (qv) was at the core of colonial endeavours. French political and social ideology followed the flag into the empire. In the 1880s and 1890s new French imperialists like Eugène Etienne (qv) and many members of the *Comité de l'Afrique française* (qv) rejected colonial assimilation, preferring association (qv), a different colonial-social philosophy.

Association In the 1880s and 1890s the new French imperialists rejected assimilation (qv) and the immediate application of the *mission civilisatrice* (qv) for a new concept called association. According to the associationists, the colonial subjects were the least important group in any colony. They were almost an unwanted element, merely associated with the process of empire building. The natives were to be left alone, allowed to develop along their traditional tribal and cultural lines. Most associationists were social Darwinists who firmly believed that the natives had not evolved sufficiently to warrant great emphasis on cultural instruction for them. They believed that the governments of the colonies should be paternalistic, but not be too dedicated to a process of Frenchification. While the advocates of associationism preferred to place their reliance on immediate industrial-commercial exploitation, they did profess a desire to see hospitals, roads and sanitary facilities built for the natives as a propaganda device. Associationism was in vogue in French colonial circles from 1880 to about 1920. The patriotic participation of the native elements in World War I and World War II altered the attitudes of French political leaders in favour of assimilation.

Association, Law of Article 29 of the Penal Code of 1810 stipulated that a gathering of more than twenty people meeting for religious, political, literary, or other purposes must have a permit from the government. This article was repealed in July 1901, by the Law of Association, which applied to all associations in French society except for those 'sharing profits', such as a company of stockholders in a commercial business venture. People wishing to associate themselves for legal purposes could seek to obtain a charter. However, Section III of the Law of Association set forth requirements for the legal association of religious congregations and gave the Council of Ministers the right to close churches and dissolve congregations at will, by decree. It was ruthlessly used against the Catholic church and religious orders; many churches, church-sponsored hospitals, schools, and orphanages were closed by the state. A byproduct, however, was the beneficial effect on legalising and aiding the formation of French trade unions. René Waldeck-Rousseau (qv), president of the Council of Ministers, in July 1901, had promised the Pope that such a law would not be harshly applied, but when Emile Combes (qv) became president of the council in 1902, the law was strictly applied. Almost no Catholic religious group could get a charter to operate. France was torn asunder by the rupture in the century-old state–church relationship. The army was rent by discord over the spying techniques of General André (qv). The Law of Association under Combes was applied with vigour, and it left a nasty scar on the body politic in France.

Audiffret-Pasquier, Edme Gaston, Duc d' (1823–1905)

Elected deputy from the Orne in 1871, he served as chief of the Orléanist group and opposed Thiers (qv). In 1873 he became the chief architect of the coalition of monarchist deputies. Slowly Audiffret-Pasquier moved to the left and in 1875 supported the national constitution. From 1876 to 1879 he presided over the Senate, and in 1879 he retired from politics. He remained a close advisor to the Orléanist Count of Paris, and staunchly opposed the strictly conservative position taken by Chambord, the head of the Bourbon house.

Augereau, Charles (1757–1816) Born in Paris on 21 October 1757 of humble origin, Augereau became a professional soldier. In 1777 he served in the Prussian army, and in 1786 he entered the military service of Naples. Augereau decided to return to France in 1790, and he saw service in the Vendée, rising to the rank of general. From 1793 to 1794 he commanded the Army of the Pyrénées-Orientales. In 1795 he served in Italy and became well known as a competent officer. Augereau was elected as a member of the Five Hundred in 1799 and rallied to the Consulate. Napoléon Bonaparte (qv) made him a marshal of France and in 1808 conferred on him the title of Duc de Castiglione. A loyal supporter of Bonaparte, he fought at Leipzig. However, he joined the Bourbons in 1814, and Louis XVIII (qv) made him a peer and governor of Lyon. During the Hundred Days (qv), Augereau supported Bonaparte's return, and after Waterloo, Louis XVIII retired him from active command in semi-disgrace. Augereau died at La Houssaye, Sambre et Meuse, on 12 June 1816.

August Decrees The decrees of 5–11 August 1789 were passed in an atmosphere of confusion. The Bastille (qv) had fallen, attacks against feudal privilege continued, and France was in the grip of violence. The Great Fear (qv) swept the rural areas of France, and the peasantry, agitated by rumours of brigands, attacked all symbols of the old regime. When news of such violence reached Paris, a number of nobles, including the Duc d'Aiguillon, gathered at the Breton Club (qv) on 3 August and decided that on the morrow a resolution would be introduced that feudal rights, payments and rents should be abolished at once. Once these rights were surrendered, the nobility would receive monetary compensation, since the privileges and dues were private property. During 4 August, with the urging of d'Aiguillon and the impoverished Viscount Louis de Noailles (qv), the nobles arose to renounce personally all feudal rights, in a frenzy of patriotic self-sacrifice. While the final decree which was presented to Louis XIV was conservative and modified, the August Decrees marked a new day in France. They also helped to calm the countryside, lessening the effects of the Great Fear.

August 1792: Insurrection of 10 After Louis XVI's (qv) escape attempt, tensions in Paris were extremely high, and radicals agitated the mobs, demanding that the king be deposed. The insurrectionary commune, seizing the moment, directed an attack against Louis XVI in residence at the Tuileries. On the night of 9–10 August 1792 an insurrection broke out, a hostile crowd attacked the Tuileries and the king was forced to flee for his life. The Swiss Guards were massacred as National Guardsmen deserted their posts. The position of commander of the National Guard was filled by an insurrectionist. The revolutionary commune directed events in Paris, including the violence of 10 August, while the supporters of the commune demanded the trial of the king and a radical, equalitarian revision of the constitution. The commune then took control of the royal family and placed them in the Luxembourg Palace, and for all practical purposes the throne was vacant. On 30 August the Assembly, trying to reassert their authority, ordered the commune dissolved, but in early September there was a systematic slaughter of royalist and suspected royalist prisoners in France. Eventually the commune was weakened by the Terror, and the Thermidorians outlawed the commune and its leaders. In practice, however, the insurrection of 10 August 1792 marked an abrupt shift to radicalism and republicanism.

Aumale, Henri, Duc d'Orléans (1822–1897) The fourth

son of King Louis Philippe (qv), d'Aumale, who was born in Paris on 16 January 1822, served as a general in Algeria. After the revolution of 1848 he resided in Britain, but returned to France in 1871 and served as an Orléanist deputy. In 1873 he presided over the tribunal which tried General Bazaine (qv). Retiring from public life in 1883, he devoted the remainder of his life to scholarly research and writing. He died in Zucco, Sicily, in 1897.

Auriol, Vincent (1884–1965)   A socialist deputy from 1910 to 1940, he rose quickly in the estimation of leftist leaders. Finance minister in the first Léon Blum (qv) government, Auriol returned to that post during the Chautemps (qv) administration in 1937 and again under Blum in 1938. He refused to vote full powers to Marshal Pétain (qv) in 1940 and fled to England. In 1946 Auriol, who was known as a moderate socialist, was elected president of the Constituent Assembly, and in January 1947 he became the first president of the Fourth Republic and named Paul Ramadier as his premier. Auriol was faced during his presidency, 1947–54, with the grave problems of French economics, decolonisation, the war in Indo-China, and parliamentary instability. He tried to come to grips with Indo-China by negotiating the Auriol-Bao Daï Accords of 1949 (qv) which maintained the façade of Vietnamese independence while maintaining a colonial presence in the area. Auriol gained the reputation of an astute politician, and he gave the position of president of the Republic unexpected strength. Hoping to rise above party politics, he stated that his great mission was to strengthen parliamentary democracy in France. In 1953 he openly criticised both extreme socialists and extreme Gaullists for blocking legislative action in the Chamber. For this criticism he was assailed by both groups. As president of the Republic, Auriol had intervened energetically to try to give some stability to republican institutions, and he gave force and meaning to his position.

Auriol-Bao Daï Accords   Vincent Auriol (qv), president of the French Republic, and Bao Daï, who had been appointed by the French to counter Ho Chi-Minh, whom Paris had previously courted, met in Paris in 1949 to discuss the future of Vietnam. The Franco-Vietnamese Accords of 1946 (qv) and the Fontainebleau Conference of 1946 tried to regularise French-Vietnamese relations, but Ho Chi-Minh, the Indo-Chinese communist leader, declared a war of national liberation against the French colonial authority from his secret headquarters in Hanoi. To reinforce the public image of Vietnamese independence and to secure permanent French influence in the area despite the promises made by Paris, President Auriol and Bao Daï signed an accord on 8 March 1949 which called for an independent united Vietnam linked to the French union. Vietnam in theory had the right to establish legations in foreign countries, and France promised to train and supplement Vietnamese troops, and to assist Vietnam in joining the United Nations. These accords, which in reality kept Indo-China in a colonial status, maintained French troops in Indo-China until 1954.

Austerlitz, Battle of Austerlitz, one of Napoléon Bonaparte's (qv) greatest victories, was fought on 2 December 1805 near the Moravian town of Austerlitz. Tsar Alexander of Russia decided to take the field against Napoléon, and the Austro-Russian force outnumbered the French army by over 20,000 men. However, Napoléon had a superior knowledge of the terrain, and he was able to guess the exact moves of the enemy forces. By the end of the day the combined Austro-Russian forces had lost almost 30,000 men while French casualties numbered 9,000. The victory of Austerlitz, which Bonaparte called the greatest battle he ever fought, was due in great part to a splendid cavalry charge which broke the enemies' will to fight on. Austerlitz weakened the Third Coalition and paved the way for the Treaty of Pressburg (qv) on 26 December 1805 between France and Austria.

Babeuf, François Noël (1760–1797) Babeuf was born at Saint-Quentin on 23 November 1760 to modest parents, but his genius carried him to the pinnacle of success. In 1790, while serving the revolution, he proposed several changes in the tax structure of France. From 1790 to 1792 he served as a financial adviser and administrator first in the city of Roye (1790–1) and then for the department of the Somme (1792). His demands for reforms cost him this position and he went to Paris as a member of the Committee of Subsistence in 1793. Babeuf opposed the Terror and wrote articles against it after 9 Thermidor (qv). In his paper *Le Tribun du Peuple* he advocated economic equality among peoples and state confiscation of wealth. Under the pen-name of Gracchus, Babeuf advocated an early form of socialism, and he is said to be the founder of modern European socialist thought. His violent attacks on wealth earned him a brief period in jail. After release, he founded the *Club des Egaux*, which advocated a rudimentary form of communism. In 1795 the Directory closed the club. Babeuf then formed a secret society to agitate against the Directory, and he was denounced in 1796, arrested and brought to trial. While some conspirators were acquitted and others deported, the Directory insisted that Babeuf be sentenced to death, and he died on the guillotine on 25 May 1797.

Bainville, Jacques (1879–1936)   Bainville was a historian of royalist sympathies. A friend of Charles Maurras (qv) and a supporter of the *Action Française* (qv), Bainville, a noted intellectual and member of the *Académie Française*, openly espoused fascism as an alternative to parliamentary government. From 1934 until 1936 he served as one of the leaders of the *Action Française*.

Ballay, Noël-Eugène (1847–1902)   A noted colonialist, Ballay was also an explorer. He served as lieutenant governor of Gabon from 1886 to 1889, and from 1890 to 1893 as lieutenant governor for the Rivières du Sud. Because of his genius he was assigned to the same post in French Guinea from 1893 to 1900. Ballay was one of the first and most energetic governors in West Africa, from 1900 to 1902. A respected member of the *Comité de l'Afrique française* (qv), he helped organise French West Africa's administrative apparatus.

Banque de Paris et des Pays-Bas   Founded in 1872, the Bank of Paris and the Low Countries was a union of the Bank of Paris (created in 1865) and the Bank of the Low Countries (formed in 1863). Known as one of the great five banks of France, this bank helped bring stability to the French stock market. It participated in the industrialisation of France, and at times manipulated politics. Never fearing the Bank of France (qv), the *Banque de Paris et des Pays-Bas* was strong enough to set its own policies and rates.

Banquet Movement   The Banquet movement was started by young French intellectuals who saw the Orléanist regime as stale and oppressive. Alphonse de Lamartine (qv) spoke at the great Mâcon banquet on 18 July 1847, sounding the call of opposition to Louis Philippe (qv), King of the French. The banquets began near Paris on 9 July 1847 and spread throughout France, and almost all speeches called for reform of the monarchist system within France. By February 1848 speakers such as Guizot (qv) and Odilon Barrot (qv) had joined Lamartine. The organisers of the movement planned a banquet for 22 February, George Washington's birthday. The government believed this a threat to national and royal honour since Washington was an American revolutionary hero. The price was extraordinarily low in order that the labouring classes could attend. Louis Philippe's government overreacted and placed a ban on the banquet. As irritation grew, crowds took to the streets, and on 22 February the revolution of 1848 began.

Barbès, Armand (1809–1870)   Born to humble parents at Pointe-à-Petre on 18 September 1809, Barbès was destined to become one of France's most consistent revolutionaries. A revolutionary and convinced republican, Barbès was active in many plots against Louis Philippe (qv). In 1834 he was arrested by the government and released, but he did not cease his revolutionary activity. In 1839 he helped lead a revolt and was again arrested; condemned to death, he was pardoned by Louis Philippe. During the revolution of 1848, Barbès became president of the *Club de la Révolution* and was elected a deputy.

For his revolutionary activity he was arrested and condemned in 1849 and imprisoned until 1854. Louis Napoléon signed his pardon warrant in 1854, but Barbès left France and spent the remainder of his life in exile encouraging a workers' revolt against the empire. Barbès died at La Haye on 20 June 1870.

Bardo, Treaty of This treaty between France and the Bay of Tunis was signed on 12 May 1881 and established a French protectorate over Tunisia. France occupied Tunisia with military forces, and Tunisia was forbidden to carry on foreign affairs. This occupation, during the premiership of Jules Ferry (qv), signalled the beginning of a new wave of French imperialism.

Barère de Vieuzac, Bertrand (1755–1841) A journalist and noted republican and born at Tarbes on 10 September 1755, Barère was elected a deputy in 1789. He served as a member of the Committee of Public Safety and survived 9 Thermidor. In 1795 he was arrested and deported, but Napoléon Bonaparte (qv) gave him amnesty after the coup d'état of 18 Brumaire (qv). Barère became loyal to Bonaparte and served him well, choosing to be exiled after 1815. In 1830 he returned to France and served the Orléanist administration. He died at Tarbes on 13 January 1841.

Barnave, Antoine (1761–1793) The son of a protestant lawyer, Barnave was born at Grenoble on 22 October 1761. A deputy from Vizille to the Third Estate in 1789, Barnave, while not a democrat, was a champion of reforms which were democratic. Basically, Barnave was a partisan of constitutional monarchy, and he opposed Mirabeau's (qv) policies. In 1791 he defended Louis XVI after the king's abortive escape attempt. He returned to his home in Grenoble to retire. However, after the violence of 10 August 1792, papers were discovered which linked him with the king and the Bourbon-royalist faction. Despite the fact that he defended himself with brilliance, he was found guilty by the revolutionary tribunal and executed in Paris on 29 November 1793.

Barras, Paul, Vicomte de (1755–1829) Born to a noble

family of modest means at Fox-Amphoux in the Var on 30 June 1775, Barras served as an army officer in the Indies. With a reckless penchant for debts and high living, he was soon destitute. Poverty-stricken, he came to Paris as an ambitious noble. In a short period of time he affiliated with the Jacobins and was elected to the Convention. In 1793 he served with distinction at the siege of Toulon. Barras attacked Robespierre (qv) during Thermidor (qv), and for his actions was made president of the Convention. He was a popular figure and the rising Napoléon Bonaparte (qv) attached himself to him and through him met Joséphine de Beauharnais (qv), Barras's mistress at the time. Barras, who was growing in power, became director in 1795 and served until 1799. During this time he moved against the royalists in 1797 and against the Jacobins on 30 Prairial, Year VII. His power was weakened by the coup of 18 Brumaire, but he continued to serve the state. Barras was allowed to reside in France during the Bourbon restoration despite being known as a regicide. He died at Chaillot on 29 January 1829.

Barrère, Camille (1851–1940) Barrère was a successful French diplomat who served as ambassador to Italy at the turn of the twentieth century. A close confidant of Théophile Delcassé (qv), Barrère was influential in working out a number of problems over Italian claims in Morocco and French claims in Tripolitania.

Barrès, Maurice (1862–1923) Maurice Barrès was one of France's leading prophets of nationalism and the Revanche. Born at Charmes-sur-Moselle on 22 September 1862, Barrès was forced to leave his native province in 1870 with his family. After attending a *lycée* in Nancy, he went to Paris in 1882 to study and entered politics and literature. Reflecting his Lorrainese heritage, he continually argued that France needed a hero to guide its destiny. In 1889 he rallied to the cause of General Georges Boulanger (qv), and later opposed the Dreyfusards. His literary efforts were considerable and were well recognised. In 1888 he published *Huit jours chez M. Renan* followed by *Monsieur Taine en voyage*. *Un Homme libre* appeared in 1889 and in 1891 he published *Le jardin de Bérénice*. *La Colline inspirée*, appearing in 1913, was one of his greatest calls for national spiritual revival. Barrès sought election to the Chamber, and served 1889–93. He lost elections in 1893 and 1896 because of his vehement attacks on French parliamentary democracy, but in 1906, as a result of a wave of nationalism, he returned to the Chamber. During World War I, Barrès, a noted member of many rightist groups, used all his influence and literary skills to support the war effort. Barrès died on 4 December 1923.

Barrot, Odilon (1791–1873) A noted lawyer and founder of the Banquet movement (qv) which helped bring on the revolution of 1848, Barrot advocated reform of the Orléanist political system. In 1845 he worked with Adolphe Thiers (qv) in an ill-fated programme of electoral or parliamentary reform. This earned for Barrot the respect of all liberal reformers in France. Barrot helped to found the Banquet movement in 1847, but he steadfastly refused to argue for a republican form of government. He believed in parliamentary supremacy under a constitutional monarch. After the violence of February and June 1848, Barrot hoped to use the rising star of Louis Napoléon (qv) to gain power for himself. From December 1848 to October 1849, Barrot was President of the Council of Ministers, appointed by Louis Napoléon, but in October 1849 Louis Napoléon dismissed Barrot's conservative ministry. Barrot spent the remainder of his life in opposition to Napoléon III.

Barthélemy, François, Marquis de (1747–1830) A noted diplomat, Barthélemy served the revolution and negotiated a number of treaties. In 1797 as a member of the Directory he opposed the coup of 18 Fructidor (9 April 1797) (qv). He was deported, but Bonaparte pardoned him and named him senator in 1808. In 1814 he turned against Napoléon and served Louis XVIII, who made him a peer. He remained loyal to the Bourbons during the Hundred Days (qv), and in 1815 Louis XVIII made him minister of state and a marquis.

Barthou, Louis (1862–1934)   Louis Barthou entered the Chamber in 1889 and remained there until 1922. From 1922 to his murder in 1934 he was a senator. His greatest contribution to French politics was his obsession with French security after World War I. He advocated and formed the Little Entente in eastern Europe as a part of French alliances surrounding Germany. Barthou first won some fame as an opponent of the Ralliement (qv). He held his first cabinet post in 1894 as minister of public works. Under Jules Méline (qv) in 1896–8 he was minister of the interior. In 1906 he was minister of public works, and under Briand (qv), in 1909, minister of justice. On 22 March 1913 Barthou formed his first cabinet, which lasted only a short period. During World War I he served as minister of state. From 1926 to 1929 he again served as minister of justice under Briand and Poincaré (qv). On 9 February 1934 Gaston Doumergue (qv) called Barthou to the Quai d'Orsay. Using eastern Europe's fear of Germany and Russia, Barthou was able to cement the series of alliances with Poland and Czechoslovakia into the Little Entente. Dynamic despite his advanced age, he pushed hard for a complete alliance system. On 9 October 1934, he was assassinated by an anarchist, and after Barthou's death the alliance system which he had so carefully constructed began to deteriorate.

Basle, Treaty of   Signed 5 April 1795, between France and Prussia, this treaty took Prussia out of the First Coalition and removed French troops from Prussian territory on the east bank of the Rhine. By secret agreements in the treaty, it was agreed that if France held territory on the west bank of the Rhine, Prussia would later receive suitable compensation elsewhere in Europe. This treaty, of value to both states, enabled Prussia to withdraw from the fighting and to participate in the Third Partition of Poland. It also showed a definite decline in France's commitment to the spread of revolutionary ideals to other areas of Europe.

Bastiat, Frédéric (1801–1850)   Bastiat was born in Bayonne on 29 June 1801. A consistently frustrated office-seeker, Bastiat was an advocate of British economic liberalism. In 1848 he was elected deputy and quickly became a leading advocate of liberalism and an open opponent of Proudhon (qv). As a deputy, Bastiat opposed socialism, and he argued for economic liberalism and economic reforms. He died in Rome on 24 December 1850.

Bastille, Fall of the   The situation in Paris in July 1789 was unsettled, and on the morning of 14 July mobs were roaming the streets in search of weapons. The news that Louis XVI (qv) had dismissed the popular finance minister Jacques Necker (qv) had spread throughout Paris and had caused great state unrest. Because of rumours, the Parisians believed that the Bastille, an old unused fortress, was filled with rifles, powder and shot. Rumours were also rife that the old fort was used to torture and kill prisoners of the crown. While basically untrue, the mobs believed the tales, and the Bastille became a symbol of all that they hated in the *ancien régime*. Owing to a breakdown of orders, the troops inside the old fort, which held only seven prisoners, fired into the mobs. A siege of the fortress began, and the mobs were joined by the French guards. The commander of the garrison, fearing a mutiny among his own troops, tried to capitulate to the French guards, but the mob stormed the fort and slaughtered its defenders. The fall of the Bastille on 14 July 1789 marked, for the French, the assault of the people on the oppression and wrongs of the old regime, and as such was vitally important, not only for France, but for all of Europe.

Batavian Republic   The Batavian Republic was the name applied to Holland after it was conquered and occupied by French troops during the campaign of 1794–5. Holland was reorganised with a Directory-styled government in late January 1795 and was bound to France by an alliance. However, in June 1806 Napoléon Bonaparte (qv) re-established the kingdom of Holland and placed his brother Louis on the throne. Napoléon believed that Holland would serve as a vassal state, subordinated to French interests, but Louis began to manifest signs of governing the kingdom for the benefit of his subjects. In 1810, Napoléon forced Louis from the throne and annexed Holland into the empire.

Bazaine, Achille (1811–1888) Born at Versailles on 13 February 1811 and entering the army in 1831, Bazaine served in Africa, and by 1855 was promoted to general. After seeing service in the Crimea, Italy and Mexico, he was promoted to marshal of France. In Mexico Bazaine manifested an inclination toward schemes and intrigue. In 1870 he was named commander in chief of the French armies opposing Prussia, but allowed the army to be encircled at Metz after a siege of two months. There was a distinct feeling that Bazaine had plotted against the French state at Metz, and in 1873 he was brought to trial for treason and condemned to death. However, his sentence was commuted and he fled to Spain in 1874 where he remained until his death in Madrid.

Beauharnais, Alexander, Vicomte de (1760–1794) Alexander de Beauharnais, who was born in Martinique, married Joséphine (qv) in 1779. Known as a liberal noble in 1789, he rose in government administration. By 1791 he presided over the Constituent Assembly and served with gallantry in the army. The Convention, impressed by his intelligence and patriotism, offered him the position of war minister in 1793. However, on 23 June 1794 he was executed during the Terror.

Beauharnais, Eugène de (1781–1824) Eugène de Beauharnais, who was born in Paris on 3 September 1781, benefitting from his relationship with Napoléon Bonaparte, was named general in 1804. The son of Joséphine de Beauharnais (qv), he was adopted by Napoléon in 1805 and became vice-king of Italy in the same year. In 1806 he married the daughter of the king of Bavaria. He served with the Grand Army in Russia, and after the retreat from Moscow he returned to Italy to defend his holdings against Austria. However, after 1815 he was forced to remain in Bavaria while most of his Italian lands passed to Austrian control. He died in Munich on 22 February 1824.

Beauharnais, Hortense de (1783–1837) Born in Paris on

C   33

10 April 1783, Hortense became queen of Holland and married Louis Bonaparte, brother of Napoléon; but her many love affairs produced two French leaders—the Duc de Morny (qv), who was illegitimate, and Napoléon III (qv), who was legitimate. In 1815 Hortense rallied to Napoléon during the Hundred Days (qv), and for her loyalty to the Bonapartist cause she was exiled to Savoy. She died at Arenenberg, Switzerland, on 5 October 1837.

Beauharnais, Joséphine de   qv Joséphine.

Belleville Manifesto   In the fall of 1869 Léon Gambetta (qv), a republican and an opponent of the Second Empire, decided to stand for election in the workers' district of Belleville in Paris. During the campaign, Gambetta issued the Belleville Manifesto calling for universal suffrage, trial by jury, freedom of the press and assembly, suppression of the church's privileges, separation of church and state, free education, reform of tax laws, election of all functionaries, reduction of the professional army, and abolition of monopolies. Gambetta reacted to *cahiers* from the Belleville labourers by issuing his Manifesto which became a blueprint for republicans, especially for the Radical Party.

Béranger, Pierre Jean de (1780–1857)   Béranger arrived in Paris after 9 Thermidor (qv) and became a protégé of Lucien Bonaparte (qv). He survived the restoration and in 1821 took a post at the University of Paris. His poetry displayed liberal and patriotic sentiments which earned him three months in prison. In 1828 his *Chanson inédites* earned him another prison term. After 1833 Béranger turned his attention toward social questions. Elected to the Assembly in 1848, he lost a great deal of influence because of his inability to guide the Assembly toward meaningful social reforms. He left it and retired to obscurity, refusing to recognise Napoléon III (qv).

Bernadotte, Jean-Baptiste Jules (1764–1844)   A career soldier who was born in Pau on 26 January 1764, Bernadotte, who rose through the ranks, became a general in 1794. In 1799 he became minister of war and was known as an energetic administrator. From 1800 to 1804 he commanded the armies of the west with dash and brilliance, and for his service Napoléon named him marshal of France in 1804 and prince in 1806. After a bitter dispute with Bonaparte in 1809 he retired from the army. Bernadotte was elected hereditary prince of Sweden and in 1813 cast his lot with the allies against France. In 1818 he became Charles XIV, King of Sweden. He died in Stockholm on 8 March 1844.

Bernier, Etienne-Alexandre (1762–1806) A brilliant doctor of theology, Bernier refused to take the oath to the Civil Constitution of the Clergy in 1791. However, from 1795 to 1799 he worked to aid church-state relations. Finally he participated as a major figure in the negotiations over the Concordat (qv). In 1802 he was made bishop of Orléans.

Berry, Charles-Ferdinand, Duc de (1778–1820) Second son of the Comte d'Artois, who was born at Versailles on 24 January 1778, de Berry served against revolutionary France in the Vendée. During the restoration he was made a general. He married Marie-Caroline, daughter of Ferdinand I, King of Naples. However, his ultra-royalist tendencies gained him many enemies, and he vehemently opposed the policies of Louis XVIII. He was murdered on 13 February 1820. Seven months after the death of the Duc de Berry, Marie-Caroline gave birth to a son who was called the miracle child. This child, Henri, the Comte de Chambord (qv), became in 1836 the head of the house of Bourbon and Bourbon pretender to the throne of France.

Berry, Marie-Caroline, Duchesse de (1798–1870) Marie-Caroline, born at Palermo on 5 November 1798, was the daughter of Ferdinand I of Naples. She married Charles-Ferdinand, Duc de Berry (qv), who was the second son of King Charles X (qv). Seven months after the murder of her husband, Marie-Caroline gave birth to a son called, by the Bourbons, the 'miracle child'. This child, Henri, Duc de Bordeaux, later the Comte de Chambord (qv), became in 1836 head of the house of Bourbon and pretender to the Bourbon throne. The

Duchess de Berry with her son followed Charles X into exile in 1830, but in 1832 tried, without success, to place her son on the throne. Betrayed in Nantes, she was imprisoned in the fortress at Blaye. Humiliated by King Louis Philippe (qv), she was released from prison, departed from France and spent the remainder of her life working for the political future of her son. She died in Austria at Brunensee on 16 April 1870.

Berryer, Antoine-Pierre (1790–1868)   Berryer was one of the most famous lawyers in France during the restoration era. He gained a national reputation for his brilliant, but unsuccessful, defence of Marshal Ney (qv) in 1815. Elected deputy in 1830 he rose to the head of the liberal opposition to King Louis Philippe (qv). Berryer refused to recognise Napoléon III (qv) and retired from public life in 1851. Until his death Berryer defended people who were accused of an offence against the empire.

Bert, Paul (1833–1886)   A scholar and administrator, Paul Bert was one of the Third Republic's leading opponents of the Catholic church. Bert had degrees in law and medicine, and held a post as professor of general philosophy at the Sorbonne. As a deputy in 1872 he played a major role in the debates on education, and in 1881 led the successful fight for the Ferry Education Bill (qv). Léon Gambetta (qv) named him as minister of public instruction. In 1886 Bert accepted a mission to Indo-China with orders to reorganise the colony. Soon after completing this he died of cholera.

Berthelot, Pierre-Eugène Marcelin (1827–1907)   An outstanding example of a famous man of science who also pursued a career in politics in the Third Republic. The son of a doctor of medicine, Berthelot in 1850 presented a well-received paper on the liquefaction of gas to the Academy of Science. In 1853 he began serious research on glycerine, and by 1864 was experimenting with explosives. His books were considered milestones in science, and he held several chairs of chemistry. In 1873 Berthelot was elected to the Academy of Science, and in 1889 he replaced Louis Pasteur as its permanent secretary. In 1881 he began his political career, being elected senator. He held the portfolio of Public Instruction in 1886, and was chief of the Quai d'Orsay in 1895. After his death in 1907 his remains were placed in the Panthéon.

Berthier, Louis-Alexandre (1753–1815)   Berthier served in America in 1780 and returned to France and served the revolution. In 1792 he fought in the Vendée against the royalists and was promoted to general. He served under Bonaparte as chief of staff, and in 1804 was made a marshal of France and named prince of Wagram. After his marriage to a Bavarian noblewoman his attitude towards Bonaparte changed, and in 1814 he rallied to the restoration. His loyalty to the Bourbons motivated him to fight against Napoléon during the Hundred Days (qv), and for his service to Louis XVIII he was made a peer. Berthier retired to Bavaria where he died on 14 June 1815 under mysterious circumstances.

Bertin, Louis-François (Bertin l'Aîné) (1766–1841)   Bertin, during the revolutionary period, remained a moderate, and while not happy over the coup of 18 Brumaire (qv), he did not attempt to alienate Bonaparte. After Brumaire Bertin went into journalism, and in 1804 founded the *Journal des débats*. This became the *Journal de l'empire*, which was confiscated by the state in 1811 because it espoused the cause of the liberal opposition to Bourbon policies. The restoration authorities allowed Bertin to re-establish it. Bertin has been called the founder of modern French journalism.

Beyle, Marie Henri (Stendhal) (1783–1842)   Of middle-class background, Henri Beyle exhibited, from his youth, a liberal, philosophical and critical nature. He quickly earned a reputation as a brilliant student and chose a career in engineering. In 1800 he entered the army as an officer, but left in 1802. He served the state in various positions and served again in the army in 1809. In 1814, in Italy, he published *Histoire de la peinture*, and in 1817 he wrote *Rome, Naples, et Florence en 1817*, using the name Stendhal for the first time. He joined the Carbonari in 1818 and had to flee Italy. From 1818 to 1830 he

37

continued to write. His famous *Le Rouge et le noir* was completed in 1830; a brilliant commentary on French society under the restoration, it brought Stendhal great fame. He entered the French diplomatic service, holding posts in Italy. However, in 1841, he was forced to give up his position and returned a rich man to France where he died of a heart attack on 23 March 1842.

Bidault, Georges (1899–   ) Georges Bidault came to national prominence as the President of the National Council of Resistance in World War II. A hero and excellent politician, Bidault was a conservative, and from 1949 to 1952 he served as president of the *Mouvement Républicain Populaire* (MRP) (qv). From June to November 1946, he served as premier, and again from October 1949 to June 1950. In 1945 to 1946 he supported the policies of General Charles de Gaulle (qv) and led the MRP to support the general. In June 1946, Bidault headed the largest party in France, but its strength waned. In 1958 Bidault was one of the strongest voices in favour of de Gaulle. Bidault advocated a militant policy of support for French Algeria. Excluded from participation in the Fifth Republic, Bidault became embittered and in 1962 led the fight to keep Algeria French. He was exiled in 1962 because of his opposition to de Gaulle's solution to the Algerian problem.

Billaud-Varenne, Jacques Nicolas (1756–1819) A revolutionary, Billaud-Varenne was a participant in the violence of 10 August 1792 (qv), and after the events of that August he was elected as a deputy to the Convention. In 1793 he became a member of the Committee of Public Safety, and as an outspoken enemy of Danton (qv) and Hébert (qv) gained a reputation as a staunch republican. He was able to work against the policies of Robespierre (qv) because of his position. Billaud-Varenne feared Robespierre's dictatorial tendencies and the extremist violence of the Terror. He became a member of the anti-Terror opposition and was a factor in the fall of Robespierre on 9 Thermidor (qv). However, Billaud was ousted after Thermidor and was deported. Refusing a pardon offered by

Bonaparte, he spent the remainder of his life serving the Republic of Haiti.

Blanc, Louis (1811–1882) Born on 29 October 1811 in Madrid, Spain, where his father was a soldier attached to Joseph Bonaparte (qv), Blanc founded in 1839 *La Revue du Progrès*, a journal dedicated to republican and democratic ideals. In 1840 he published his famous work *De l'Organisation du Travail*, in which he advocated his most famous concept, 'To each one according to his needs, from each according to his talents.' In his *Organisation*, Blanc attacked the concept of class struggle and argued that both the sick and the poor had much to gain from cooperation. Competition and free trade, to Blanc, were the source of unbelievable evil. Labour needed to be organised into social workshops, producers-workers' cooperatives where all men would be allowed to work. When the revolution of 1848 broke out, Blanc was named a member of the provisional government, and he became president of the Luxembourg Commission, which reduced workers' hours to ten in Paris and eleven in the provinces. Workers' delegates were to attend its meetings. Some local cooperatives were established, and Blanc advocated building workers' housing complexes. But he was unable to implement many of his ideas, due to governmental hostility and the confusion growing out of the revolutionary days. In the critical election of 1848, Blanc supported Louis Napoléon (qv) for the presidency of France. In June 1848 the Luxembourg Commission was dissolved; Louis Blanc fled to Belgium and later to England, where he began work on his monumental *Histoire de la Révolution*, which was finished in 1862. He returned to France and was elected deputy for the Seine in 1871 after he had turned his back on the Commune (qv). However, until his death at Cannes on 6 December 1882 he continued to associate with the extreme left.

Blanqui, Auguste (1805–1881) Born at Puget-Theniers on 14 February 1805, Blanqui, son of a minor official, became an advocate of violent revolution. A romantic at heart, Blanqui studied law and medicine. He affiliated with the *Charbonnerie*, became an advocate of revolution and associated himself with the *Société des Amis du Peuple* in 1831, and the *Société des Saisons* in 1839, the year the *Société* tried to revolt against the government, but failed. In 1848 Blanqui advocated class warfare, Saint-Simonian types of associations, as a way toward communism. For him, revolution against the system could only benefit the proletarian class. He participated in many plots and was frequently jailed. In 1839 he was imprisoned by the Orléanist monarchy, but was released in 1848 by the revolutionary government. He immediately founded the Central Republican Society to work against the government which freed him. Jailed again, he was deported from France. In 1859 Napoléon III (qv) granted Blanqui a pardon, but did not allow him to return to France for a few years. In 1869 the imperial government arrested Blanqui and deported him; again he was allowed to return to France, where he agitated against Léon Gambetta (qv) and the government of National Defence. Arrested, he remained in jail until 1879. Basically Blanqui believed that the equality of the working class was linked to perpetual struggle, which had to be violent. He died in Paris on 14 February 1881.

Bloc National The elections of 1919 swung the Chamber to the centre and to the right. The *Bloc National*, associated with the leadership of Aristide Briand (qv) and Raymond Poincaré (qv), was in the main far more interested in foreign than in internal affairs. In the foreign area, *bloc* politicians were generally conservative as far as Germany and security were concerned. Until 1924 the *bloc* was able to maintain control of politics by not distressing the electorate with high taxes or internal political, social or religious questions. One of the main failures of the *Bloc National* was its inability to stop inflation, stabilise the franc and arrest France's general economic decline. As the area of foreign affairs caused consternation, for example over the occupation of the Ruhr valley, the *bloc*'s prestige fell. In May 1924 it was toppled from power by the *Cartel des Gauches* (qv). After 1926 the *bloc* ceased to be a force in French politics, being replaced by the *Union Nationale* (qv).

Bloch, Marc (1886–1944)   One of France's greatest historians, dealing primarily with the medieval era, Bloch served in two wars. After demobilisation he joined a resistance force and was executed by the Germans on 16 June 1944. Bloch is best known for his works on Europe in the Middle Ages such as *La Société feodale* (2 vols) published in 1939, and his many articles on French society, both urban and rural, during the Middle Ages. In 1940, Bloch wrote *Strange Defeat: A Statement of Evidence Written in 1940*, which questioned why France fell to the Germans.

Blum, Léon (1872–1950)   Blum began his career in politics in 1914, but was not elected deputy until 1919. After the ideological split between the communists and socialists in 1920, Blum became one of the principal leaders of the *Section Française de l'Internationale Ouvrière* (SFIO) (qv). In 1936 he became premier of the Popular Front (qv) government. For a year Blum, a Jew, led the highly controversial government which set in motion several leftist proposals, such as compulsory labour-management arbitration and a reduction of the work week. After a year out of power, Blum returned to office in 1938. By his actions in 1936 over the Spanish civil war, he had alienated much of the French centre and all of the right. Many members of the right violently assailed Blum because of his Jewish background. In 1938 Blum, again out of power, supported the Munich agreements which began the process of dismembering Czechoslovakia. In 1940 Blum was arrested by the Vichy government, tried at Riom (qv) and deported to Germany. After the war he served as president of the Council of Ministers from 1946–7.

Bonaparte, Caroline (1772–1839)   In 1800, Caroline, a sister of the Emperor Napoléon, married Joachim Murat (qv), and in 1808 she became queen of Naples. Ambitious, she urged her husband to approach Austria with the possibility of Naples joining the allies against Bonaparte. As a result of these offers Austria permitted Caroline and Murat to remain as sovereigns in Naples. During the Hundred Days (qv), however, Caroline switched her loyalties back to her brother, and for this the British incarcerated her. She was later released and allowed to live in the city of Trieste. She died in Florence on 18 May 1839.

Bonaparte, Eugène-Louis (1856–1879) Known as the Prince Imperial, Eugène-Louis was the son of Napoléon III (qv) and Eugènie (qv). After 1870 he resided in Britain, served in the British army and was killed in a skirmish with the Zulus in South Africa.

Bonaparte, Jérôme (1784–1860) A brother of Napoléon born on 15 November 1784, Jérôme incurred his family's displeasure by marrying an American woman. The family recalled him to France and had the marriage annulled. In 1806 Jérôme became an admiral, and a year later Napoléon made him king of Westphalia (qv). He married Catherine of Wurtemberg, but this did not save his throne. Jérôme fought at Waterloo and was exiled by the restoration administration. Under Napoléon III he was made a marshal of France in 1850 and presided over the Senate from 1852 to his death on 24 June 1860.

Bonaparte, Joseph (1768–1844) Brother of Napoléon Bonaparte (qv), Joseph was born on 7 January 1768. A lawyer by profession, Joseph was driven from Corsica to France in 1792. In 1797, he became ambassador to Rome. A member of the Five Hundred (qv), Joseph was known as a man of diplomatic ability, and he played a great role in the negotiation of the Treaty of Lunéville (qv) in 1801, the Treaty of Amiens (qv) in 1802 and the Concordat (qv) of 1802. For his service and because he was the brother of Napoléon Bonaparte, in 1805 he was made king of Naples by Napoléon. In 1808 he became king of Spain, but failed to hold the country for France. By 1814 he was a general, fought against the allies and exiled himself to Switzerland during the Hundred Days (qv). After

Waterloo he fled to the United States where he lived in exile from 1815 to 1841. In 1841 he was permitted to take up residence in Florence where he died on 28 July 1844.

Bonaparte, Lucien (1775–1840) During the early years of the French revolution, Lucien Bonaparte, who was born at Ajaccio on 21 May 1775, was known as an ardent Jacobin, but he survived Thermidor by turning his back on old Jacobin colleagues. Elected to the Five Hundred (qv), he presided over the Directory during the coup d'état of 18 Brumaire (qv) in which he played a vital role. Lucien Bonaparte was instrumental in moving the Directory to assemble out of Paris, and during the confusion of 18 Brumaire he guided the fortunes of his brother. Named as minister of the interior from 1799 to 1800, Lucien helped prepare the way for the Napoléon's assumption of power. In 1800 he was named ambassador to Spain. Slowly, however, he became disenchanted with his brother's policies and left France in 1810. The British interned him until 1815, and after Napoléon's downfall allowed him to live in Italy where he died in Rome on 29 June 1840.

Bonaparte, Napoléon (1769–1821) Napoléon Bonaparte was born in Corsica on 15 August 1769, to a family of Corsican petty nobility. He chose a military career, and at the military academy at Brienne he excelled in history and mathematics. He also made friends there, for he was not a social outcast as some biographers reported. He entered the army, and in 1789 returned to Corsica to agitate for the revolutionary cause. In 1791, his commission in danger, he returned to France. During the siege at Toulon, Bonaparte distinguished himself and in 1793 he was promoted to captain and, on 22 December 1794, to the rank of general. A friend of Robespierre's brother, Napoléon almost fell with the Terror government, but survived. In October 1795 he won fame when he saved the convention during the coup of 13 Vendémiaire (qv). After a brilliant campaign in Italy in 1796–7 and a campaign in Egypt in 1798–9, Bonaparte returned to France and participated in the coup d'état of 18 Brumaire (1799) (qv), which made him

43

first consul of France from 1800 to 1804. On 2 December 1804, he was crowned emperor of France. In 1805 Bonaparte reorganised his empire, annexing territory to France and making plans for a campaign against Prussia and Austria. In the late fall of 1806 he defeated Prussia at Jena (qv), and in December French troops occupied Berlin. In July 1807, Napoléon and Tsar Alexander I signed the Treaties of Tilsit (qv) which drew Russia into the Continental System (qv) with France. From 1808 to 1813 French armies were weakened in Spain. In 1810 Napoléon divorced Joséphine de Beauharnais (qv), and on 1 April 1810 married Marie Louise (qv) of Austria. However, in 1810 Tsar Alexander I broke with Napoléon; in 1812 Napoléon invaded Russia. The Russian invasion ended in the terrible retreat from Moscow. From 1813 to 1814 Napoléon fought against the allies, but in April 1814 he abdicated as the allies demanded. He departed for exile on Elba on 20 April 1814. In February 1815 he decided to return to France, and from 1 March 1815 to 22 June 1815 tried to re-establish himself as French emperor during the Hundred Days (qv), but lost at the battle of Waterloo (qv). He abdicated again on 22 June 1815, surrendered to the British and was transported to the island of Saint Helena where he died on 5 May 1821.

Bonaparte, Napoléon Jérôme (1822–1891) The son of Jérôme Bonaparte known as Prince Jérôme, Napoléon became a deputy after 1848. A leftist and anti-clerical, he advocated social legislation which attracted the attention of Napoléon III (qv). After the establishment of the Second Empire, Napoléon III used him as a mediator between the government and the left.

Bonaparte, Pauline (1780–1825) Born at Ajaccio on 20 October 1780, this sister of Napoléon married General Leclerc but was widowed in 1802. At the insistence of her brother she married Prince Camille Borghese—a dynastic marriage, arranged in the interest of the state by Bonaparte and ending in failure. She lived in Rome until 1814, and during Napoléon's first exile moved to Elba, trying to reconcile Napoléon, Murat (qv) and Lucien Bonaparte (qv). Exiled after the Hundred Days (qv), Pauline was allowed to rejoin her husband in 1821. She died in Florence on 9 June 1825.

Bonchamps, Charles, Marquis de (1760–1793)   Charles Bonchamps, a career officer, served in the Indies during the American revolutionary war. However, when the French revolution broke out in 1789, he retired from the army, refusing to serve the revolutionary cause. The royalists of the Vendée asked him to take command of their forces against the republicans, which he did, serving mainly as a technician. He constantly suffered from bad advice and poor discipline in the armies. On 17 October 1793 he was mortally wounded at Beaupreau, but before he died he ordered the pardoning of 5,000 republican prisoners.

Bonnet Rouge   In 1911, in the wake of the Second Moroccan crisis (qv) and serious political scandals, Joseph Caillaux (qv) and his supporters launched a new, left-wing newspaper, *Le Bonnet Rouge*. In 1915 the paper began an active campaign against the French war effort. In 1917 it supported the mutinies which took place in the French army. It was felt in government circles that the *Bonnet Rouge* was more than a newspaper. Georges Clemenceau (qv), for example, argued that it was really a front for subversive German agents. This was never proved, but the government under Clemenceau took steps to suppress the newspaper and to arrest many of its contributors and editors.

Borodino, Battle of   On 7 September 1812 Napoléon engaged Russian forces, under General Kutusov, at the village of Borodino. While Borodino was not a French victory, the staggering losses forced the Russians to retreat, and this opened the way for Napoléon to advance on Moscow.

Boulanger, Georges (1837–1891)   Boulanger was born at Rennes on 29 April 1837. He entered the military academy at St Cyr in 1855, and in 1857 was posted to Algeria. He served in Italy in 1859, in Cochin-China in 1862, distinguished himself during the fighting in 1870, and later served against the

Paris Commune. By 1880 he was a general, and by 1884 Boulanger commanded a division in Tunisia. Boulanger's popularity rose, and in 1886 he became minister of war. The war minister gained immense favour by riding a wave of public indignation against Germany in 1887. Boulanger's sudden attraction to the revanchards motivated Prime Minister Maurice Rouvier (qv) to order him to a small army post at Clermont-Ferrand. Boulanger's exile did not dim his popularity, and the revanchards in Paris demanded that he return to the capital to seize power. His support came from both the workers and the bourgeoisie of France. Boulanger had taken steps to republicanise the army by ousting royalists, and these measures pleased some middle-class republicans. The difficult economic conditions of 1887–8 brought him labour and peasant support because these groups saw Boulanger as a man who could, by personality and force, bring economic relief to France. In 1887 Boulanger was elected deputy from a number of districts, and in 1889 he was re-elected. However, when in 1889 he had the opportunity to seize the government, he lost his nerve and fled to Belgium. On 30 September 1891 Boulanger shot himself beside the grave of his mistress, Marguerite Vicomtesse de Bonnemains. The Boulangist threat, a direct outgrowth of the Revanche and political frustrations, represented a definite tendency toward the Revanche and nationalism within French society.

Bourgeois, Léon (1851–1925)   Léon Bourgeois entered the Chamber as a deputy in 1888 and served until 1905. From 1902 to 1904 he was president of the Assembly. Named senator from the Marne in 1905, he continued in that post until his death, and from 1920 to 1923 was president of the Senate. In 1890 he held his first cabinet post as minister of public instruction in the de Freycinet (qv) government. Under Alexandre Ribot (qv), Bourgeois was minister of justice. On 1 November 1895 he formed the first radical ministry which lasted one year. Foreign minister in the 1906 Jean Sarrien cabinet, he tried to strengthen France's alliances in the face of growing German might. During World War I he held numerous cabinet posts and served on the war committee in 1917. After 1917 Bourgeois refused to join a cabinet, preferring to continue his duties in the Senate.

Bourgès-Maunoury, Maurice (1914–   ) A radical deputy, first elected to the Chamber in 1946, Bourgès-Maunoury became known as a close ally of the socialist party. As a radical deputy from the Haut-Garonne, he was attacked by other radicals for his nearness to socialist principles. Despite such opposition, Bourgès-Maunoury gained a reputation as a man of fighting qualities and great ability in the Chamber. He was instrumental in toppling a number of governments. In 1957 he became minister of defence at a time when the war in Algeria had seriously weakened the republic. Bourgès-Maunoury promised moderation in dealing with the issue of Algeria. In June 1957 he became premier with only the slightest margin of support, but almost from the first day he was aided by a Chamber which voted to ratify the Common Market Treaty and the Euratom Treaty. However, on the Algerian issue there could be no sense of moderation in the Chamber, and because of the colonial question Bourgès-Maunoury was ousted in September 1957.

Bourget, Charles-Joseph Paul (1852–1935) A well-known nationalist, Bourget was involved with the *Ligue de la Patrie* (qv). In 1898 he helped found the organisation which was basically anti-Dreyfusard. A friend of Renan (qv), he called for a moral revival in France.

Brazza, Pierre Savorgnan de (1852–1905) An Italian who was naturalised in 1874, de Brazza became one of France's greatest explorers. In 1874 he began a detailed exploration of the region known later as the French Congo. In 1877 he completed his work with the founding of Brazzaville. From 1881 to 1884 he continually explored that region, and as a reward was made commissioner general of the colony. De Brazza became a respected member of the *Comité de l'Afrique française* (qv) and an intimate friend of Joseph Chailley-Bert (qv) and other leading

47

imperialists in Paris. In 1897 de Brazza returned to France after having opposed the establishment of governmentally sponsored commercial concerns. From 1897 to 1905 he lobbied for reforms and used his prestige to forward French imperial efforts in equatorial Africa. He died during a visit to Dakar in Senegal in 1905.

Breton Club, The One of the first of the revolutionary clubs, the Breton Club was established by deputies from Brittany to provide a forum for discussion. After July 1789 it moved its headquarters to Paris. It was members of this club who decided, in early August 1789, to demand an end to all feudal rights in France. On the night of 3 August, the Breton Club decided to bring the question of feudal rights before the assembly, and on the night of 4 August, a Breton deputy, dressed as a peasant, added his voice to the emotionalism that led to the surrender of feudal privileges. In the fall of 1789 the Breton Club allowed members from areas other than its original constituency, and this set a pattern for the other clubs centred at Versailles. By the end of 1789 the *Club Breton*, with its enlarged membership, became known as the *Société des Amis de la Constitution*, its new nickname being the Jacobin Club.

Briand, Aristide (1862–1932) Twenty-six times a minister, Briand, born at Nantes on 28 March 1862, was first elected a deputy in 1902. In 1906 he held his first post as minister of public instruction. By 1909 he was known as one of France's most popular politicians and in that year he became president of the Council of Ministers. In 1913 he pushed for electoral reforms, and in 1915 formed a government with himself as minister of foreign affairs. He held the premiership until 1917. After World War I, Briand formed a ministry from 1921 to 1922 by promising to maintain strictly the Versailles Treaty and the spirit of the 1904 Anglo-French Entente Cordiale (qv). The Locarno Pact (qv) 1925 and the Pact of Paris (Kellogg-Briand Pact) (qv) of 1928 were two of his major accomplishments during this period of his life. Briand worked well with Gustav Stresemann of Germany, Austen Chamberlain of

Britain, and Frank B. Kellogg of the United States. Moderate in politics, Briand wished for some sort of United States of Europe, but the worldwide depression and the hostility of President Paul Doumer forced him, now ailing, to retire from public life in 1931. He died in Paris on 7 March 1932.

Brinon, Comte Ferdinand de (1892–1947)   De Brinon was known as a pro-German advocate of rightist causes. He was leader of the Franco-German Friendship Committee, and during World War II was Vichy ambassador to Berlin.

Brisson, Henri (1835–1912)   Lawyer and journalist, Brisson served as a deputy from 1871 to his death in 1912. He was elected president of the Chamber 1881–5, 1894–8, 1904 and 1906–12. In 1885 he served as president of the Council of Ministers, holding the same position 1898–9. Brisson, as president of the Council, decided in August 1898 to reopen the Dreyfus (qv) case and to re-examine the evidence against the wrongly accused captain. There was growing opposition to Brisson's activities on behalf of Dreyfus, and in 1899 the Chamber forced Brisson to resign as president of the Council of Ministers. However, he continued to maintain that his support for Dreyfus was correct regardless of the consequences. A Gambettist, he served as a constant mediator between the opportunists and radicals.

Brissot, Jean-Pierre (1754–1793)   Brissot was born in Chartres on 15 January 1754 and began his career in an unspectacular manner as a clerk to a local notary. He began his rise to fame as the author of *Théorie des lois criminelles*, which appeared in 1781. After extended voyages to other European nations and to the United States, he became interested in the slavery question, and in 1788 founded the society *Les amis des noirs*, which demanded an end to slavery. When the revolution broke out in 1789, Brissot turned his considerable literary talents towards journalism. At first he espoused political moderation, and with Mirabeau (qv), edited *Patriote français*, which reflected Brissot's drift toward republicanism. As a deputy from Paris, Brissot became one of the major leaders of

D   49

the Brissotins (qv), who later became known in history as the Girondins (qv). It was Brissot who advocated a militant policy towards Austria in 1792. He left Paris and returned to the Convention as a deputy from Eure-et-Loir. Retaining his position of leadership, he advocated with great reluctance the execution of Louis XVI (qv). Brissot, the theoretical republican, feared the growing drift to what he saw as a dangerous republican anarchy. The Jacobins (qv) marked Brissot and his Brissotins for purging in 1792. Despite his urging of war against England and Holland in 1793, the new forces within the Convention were determined to topple him and the remainder of the Girondist leadership. During the period of massive arrests of Girondins, Brissot fled to Switzerland. He returned to France in June 1793 and was arrested at the town of Moulins. Maximilien de Robespierre (qv) and the Jacobins, now in control of the Convention, saw to it that Brissot and his political allies were put to death. Brissot was a man who theorised about republicanism but failed to see the final excesses of the concept. Once associated with the early Jacobins, he abhorred their later tendencies to extremism. Brissot was arrested on 11 June 1793 and remained in prison until his execution on the guillotine on 31 October 1793.

Brissotins, The   The Brissotins were the followers of Jean Brissot (qv) in the Assembly and Conventions from 1789 to 1793. They are best known as the Girondins (qv), a name applied to them much later. The Brissotins had some very specific policies, likes, and dislikes. For example, they disliked Paris. They were not agrarians or ruralists, being from many of the larger cities of France, but they distrusted the volatile nature of the Paris mobs and their possible influence on the assembly. Basically republicans, the Brissotins supported the war against the autocratic powers in 1791–2. In 1792–3 they controlled the assembly, electing many of their numbers as president and as secretary of the Convention and in 1793 tried to save the life of Louis XVI (qv) but were unable to do so. Dependent on some conservative support, they looked with disfavour on radical economic proposals such as the price and wage restrictions that were enacted in 1793.

Broglie, Albert, Duc de (1821–1901) Author and diplomat, de Broglie, who was born in Paris on 13 June 1821, began his career as a deputy in 1871. Like his father Victor de Broglie (qv), he sought a diplomatic career. His first opportunity came when he accepted a post as ambassador to Britain from 1871 to 1872. However, de Broglie became identified with the monarchist opposition to Thiers (qv), earning the enmity of Thiers and the republicans. For a brief period in 1873 he was foreign minister but his growing opposition to the policies of the extreme right cost him his post. From 1874 to 1877 he was a senator. In 1885 he tried to win a seat in the Chamber but lost and retired from politics. He remained in Paris where he died in 1901.

Broglie, Léonce-Victor, Duc de (1785–1870) The Duc de Broglie served France as a conservative diplomat and cabinet minister. A peer of France in 1814, he rose in the estimation of moderate conservatives who supported Louis Philippe (qv). In 1830 he became minister of public instruction and in 1832 minister of foreign affairs. In 1835–6 was president of the Council of Ministers. During the revolution of 1848 he was ousted from power, and until 1851 remained in retirement. In 1851 he returned to the Assembly and remained aligned with the monarchists. He died in Paris on 25 January 1870.

Brumaire, Coup of 18 By 1799 the Directory government in France had failed. A foreign war, crushing debt and unsettled social conditions were pushing France toward an international upheaval. In the Directory, Abbé Sièyes (qv) planned a coup d'état with the help of Napoléon Bonaparte (qv), who had returned from the illfated Egyptian campaign. On 9 November 1799 the Council of Ancients (qv), under Sièyes, voted to meet at Saint Cloud because of alleged Jacobin (qv) intrigue in Paris. Lucien Bonaparte (qv), brother of Napoléon presiding over the Council of Five Hundred (qv), also supported the move to Saint Cloud. Napoléon was given command of the troops to protect the *Corps Législatif*, and Sièyes and Ducos (qv) resigned from the Directory. During the coup Napoléon Bonaparte began to lose his nerve before the Five Hundred, and he appeared to shrink from the goals of the day. In fact, when deputies called out to outlaw Napoléon he fled from the hall. Lucien Bonaparte then took command of his faltering brother and the coup attempt. After bitter debate, Bonaparte used his troops to 'restore order' at Saint Cloud and to seize the assembly hall. The remaining councils approved of a leadership comprised of Bonaparte, Sièyes and Ducos. The three men were named provisional consuls with equal authority, but it was clear that Napoléon had greater ambitions. Soon Ducos and Sièyes were eased out and Napoléon Bonaparte ruled France as first consul. The two weak consuls added to the consulate form of government, by the end of 1799, but Bonaparte was in firm control of France.

Buchez, Philippe-Benjamin (1796–1865) Buchez, a toll collector in Paris, began his career as a leader of French socialism in 1821 when he helped found the *Charbonnerie*. He was granted a doctorate of medicine in 1825. His mind, however, constantly turned to the plight of the poor, and he began to combine his medical practice and early socialist ideology. Buchez founded the *Journal des Progrès des Sciences et Institutions Médicales*, which attempted to reconcile medicine and philosophy. He argued for state-financed medical services, and, a disciple of Saint-Simon (qv), argued that religion and socialism went hand in hand. His massive 40 volume *Histoire parlementaire de la Révolution française*, written 1833–8 tried, in many ways, to bring his catholicism and socialism together. Buchez participated in the revolution of 1830, and from 1831 to 1848 he wrote for the *Revue nationale*. He brought together Catholics who were socialists and helped form the first coherent Catholic, Christian, socialist group in France. Elected deputy in 1848, Buchez served as president of the assembly in that year. He was not re-elected to the assembly, and, in disappointment, retired from public life.

Bugeaud de la Piconnerie, Thomas Robert (1784–1849)
A professional soldier, Bugeaud de la Piconnerie served at
Austerlitz and in Spain. He remained loyal to Bonaparte during
the Hundred Days (qv) and his loyalty cost him his military
career. Reinstated by the Orléanists in 1830, he was elevated
to general in 1831. In 1831 he was elected deputy, but was
sent to Algeria to fight against the Muslim rebel leader Abdel
Kader (qv). As a result of his victories he was made a marshal
of France in 1847. Distrusted by the revolutionaries of 1848,
Bugeaud lost his command, and Louis Napoléon, who also
distrusted the popularity of the soldier, failed to offer him a new
post. However, he was honoured as the military conqueror of
Algeria.

Cabet, Etienne (1788–1856) A lawyer and political acti-
vist, Cabet, born in Dijon on 2 January 1788, first emerged as
a controversial figure in 1827 when he became director of a
militant coalminers' committee. After 1830 he was elected
deputy and fought against the conservative policies of Thiers
(qv) and Guizot (qv). Cabet, who served as a deputy for the
Côte d'Or, founded a journal, *Le Populaire*, to serve as a vehicle
for his ideas which caused Louis-Philippe (qv) to exile him.
During a period of exile in England, Cabet met the British
social philosopher Robert Owen, and by 1840 he was writing
tracts and books heavily laced with Owen's philosophy and
communalist idealism. He published in 1840 *Voyage en Icarie*,
and he advocated a communist-style community, with a religious bias, called the *communauté icarienne*, set up in Texas in
1848 but short-lived. After a visit to the United States, he returned to France in 1848 to advocate his ideas and to raise
funds but was soon disgusted with the rise of Bonapartism and
returned to America, to Illinois. However, internal dissension
soon forced Cabet's retirement, and he died in Saint Louis,
Missouri, on 9 November 1856.

Cagoule, The A secret, masked terrorist organisation with
definite fascist sympathies, it was set up in the 1930s to support
extreme right-wing causes. Organised by Henri Dorgeres, the

Cagoule opposed parliamentary government, the Third Republic and Jewish politicians like Georges Mandel (qv); during the late 1930s they became open admirers of Nazi Germany.

Caillaux Affair   In March 1914 Henriette Caillaux, second wife of the controversial premier Joseph Caillaux (qv), shot and killed Gaston Calmette, the outspoken critical editor of the *Figaro*. On 16 March 1914 Calmette, a political enemy of Caillaux, had printed some old intimate love letters sent by Joseph Caillaux to Henriette when she was his mistress. Her resentment of the letters being used for political purposes sparked off the murder, for which Madame Caillaux was tried and acquitted. Not only did this scandel effectively remove Joseph Caillaux from his position as minister of finance in the Poincaré government, it also occupied the attention of the French public during the critical month of July 1914, when war clouds were gathering in Europe.

Caillaux, Joseph (1863–1944)   Caillaux was born at Mans on 30 March 1863. Elected deputy in 1898, Caillaux emerged as a champion of the Radical Party. From 1899 to 1902 he served as minister of finance, and he held the post again in 1911. Caillaux was president of the Council of Ministers from 1911 to 1912, and had to deal with the Second Moroccan Crisis (qv). The Radical Party named him as their leader in 1913, and Caillaux began to work for peace as it became clear that Europe was headed for war. In 1914 his wife was tried for the murder of a newspaper editor, and this trial removed Joseph Caillaux from public office but not from public view. Caillaux's outspoken views on the necessity for world peace, at a time in July 1914 when Europe was preparing for war, kept him from capitalising on this brief period of notoriety. Georges Clemenceau (qv), who became premier in 1917, had Caillaux arrested for treason in December of that year because of his outspoken criticism of the war effort and of French military failures, and in 1920 he was convicted. However, in 1924 the government of the *Cartel des Gauches* (qv) granted him amnesty. In 1925 he accepted the post of minister of finance. Moderating his radicalism, from 1925 to 1940 Caillaux sat in the Chamber advocating mildly radical financial programmes. He died at Mamers on 20 November 1944.

Caillié, René (1799–1838)   One of the first French explorers of Africa, Caillié in 1824 dressed himself as an Arab and explored the Niger river region, reaching Timbuktu in 1828. From Timbuktu he went to Tangiers; his extensive memoirs concerning his trip helping prepare the groundwork for French claims in West and North Africa.

Calonne, Charles Alexandre de (1734–1802)   Appointed by Louis XVI to the position of controller general of finance, Calonne tried to restore confidence in the French financial system by giving it at least the appearance of stability and prosperity. Casting all caution to the wind he borrowed vast sums of money. In 1783–7 France went deeper into debt, and Calonne was unable to arrest the decline. By 1786 he convinced the king to call the Assembly of Notables, which had not met since 1626, to discuss far-reaching reforms. Calonne proposed the abolition of the *Corvée* (qv), certain taxes and outdated financial procedures. He advocated the creation of a truly centralised state bank. He suggested to the Assembly of Notables that the nobility be taxed and even tried to convince the notables that taxation of their class was necessary to salvage the rapidly declining situation. Queen Marie Antoinette (qv) led a court group which fought against any reform Calonne advocated. In 1787 he tried to convince the king of the correctness of his proposals, but was ousted by a court clique. During the revolutionary period he continued to campaign for financial reforms and a sound fiscal policy.

Cambacérès, Jean-Jacques, Duc de Parme (1753–1824)   In 1792 Cambacérès was elected deputy to the Convention and served on the Committee for Legislation. Later he was a member of the Five Hundred (qv) and minister of justice in June 1799. Napoléon Bonaparte picked him as second consul, and he played a vital role in the publication of the Napeolonic Code (qv). In 1808 he received the title of Duc de Parme.

During the Hundred Days (qv), he remained loyal to Napoléon and during the Bourbon restoration he was banished from France.

Cambon Jules (1845–1935) Jules Cambon, brother of Paul Cambon (qv), became a lawyer in 1866. He manifested republican tendencies, and in 1871 worked for the establishment of the young republic. In 1874 he served in the administration of Algeria, and three years later earned the position of prefect of Lyon. After a successful tenure in Lyon, Cambon was named governor general of Algeria, a post which he held from 1891 to 1896. A friend of Gabriel Hanotaux (qv), the French foreign minister, Cambon was, like his brother Paul Cambon, singled out for a high diplomatic post, and in 1897 he was named ambassador to the United States. In 1906, after the critical Algeciras Conference (qv), Cambon was sent to Berlin as the French ambassador. He held that post until the outbreak of World War I in 1914. During the war Jules Cambon served in the Quai d'Orsay, and in 1919 he was instrumental in drafting the Versailles Treaty (qv). From 1919 to 1922 he was the French representative to the internal conference which attempted to enforce the Versailles Treaty. In 1922 Cambon retired from public life.

Cambon, Paul (1843–1924) Paul Cambon began his career as *chef du cabinet* for Jules Ferry (qv) and as a member of the Government of National Defence. In 1882 he served as resident general in Tunisia, and in 1886 was named as ambassador to Madrid. After a period of service as ambassador to Constantinople, he was sent, in 1898, to London as French ambassador. He negotiated and supported the Anglo-French Entente Cordiale of 8 April 1904 and was instrumental in maintaining good relations between London and Paris during the years of World War I. Retiring in 1920, Cambon began a systematic publication of his letters. He is often called France's master diplomat, because of his work in 1904.

Camelots du Roi Street gangs associated with the *Action Française* (qv), they engaged in violent acts. They took their ideas from Charles Murras (qv) who believed that the Third Republic was decadent and must be overthrown. Anti-semitic in nature, the *Camelots du Roi* believed that Jews like Georges Mandel (qv) were too closely tied to the parliamentary republic and they fought against socialists, communists and republicans alike. In the late 1930s the group became openly associated with support for a rapprochement with Nazi Germany.

Campo Formio, Treaty of This treaty was signed on 17 October 1797 to assure Austrian consent for the French annexation of Belgium and the establishment of the Cisalpine Republic (qv) of Northern Italy. The Austrians were given huge tracts of land which belonged to the moribund Republic of Venice. France also received the Ionian Isles, again at the expense of Venice, plus territory on the eastern side of the Adriatic. Napoléon Bonaparte also secretly promised to try to obtain compensation for Austria in Germany. Basically the treaty lasted only two years when war broke out again in 1799.

Cannes, Conference of (January 1922) See Locarno Pacts.

Carnet B This carnet was a list of suspected subversives and outspoken defeatists which the French government kept during World War I. Such a list existed in 1914 when the war broke out, but Louis Malvy (qv), the controversial minister of the interior refused to use it. Georges Clemenceau (qv) did, however, make use of Carnet B after 1917, and a number of alleged dangerous subversives were arrested.

Carnot, Lazare-Hippolyte (1801–1888) Born at Saint-Omer on 6 October 1801, a noted Saint-Simonian, Carnot served as president of the Society for Elementary Instruction which had been founded by his father Lazare-Nicolas Carnot (qv) during the Hundred Days (qv). Elected deputy in 1839, he became minister of public instruction in 1848. Out of office during the Second Empire, he returned to public life as a deputy in 1871 and was elected senator in 1875. Carnot continued until his death in Paris on 16 March 1888 to be interested in the question of public instruction in France.

Carnot, Lazare-Nicolas (1753–1823)   A noted army officer and engineer, born at Nolay on the Côte d'Or on 31 May 1753, Carnot was first elected deputy for the Pas de Calais in 1791, and sat among the Montagnards (qv) in 1792. On 14 August 1793 he became a member of the Committee of Public Safety (qv) and concerned himself with military affairs. Carnot developed the concept of the *levée en masse* (qv) which served as the basic premise for an entire nation at war. Because of his tireless efforts Carnot is sometimes called the saviour of the revolution. In 1794 he became president of the Convention and openly opposed the policies of Maximilien de Robespierre (qv). Despite his Thermidorian affiliation he defended many Jacobins who were old friends after the fall of Robespierre. Later as a member of the Directory (qv), Carnot retained all of his interest in military affairs. In 1797 he fled into exile as a result of the coup of 18 Fructidor (qv), but returned to France in 1800 to become minister of war. He opposed Bonaparte until the restoration became a real possibility, but he believed that the conservative restoration would be worse for France than a continuation of the empire under Napoléon. Napoléon named Carnot a general, and in May 1814 he defended Anvers with great gallantry. During the Hundred Days (qv) he served as minister of the interior, and was made a peer and a count. The Bourbons exiled him in 1815. On 2 August 1823 he died at Magdebourg, Prussia, and in 1889 his remains were deposited in the Panthéon in Paris.

Carnot, Marie-Sadi (1837–1894)   Sadi Carnot, born to a well-known political family of Limoges, began his career as a civil-servant engineer. A staunch republican, Carnot manifested a definite opposition to the Second Empire. In 1871 he was elected to the National Assembly from the Côte d'Or, and held that post until 1876. From 1876 to 1887 he held the position of deputy from the same region, until he was elected president of the Republic in 1887. Carnot served as undersecretary for public works in 1879 under William Waddington (qv) and again under Charles Louis de Freycinet (qv) in 1879; Jules

Ferry (qv) gave him the portfolio of public works in 1880, and he held the same ministry under Henri Brisson (qv). In the wake of the Wilson affair (qv) Carnot became president of the Republic in 1887. He tried to become a symbol of stability, law and order in France, but he was murdered by an anarchist fanatic in 1894.

Carrel, Armond (1800–1836)   Carrel began his career at the military school at St Cyr but resigned from the French army in 1823 in protest against Bourbon policies. He fought in Spain, in the Spanish Legion, against Bourbon forces and was captured, condemned to death, and then pardoned. He then became personal secretary to Augustin Theirry, the noted journalist. During the revolution of 1830 Carrel helped establish the *National*, a paper devoted to liberal causes. He soon left this to devote his time to politics, becoming one of the leaders of the republican party. Before his death in a duel, Carrel published his principal work, *Histoire de la contre-révolution en Angleterre* in 1827.

Carrier, Jean-Baptiste (1756–1794)   A lawyer by profession, Carrier started a small practice at Aurillac in 1785. In 1792 he was elected deputy from Cantal to the convention and played an important role in the establishment of the Revolutionary Tribunal in March 1793. In May that year he helped to purge the Girondins (qv) from the assembly. He was sent to Normandy in September 1793 and to Nantes in October 1793 to stamp out revolutionary activities. He achieved a reputation in the Vendée as a merciless individual, and by early 1794 had over 3,000 prisoners executed on various charges. The Jacobin party (qv) in Nantes, repulsed by such violence, demanded Carrier's recall. Carrier, who was a personal enemy of Robespierre (qv), was brought back to Paris in January 1794. In November 1794 Carrier was arrested by the Thermidorians, and he was sent to the guillotine in Paris on 16 November 1794 by the revolutionary tribunal he had helped to create.

Cartel des Gauches   After World War I, France faced political and economic stagnation at home and over-aggressiveness in foreign affairs. The conservatives in power seemed determined to maintain an unsatisfactory status quo in the face of rising criticism and demands for an improvement in the quality of life in France. In 1922 the parties of the left combined into the *Cartel des Gauches* to present a united front in the Chamber elections of 1924. The combination of radicals, socialists and other minor leftist parties secured a majority in the Chamber and Edouard Herriot (qv) became premier. In the area of internal legislation the *cartel* was able to accomplish little, but in foreign affairs it secured an evacuation of the Ruhr area of Germany and negotiated the Locarno Pact (qv) of 1925. The *cartel* was able to force the resignation of President Alexandre Millerand (qv). In the economic sphere the *cartel* was a dismal failure and the franc fell to an all-time low during the two-year period of its administration. In 1926 Herriot and the *Cartel des Gauches* were ousted, but the *cartel* returned to power during the chaotic period of 1932 to February 1936. It held the reins of government only periodically during that confusing time.

Castiglione, Virginia Oldoini, Comtesse de (1837–1899) Reputed to be one of the most beautiful women in Europe, the Countess Castiglione was intelligent, but vain. She was dispatched by Count Cavour, the Piedmontese prime minister, to Paris to win Napoléon III's favour and in turn influence him to aid in the cause of Italian unification. In 1855 she met Napoléon, who was instantly captivated by her beauty, and in 1856, now Napoléon's mistress, she separated from her husband. She used her influence to aid her family, and totally rejected her weak-willed husband. By 1857 Napoléon III and the countess visited with great frequency, and she, faithful to her mission, pressed the emperor to help Italy. After the armistice of Villafranca (qv) in 1859, which ended French participation in the Italo-Austrian War, Castiglione openly assailed Napoléon III and was expelled from France. Allowed to return in 1861, she was involved with the social whirl, but never again had a liaison with Napoléon III. After 1870 she lived in Paris and once plotted an Orléanist coup which never materialised. The Countess Castiglione was a perfect representative of the glamorous social world of Napoléon III, an example of how the social life surrounding Emperor Napoléon III affected his diplomatic decisions.

Caulaincourt, Armand Louis de (1773–1827)   Caulaincourt served Napoléon Bonaparte as a personal secretary from 1804 to 1814 and was one of his advisors who opposed the Russian invasion. After the battle of Leipzig he became minister of foreign affairs, but Napoléon's changing attitudes towards peace kept Caulaincourt from effectively dealing with the allies. Caulaincourt refused an offer to serve the Bourbons during the restoration and retired from public life when Bonaparte was exiled to Elba. During the Hundred Days (qv) he again served Bonaparte as foreign minister and, after surrendering to the allies, he was allowed to retire to private life. Caulaincourt wrote a series of memoirs about his service with Napoléon Bonaparte which serve as a vitally important source for the period.

Cavaignac, Louis Eugène (1802–1857)   Born in Paris on 15 October 1802 he became an officer in 1830 but Cavaignac fell out of favour with the Orléanists because of his outspoken republican views. After service in Algeria, he was made a general in 1848. Elected deputy in 1848, Cavaignac was charged with crushing resistance in Paris during the June Revolt of 1848. His brutal methods cost him popularity, but he won over a million votes for president in the elections held in December 1848. In 1852 and again in 1857 he was elected a deputy, but refused to take the oath to the emperor and retired from public life to Ourne (Sarthe) where he died on 28 October 1857.

Chaban-Delmas, Jacques (1915–   )   A career civil servant, Chaban-Delmas served in various posts prior to 1940. When France fell in 1940 he was deeply moved and rallied very early to General Charles de Gaulle (qv). Serving in the resistance in France, Chaban-Delmas played a vital role in the August 1944 liberation of Paris. In 1944, at the age of twenty-nine, he was promoted to brigadier general and served de Gaulle in France. After 1946 he served in the Mendès-France (qv) cabinet of 1954 as minister of public works, in the Mollet (qv) cabinet of 1956 as minister of state, and in the Gaillard (qv) cabinet of 1957–8 as minister of defence. In 1958 Chaban-Delmas was chosen by de Gaulle as a leader of the *Union pour la Nouvelle République* (UNR) (qv). Elected president of the Assembly in 1958, he served in that capacity until 1968 when he became premier. Chaban-Delmas had also held the position of mayor of Bordeaux since 1947.

Chailley-Bert, Joseph (1854–1928) Born Joseph Chailley, he pursued a career as an economist until he became interested in the cause of imperial expansion. Chailley-Bert became his official name after his marriage to the daughter of the colonial administrator Paul Bert (qv). In 1890 he joined the *Comité de l'Afrique française* and in 1893 the *Union Coloniale française*. By 1897 he was working as the chief editor of the *Quinzaine Coloniale*, the monthly organ for the *Union Coloniale*. In its pages, Chailley-Bert urged a sensible business-like approach to colonisation. He continued up to his death as a leading advocate of a slow, deliberate approach to colonialism.

Challemel-Lacour, Paul (1827–1896) Paul Challemel-Lacour first came into public view as an open, hostile opponent of the Second Empire. His attacks against Napoléon III were so violent that the government forced Challemel-Lacour into exile until 1870. In 1870 he attached himself to Jules Ferry (qv) and to Léon Gambetta (qv) and served briefly as the French ambassador to London. At the insistence of Jules Ferry, he ran for the Senate in 1876 and won a seat which he held for twenty years. In 1883 he held the post of foreign minister in the second Jules Ferry cabinet, and from March 1893 to January 1896, despite ill health, he was president of the Senate.

Chambord, Henri, Comte de (1820–1883) The 'miracle child' sired by the Duc de Berry (qv), born in Paris on 24 September 1820, was taken into exile after the revolution of 1830. In 1830 the Duchess de Berry (qv), his mother, made an illfated attempt to place her young son on the throne of France, but she was imprisoned and humiliated by King Louis Philippe. In 1836 he became the heir to the Bourbon throne. After 1870 he was the principal claimant to the throne, but his absolutist views, as expressed in Chambord's Manifesto (qv), kept him from becoming the king of France. Known as Henri V by his supporters, Chambord failed to recognise the anti-absolutist tendencies of the early Third Republic. He left France and went to Austria where he died at Frohsdorf on 24 August 1884.

Chambord's Manifesto This manifesto was issued by the Comte de Chambord (qv) to the French people on 5 July 1871, setting forth the Bourbon pretender's conditions for coming to the throne as Henri V. While moderate in its approach to the relationship of the king vis-à-vis the state, the document did state that, as a Bourbon, Chambord could not accept the revolutionary tricolour. He claimed to repudiate 'privilege, absolutism . . . intolerance . . . titles, feudal rights . . .', but argued that the issue of the flag was a matter of principle and simply refused to compromise his position by accepting the red, white and blue flag of the revolution. Without the white Bourbon banner of pre-1789 France, Chambord refused to take the throne.

Chambre Introuvable In 1815 elections were held for the Chamber, and out of an electorate of 72,000 about 48,000 cast votes. This resulted in a reactionary, ultra-royalist and recalcitrant group of deputies. This so-called Matchless Chamber even repudiated Louis XVIII's (qv) moderate policies and caused him to despair. It embarked on a violent policy of purging anyone who was a regicide, an old Jacobin, or a collaborator with the Bonapartist regime. They demanded a return of all property to its former owners, both clerical and noble. They ousted many members of the Napoleonic bureaucracy, and reinstated a number of royalist army officers, thereby creating great discontent in the military. As a rebuke to revolutionary policy, this *Chambre Introuvable* tried to return education to the control of the Catholic church. In short, the members refused to recognise the events of a quarter century and tried to proceed in 1815 as if the events of 1789 had never happened. The Duc de Richelieu (qv) found things to be unmanageable, and in 1816 the Chamber was dissolved. In new elections Louis XVIII and Richelieu, much to the disgust of the extremists, formed their working moderate majority.

Champs de Mars, Massacre of   In July 1791 the *Club des Cordeliers* (qv) agitated against King Louis XVI (qv), demanding that he be tried for treason to the state. On 15 July the deputies absolved the king of guilt in connection with his attempt to escape and restored him to his office. The radicals were furious and placed petitions against the king on the Altar of the Fatherland on the Champs de Mars. On 17 July 1791 two men were discovered under the altar and were torn apart by a mob, who believed them to be spies. Lafayette and the National Guard fired on the mob, killing about two dozen people. After this, the republicans, and especially the radicals, were repressed, and leaders of the clubs were brought to trial. The Assembly, after the violence, seemed to be less inclined to allow the clubs the right to agitate the populace of Paris openly.

Chapelier Law   The Chapelier Law of 14 June 1791 was a middle-class response to deteriorating economic conditions and a rising demand for political equality. Employers and workers were forbidden to form any defensive trade or craft associations. This was done to keep groups, radical or potentially so, from forming against the Assembly. This law set the tone for the official governmental position in the rights of labour in France until the last decade of the nineteenth century. The Law of Association (qv) of July 1901 finally had the effect of legalising and in fact aiding the formation of French trade unions.

Charette de la Contrie, François (1763–1796)   An ultra-royalist from the Vendée, he commanded royalist Catholics in that province from 1793 until his death in 1796. Charette served also as an advisor to Louis XVIII (qv) while he was Comte de Provence.

Charles X, Comte d'Artois (1757–1836) Born at Versailles on 9 October 1757, Charles X was a brother of Louis XVI (qv) and Louis XVIII (qv). He emigrated on 17 July 1789 and agitated against republican and imperial France. In 1814 he prepared the return of the Terror. Opposed to moderation, he led the forces of ultra-royalism in the Chamber, and he even attacked Louis XVIII and his minister Decazes (qv) as being too weak in dealing with Jacobins, Bonapartists and regicides. Upon the death of Louis XVIII in 1824, d'Artois became King Charles X, a king pledged to ultra-conservative policies. In 1829 he placed the Prince de Polignac (qv) at the head of an ultra ministry which sparked the July revolt. Charles was forced to flee after abdicating on 2 August 1830. He spent the remainder of his life in travel. He died at Goritz, Austria, on 6 November 1836.

Charter of 1814 Louis XVIII (qv), the restored Bourbon king of France, issued the Charter of 1814 to reassure France that his return signalled no Terror or reverse repression. Issued at Saint-Ouen, the charter promised that no one would be persecuted for his support of the revolution or Napoléon (qv). A liberal constitution would retain most of the basic liberties won by the revolution. The Napoloenic civil code, if it did not run counter to the charter, would be held intact in order to maintain some semblance of continuity in French life. Land confiscated from the nobles and church remained in the hands of the new owners. This, of course, recognised the right of property, but this part of the Charter of 1814 was bound to cause ill-will, especially among the returning *émigrés*. While the charter proclaimed religious toleration, the document also recognised that there was a special relationship between the church and the state: Catholicism would remain the official religion. Also, the Charter of 1814 recognised the right of a free press and the right of the state to control journalistic abuses.

However, the existence of the revolution or Bonapartist era was not recognised in the charter.

Chateaubriand, François-René (1768–1848) Born in Saint Malo on 7 September 1768, Chateaubriand entered the army in 1786 and in 1787 was presented to King Louis XVI (qv). He began to write, but, disturbed by the revolution, he travelled to America during 1791–2. He served with royalist forces and in 1793 was wounded. Living in England and teaching French, Chateaubriand wrote *Essai historique, politique et moral sur les révolutions anciennes et modernes, considérées dans leurs rapports avec la révolution française,* published 1797. After the death of his mother, his thoughts turned to matters of religion, and he wrote *La Génie du Christianisme,* which appeared in France in 1802 and coincided with the Concordat (qv). Napoléon Bonaparte (qv), approving of Chateaubriand's efforts, appointed him secretary to the French Embassy in 1802. However, the Enghien Affair (qv) distressed Chateaubriand, and he failed to take up the post. In 1802 he published *René.* Chateaubriand spent the next few years in travel, visiting the Near East, Spain, Greece, and North Africa. In 1809, as a result of his voyages, he published *Les Martyrs,* and in 1811 was elected to the *Académie française.* Bonaparte refused, however, to agree to his appointment. When the allies entered Paris in 1814, Chateaubriand wrote *De Bonaparte et des Bourbons,* which Louis XVIII (qv) praised as worth an army to the royalist cause. Louis XVIII named him ambassador to Sweden, but the Hundred Days (qv) and Bonaparte's return kept him from his post. After Waterloo, Chateaubriand returned to France, but the extreme violence of the royalists repulsed him. He served as minister to London, delegate to the 1822 Congress of Verona, and in 1823 became foreign minister. During his term in this ministry (1823–4), he decided on the French intervention in Spain. Disgusted again with ultra-royalist policies, he left his post and wrote articles for the *Journal des Débats* defending the freedom of the press and the independence of Greece. In 1826 he published the first edition of *Oeuvres complètes.* From

1828 to 1829 he served as ambassador to Rome, and in 1830 he refused to recognise the revolution. In exile, he quickly lost faith in the Bourbon cause. Knowing that his political career was ruined, Chateaubriand returned to France to devote himself to literature, and in 1831 he published *Etudes historiques*, followed by *Essai sur la littérature anglaise*. He also began his *Mémoires d'outre-tombe*, which would not be published until after his death. In 1848 Chateaubriand's beloved wife died; he became deeply depressed and died on 4 July 1848.

Chautemps, Camille (1885–1963) One of the chiefs of the Radical Party during the two decades between the two World Wars, Chautemps was known as a democratic liberal. He was premier during the Stavisky affair (qv), and because of the scandal was ousted from power. After 1938 he tried, as premier, to keep alive the programme of the Popular Front (qv), but Hitler's takeover of Austria forced foreign affairs to take precedence over internal policies. A few days before Germany moved into Austria, Chautemps resigned as president of the Council of Ministers, thereby causing a governmental crisis which rendered France ineffective in world affairs. During the downfall of France in the spring of 1940 Chautemps argued for a continuation of the struggle against Germany from London, but his plan failed to carry. He later advocated an armistice with the Germans, but planned to continue the struggle against the Germans from North Africa. Appointed vice-premier, he fled France, but refused to rally to de Gaulle (qv), and actually worked, at times, against the Free French. After liberation Chautemps, whom the Gaullists and other liberation forces distrusted, retired from active public life.

Chevalier, Michel (1806–1879) A champion of free trade, Chevalier was a vocal enemy of Louis Blanc (qv). He served as an economic advisor to Napoléon III and negotiated the Cobden-Chevalier Treaty of 1860 (qv). For his work he was made a senator.

Cisalpine Republic In 1797 Napoléon Bonaparte (qv) transformed the Cispadane Republic, a few small Italian states of the southern Po valley, and Lombardy into the Cisalpine Republic. Appearing to favour a unification of Italy, he confirmed the creation of the republic by the Treaty of Campo Formio (qv). On 3 June 1800 he reconfirmed the existence of the republic while fighting the Marengo campaign. The Cisalpine Republic was firmly in French hands and was a staunch ally of the French. It ceased to have importance after Bonaparte took the iron crown of Italy in Milan in May 1805. Despite the fortunes of the Cisalpine Republic, the creation of such a state was a rallying point for Italian unificationists and it helped prepare the ground work for the Italian nationalists of the nineteenth century.

Civil Constitution of the Clergy   The Civil Constitution of the Clergy was enacted by the Constituent Assembly on 12 July 1790. Basically it emphasises the traditional independence of the Gallican church and the subordination of church to state. Also, the Assembly knew that church lands and tithes were an excellent source of wealth for the state. The issuance of the assignats (qv) to aid the land-hungry peasants in purchasing church lands caused deep alienation between clergy and state. The number of bishops and archbishops was reduced from 139 to 83, with each department being a diocese. There were to be ten metropolitan districts controlled by a bishop; these bishops would be elected at local level rather than appointed by the pope. Salaries were regulated by the state. Clerics were to swear an oath to the constitution which was, in effect, an oath to the state. This meant that eventually the clergy was divided into juring and non-juring clerics, and France was deeply divided over the issue of the Civil Constitution of the Clergy.

Claudel, Paul-Louis (1868–1955)   Born on 6 August 1868 to a middle-class family, Claudel was a brilliant student, and in 1890 began to study for a career in the foreign ministry. He had already published *Tête d'Or*, a dramatic essay, in 1889, and by 1892 his *La Jeune Fille Violaine* appeared. In 1893 he became consul in New York, and a year later was sent as consul to China. During this period he published a large number of works in the *Revue de Paris*, the *Revue Blanche* and the *Mercure de France*. After a brief period of rest in France in 1900, he was dispatched again to China from 1901 to 1909. From 1909 to 1911 he saw service in Prague and Frankfurt. In 1911 he returned to France and helped found the *Nouvelle Revue française*. In 1917 he became minister to Brazil, and in 1922 he held the same post in Denmark. Rising to ambassadorial level, Claudel served as ambassador to Japan from 1922 to 1926, to the United States from 1926 to 1933, and to Belgium from 1933 to 1935. He retired from the diplomatic service in 1935 to write, but most of his well-remembered works were composed between 1911 and 1925. He died in Paris on 23 February 1955. Claudel serves as a prime example of the French artist-diplomat.

Clemenceau, Georges (1841–1929)   Born at Mouilleron en Pareds on 28 September 1841, Clemenceau began his career as an opponent of Napoléon III (qv). Because of this opposition to the empire, he travelled to the United States and to Britain in 1862. In 1870 he was elected mayor of Montmartre and served during the bitter days of the Commune. Elected deputy to the National Assembly in 1871, he represented the Seine; in 1876 he was re-elected and he espoused radicalism. His violent attacks on the government gained him the reputation of a man who could topple governments; Gambetta (qv), Ferry (qv) and Brisson (qv) lost ministries because of him. In 1885 Clemenceau gave up his position as deputy for the Seine because of growing opposition there to his radical positions, and sought and won a seat in the Var. During the Wilson Affair (qv), he was mainly responsible for the fall of Jules Grévy (qv). An opponent of imperial expansion, the Old Tiger, as Clemenceau was known, argued that imperialism detracted from the Revanche which he advocated. In the Chamber, he constantly clashed with colonialists, arguing that the troops being used in Africa and in Asia would be better employed on the Franco-German border. As a result of the Panama Affair (qv), he lost his position as a deputy. After his defeat in 1893, he turned his hand to journalism, founding the newspaper *L'Aurore*. In 1902 Clemenceau became a senator for the Var, and in 1906 took the portfolio of the interior ministry. The same year he formed his own government, basically a traditional one which enforced anti-clerical laws moderately and maintained a continuity in colonial affairs. He clashed with French labour over several key issues, not the least of which was the attitudes of the *Confédération Générale du Travail* (CGT) (qv) against military conscription, service and discipline. His attitudes toward the CGT and the strike became increasingly hostile. In early 1906 he called out the French army to break a miners' strike in Pas-de-Calais, and a year later French troops were sent into Montpellier. This did not mean, however, that Clemenceau was unwilling to aid the legitimate demands of labour, and in his 1906 government, he placed René Viviani (qv), a socialist, at the newly created ministry of labour. By 1909 he had become a foe of Joseph Caillaux (qv), and the Old Tiger also basically opposed Poincaré's (qv) policies during the first years of World War I. He accused Caillaux and Interior Minister Malvy (qv) of treason. On 16 November 1917 Clemenceau became premier. At the pinnacle of his popularity, he attended the Versailles Conference in 1918 and pushed France's claims for reparations and a harsh policy towards defeated Germany. In 1920 he was defeated for the office of president, for which he did not actually campaign. Clemenceau retired from the senate post for the Var and from public life. He devoted the remainder of his life to travel, lecturing and writing, and died in Paris on 25 November 1929.

Cobden-Chevalier Treaty   This treaty was of special interest to Napoléon III (qv), who seemed to favour free trade. In signing it with Britain on 23 January 1860, France pledged a massive reduction of tariffs on British goods. This treaty followed Napoléon's efforts in Belgium, Switzerland and the German Zollverein, but ironically it alienated French industrialists and British commercial interests. In the long run, the treaty proved to be a failure, because of the antagonism within Britain and France.

Cochin, Denys (1851–1922) A conservative republican, Denys Cochin entered the Chamber as a deputy for the Seine in 1893 and held that post until 1919 when illness forced him to resign. Active in colonial affairs, Cochin also held posts within various ministries. In 1915 he was a minister of state in the Briand (qv) cabinet, and in 1916 he served as undersecretary of state for foreign affairs under Briand. He held the same post in 1917 under Alexandre Ribot (qv). Ill-health forced him to refuse future positions, and in 1919 he retired from public life.

Code de la Famille After World War I the birthrate in France began to drop seriously. In July 1939 the Chamber passed the *Code de la Famille* as a response to the situation. The code aimed specifically at increasing the size of French families and at helping to preserve the traditional family unit. The state began, under the code, to supplement the wages of a man who had children: for example, a father with four children received a subsidy equal to his earned wages. The more children in a family, the higher went the stipend. After World War II the Fourth Republic raised the benefits. However, it appears that the *Code de la Famille* did little to contribute to the upward trend of births after 1945. Despite the debate, which still rages, over its effects, it is clear that the *Code de la Famille* of 1939 stands as a major piece of social legislation in France.

Collot d'Hérbois, Jean-Marie (1750–1796) A successful professional actor with a crude personality but brilliant mind, Collot d'Hérbois resented his low social standing because of his profession. He became a violent revolutionary, and in 1793 entered the Committee of Public Safety. He tended to be excessively violent, and his actions in suppressing counter-revolutionary activity in the city of Lyon distressed the Assembly. Collot d'Hérbois survived Thermidor but was deported in 1794 because of the many excesses during his tenure on the Committee of Public Safety.

Combes, Emile (1835–1921) A student of philosophy and

Catholic theology, Combes displayed a brilliant but argumentative mind. In middle age he turned his attention toward politics and entered the legislature in 1885 as a senator, a position he maintained until his death in 1921. In 1895 he held the post of public instruction in the first Léon Bourgeois (qv) cabinet. Combes formed his own ministry in June 1902, taking for himself the portfolio of the interior ministry. He demanded legislation to separate church and state from 1902 to 1905, when the Chamber passed a series of laws separating the two. His actions, and the vigorous application of the laws by General Louis André (qv), the war minister, caused distress and civil disturbances in France. After Combes's fall in 1905 there was an attempt to undo some of the basic laws in order to restore calm. In the Aristide Briand (qv) cabinet of 1915, Combes assumed the portfolio of a minister of state. Owing to age and ill health he retired from cabinet politics and, after 1915, devoted himself to his senatorial duties.

Comité de l'Afrique Française The committee for French Africa, dedicated to the cause of imperial expansion in Africa, was founded in Paris in 1890 by Eugène Etienne (qv) and other major colonialists. Dedicated to militant expansion, the *comité* influenced expansionist and diplomatic policies in regard to imperialism in Africa. The *comité* became France's most influential imperialist lobby and served as a parent group for other organisations such as the *Comité du Maroc* (qv).

Comité de l'Asie Française In 1901 Eugène Etienne (qv) and members of the *Comité de l'Afrique française* (qv) and the *Union coloniale française* (qv) founded the committee for French Asia. The main purposes of the new *comité* were basically to create interest in the French colonies in Indo-China and to stimulate colonisation in the area. The possibility of carrying the French flag into China was a definite reality for Etienne and the members. However, the *Comité de l'Asie française* was the least popular of all imperialist groups.

Comité de Salut Public A law passed during the difficult days of March and April 1793 established a committee to prosecute the war against the autocratic invaders. Jacobin-controlled, this committee had executive functions. Created on 6 April 1793 by the Assembly, it fell under the control of Danton (qv), but Danton and his followers failed to halt rising prices or master the military situation. With the addition of Robespierre (qv) and Saint-Just (qv) to the committee, radicalism appeared to be taking over. In late May 1793, the *comité* began a small, but systematic purge of the Convention. By August 1793 (Robespierre had joined the committee on 27 July 1793), the extremists were in full control of the committee, although not all its twelve members were in full sympathy with its terrorist methods. Under the *comité* the *levée en masse* (qv) was decreed, and after 5 September 1793 the Terror was introduced as an official *comité* policy. Purging France of royalists, hoarders, Girondins (qv) and finally Jacobins, Robespierre and the Committee of Public Safety brought a wave of fear which culminated in the reaction of 9 Thermidor (qv). Robespierre died on 27 July 1794 and attacks began on the committee on 28 July. In 1795 the Committee of Public Safety ceased to exist.

Comité des Forges de France This organisation, a combination of steel manufacturers, was formed in 1864 and quickly became one of the most influential industrial associations in France. After the 1887 law allowing *syndicats* (qv) the *comité* reorganised itself to meet modern demands. It pressured governments to pass protective tariff laws for the benefit of the steel industry, and in the main remained opposed to socialist demands for reformist, social legislation.

Comité du Madagascar Founded in the 1890s by the French imperialists, the Madagascar committee supported French colonial efforts on the East African island. After 1896 the *comité* encouraged European colonisation on the island and supported the administration of General Joseph Galliéni (qv). The *Union coloniale* (qv) and Joseph Chailley-Bert (qv), editor of the *Quinzaine Coloniale*, gave time and money freely to the committee. Eugène Etienne (qv), a member of the *Comité du*

73

Madagascar, also helped to popularise the cause of French expansionism on the island of Madagascar.

Comité du Maroc   The committee for Morocco was founded in 1904 by the membership of the *Comité de l'Afrique française* (qv). Its primary purpose was to popularise French colonial efforts regarding the annexation of Morocco. The *Comité du Maroc* acted as a powerful lobby, pressuring the government and especially Théophile Delcassé (qv), the minister of foreign affairs, to take strong action in respect of the question of Moroccan annexation. The *comité* faded as a force in colonial affairs after the Treaty of Fez, 1912 (qv), which brought Morocco into France's North African empire.

Comité Français de la Libération Nationale (CFLN) The CFLN took the place of the *Comité National Français* (CNF) (qv) in 1943. It was created in Algiers by General Charles de Gaulle (qv) and General Giraud on 3 June 1943; by August Russia, Britain and the United States established official relations with the CFLN. By June 1944 de Gaulle had emerged as the head of the CFLN. In May 1944, without the approval of the allies, the committee decided to reconstitute itself as Provisional Government of the French Republic. The allies continually refused to recognise the Provisional Government, and maintained that in 1944 France had no governmental structure. In reality, however, the Provisional Government of 1944 (qv) was the government of France.

Confédération Générale de la Production Française (CGPF) In the 1920s a group of industrialists banded together in the CGPF. These bosses, conservative in political and social philosophy, were known as the *Patronat*, and they were forced to negotiate the Matignon accords (qv) in 1936. Especially repugnant to the *Patronat* were the sections of the Matignon accords which provided for collective bargaining (section I), for the recognition of a labourer's right to membership in a union (section III), for an immediate rise in pay beginning on the day the workers went back to the plants (section IV), and for the receiving of grievances by shop stewards (section V).

74

By 1936 the *Patronat* were openly fearful of the left, especially the CGT (qv), and they made great concessions. However, these industrialists were openly hostile to parliamentary government after the 1936 accords.

Confédération Générale du Travail (CGT)   The CGT, the French national labour union organisation, was set up in 1895. This union was not adverse to violent strikes and even sabotage to help the position of French workers. After World War I the CGT was divided over the question of participation with the French communists and openly preferred not to act with them, despite the failure of some CGT-led strikes in 1919. In 1920 the CGT split into two factions, the traditional labour unionists and the communists. The CGT leadership participated in the riots of 6 February 1934 (qv), and promised to participate in joint political action with the socialists and even the communists. In 1936 the CGT supported the election of Léon Blum (qv) and his Popular Front (qv) government. In 1936 the CGT participated in the widespread strikes which brought about a standstill in French production. Labourers occupied the factories, and the leadership of the CGT called on Léon Blum to aid them since they had aided Blum in the elections of 1936. The resultant Matignon accords (qv) were called a charter for labour in France. The CGT supported the concept of compulsory arbitration, the forty-hour week and the paid annual vacation which became law under the Popular Front. In 1939 general strikes were called by this union which in turn alienated the right wing. During the Vichy period the CGT, socialists and communists united to oppose the Nazis, but in 1946 after liberation violent ideological conflicts between the CGT and communists broke out again. However, after 1950 the CGT began to lose votes and influence as a political action force because of a divided labour movement and weak leadership. In May 1958 when General Charles de Gaulle (qv) came to power the CGT shunned violent action, but did call a general strike against de Gaulle's assumption of power. After 1945 it was controlled by the Communist Party. The

CGT lost some influence during the first year of the Fifth Republic, but it has since shown strong signs of revitalisation.

Comité National Français (CNF)   On 23 September 1941 in London, General Charles de Gaulle (qv) proclaimed the formation of the CNF, which had two basic goals: the liberation of France and the restoration of civil government in France during and after liberation. By January 1942 the CNF had been recognised by twenty-one sovereign states and by those European governments in exile residing in London. After the allied invasions of North Africa in 1942 the CNF moved to Algeria where it was replaced by the *Comité Français de la Libération Nationale* (CFLN) (qv).

Comité National de la Résistance (CNR)   The CNR was one of the major resistance organisations in France during the Nazi occupation (1940–4). In theory the CNR, founded in 1942, coordinated the various groups in France, but it continually had difficulties with the communist resistance groups. In May 1943 General Charles de Gaulle (qv) recognised that the CNR should consist of representatives of all political factions, even those who might be potentially anti-Gaullist in nature. During the liberation of Paris (August 1944) the CNR played a vital role, but again had difficulties with the communists. When de Gaulle arrived in Paris he manifested a disdain for the CNR and *Comité Parisien de la Libération* (CPL) (qv) leaders, and claimed that they had to call on him, as chief of state. De Gaulle's main aim in downgrading the CNR was to establish himself as chief of state, not as a resistance leader.

Comité Parisien de la Libération (CPL)   The Paris committee for the liberation was founded during the occupation to drive out the German forces. It participated in the August 1944 fighting, but suffered the same fate as the *Comité National de la Résistance* (CNR) (qv). The CPL was downgraded when General Charles de Gaulle (qv) entered Paris as chief of state in August 1944.

Communards, The   The name 'communard' is applied to those who supported and fought for the Paris Commune of

1871 (qv). They also called themselves federals since many believed in a federal system for France.

Communauté Européene de Défense (CED) On 27 May 1952 Italy, Belgium, Luxembourg, West Germany and France, despite great internal opposition and governmental reluctance, signed an accord in Paris which created the European Defence Community. The western European states, led by France, on 26 May 1952, had ended the inferior status of West Germany, opening the way for the signing of the CED accords. These called for an executive committee of nine members, an assembly and a council of ministers drawn from the member states. Troops and finances were to be contributed by each member state. On 1 August 1952 West Germany officially ended her post-war occupied status, and also on that date Britain adhered to the Paris protocols.

Commune of 1871 With the downfall of the Second Empire in 1870, France, especially Paris, was in a turmoil. The new Assembly meeting at Bordeaux was openly conservative in nature, and actively sought peace with the Germans. This was viewed in Paris as treason, and passions reached boiling point. In March the Assembly, fearing the volatile nature of the Paris citizens, chose to move from Bordeaux to Versailles. By 18 March 1871 Adolphe Thiers (qv) had decided to disarm Paris, and this touched off an insurrection. Paris declared itself to be a commune and called on the rest of France to follow her example. Class differences divided the Paris population into federals, or communards, and supporters of the Versailles government. Contrary to popular traditions, the Commune did not manifest radical or extreme leftist tendencies. Communard legislation included, for example, the extension of debts for three years, a moratorium on rents and price controls on bread. In May Thiers used force against the Commune, which resulted in great destruction and loss of life. The Tuileries was burned, but the Louvre was saved. Over 25,000 died in the fighting during the 'bloody week', and many thousands more were deported to Algeria and New

Caledonia. The Commune left a bitter scar which separated the working classes of Paris into a hostile group which, since the suppression of the Commune of 1871, has remained hostile to the government. The murder of hostages by the communards tinged the Commune with Jacobin terrorism.

Compiègne, Armistice of On 22 June 1940 General Hutzinger representing France and General Kietel representing Germany signed an armistice which ended the fighting between the two states. In early May 1940 German troops had smashed through Belgium into France. Within forty days the French were defeated and the Third Republic was dead. After the fall of Paris on 13 June the French brought Marshal Henri Philippe Pétain (qv) from his post as ambassador to Spain back to France to head a new government. For all purposes France was divided into an occupied and unoccupied sector, and a permanent peace was put off until the war ended.

Comte, Auguste (1789–1857) An excellent student, Comte, who was born at Montpellier on 18 January 1789, displayed an amazing memory. In 1815 he entered the *Ecole Polytechnique* where he held a brilliant record, astounding his professors of mathematics. His studies were curtailed because of the Hundred Days (qv). Between 1815 and 1817 he wrote *Mes réflexions* and served as a secretary to Casimir Périer (qv). In 1817 Comte met Saint-Simon (qv) and collaborated with him on several books. After 1821 Comte began to formulate his concept of positivism. His six-volume *Cours de philosophie positive* began to appear in 1830. His fame grew and friends contributed generously to his work which proclaimed science as a key to the positive reorganisation of society for the benefit of humanity. Like Saint-Simonism, positivism had a religious tinge. After the founding of the Positivist Society in 1848, Comte wrote, until severe ulcers of the stomach took his life on 5 September 1857.

Concordat, The On 16 July 1801 Napoléon Bonaparte accepted an agreement drawn up by French and clerical authorities in both Rome and Paris. Bonaparte felt the necessity of restoring some semblance of order to France's religious life.

While he was not a religious man, he knew that the upheavals of the revolutionary period had distressed a number of people in France. Catholicism was recognised as the religion of the majority of French people, and not the state religion. The state placed churches and chapels at the disposal of the bishops, who were now chosen by joint decision by the papacy and the French state. Bishops appointed curés. The bishops and curés, who took an oath to the state, were paid by the government. The Pope recognised revolutionary changes and the sale of ecclesiastical lands in France. The church in France was, for all purposes, subservient to the state, and the papacy recognised revolutionary civil marriages and civil birth records. The Concordat, publicly proclaimed in 1802, had a mixed reaction in France, but in the long run it was accepted and assisted Bonaparte's rise in popularity.

Condorcet, Marie Jean, Marquis de (1743–1794) Known as the last of the *philosophes*, Condorcet, who was born at Ribemont in the Aisne on 17 April 1743, was a philosopher, mathematician, journalist and revolutionary politician. He was a well-known author prior to 1789, and in 1782 he was admitted to the *Académie Française*. In 1789 he was elected to the Legislative Assembly and immediately became a leader. Condorcet tended to vote with the Girondins (qv), but he never officially sat with that group. He preferred to devote his time to the construction of an enlightened constitution for France. For his voting record he earned the hatred of the Jacobins (qv), and during the purge of the Girondins, he was arrested and sent to prison. While in prison he died on 29 March 1794.

Confédération Générale du Travail Unitaire (CGTU) This national labour union was openly dominated by communists and was allied to the platform of the French Communist Party. The CGTU was formed in 1920 when the *Confédération Générale du Travail* (CGT) (qv) split into rival factions but under Léon Blum's (qv) Popular Front they were momentarily united. The CGTU was, however, uneasy in this brief alliance. During the summer and fall of 1939 the leadership of the CGTU were openly divided on the question of Nazi Germany.

Conseil National du Patronat Français (CNPF) This council had its origins in the concept of the corporate state during the Vichy period. It was unpopular in the Fourth Republic as politicians avoided any official connection with it. However, the CNPF was known to contribute heavily to political campaigns, and the organisation was exceedingly discreet in its financial support of candidates. In 1951 the CNPF tried seriously to weaken the Coal and Steel Community of Europe and France's participation in it by treaty. The CNPF lost a great deal of respect when the treaty was ratified by a massive majority in the chamber. After this defeat the CNPF lost influence, but continued to contribute to all parties except the extreme socialists and the communists.

Considérant, Prosper Victor (1808–1893) Considérant, a socialist theoretician, was born at Salins on 18 October 1808. He entered the army but resigned in 1831 and became a follower of Charles Fourier (qv). Considérant wrote *Noveau monde* and *Réforme industrielle*. He helped found *La Phalange* and *Democratie pacifique*. In 1848 he was elected to the assembly and argued for socialist reforms for labour. However, he was exiled to Belgium in 1849. In 1853 he journeyed to the state of Texas in the United States to establish a Fourier-type commune which failed. Disgusted with his failures, he returned to France in 1869 and went into retirement until his death in Paris on 27 December 1893. His principal books, laced with Fourier philosophy and socialist concepts, were *Destinée sociale* (1834–44) in three volumes, *Le Socialisme devant le vieux monde* (1849), and *Texas* (1854).

Continental System By 1807 Napoléon I had decided to close European markets to the British in the hopes of ruining England's economy. On 21 November 1806 he issued the Berlin Decree, and he followed it with the Milan Decree of 17 December 1807. Both decrees aimed directly at British commerce. The British had, on 16 May 1806, issued an Order in Council which declared most European ports to be in a state of blockade. Napoléon countered in Berlin, stating that England was blockaded and that no European state could trade in English goods. The British reacted on 7 January 1807 by declaring that no neutral could trade with France. The Milan Decree applied to neutral ships which allowed a British search. The ships were 'denationalised', as a result of the British search and would be considered a lawful prize of war. For all practical purposes, the continent was sealed as far as British shipping was concerned, but smuggling brought English goods into Europe in vast amounts. Napoléon Bonaparte, however, did not foresee that the creation of the Continental System would force him to invade Spain to strike at England's Portuguese allies in 1807. The system also brought Napoléon to Tilsit (qv) in 1807 to negotiate with Tsar Alexander I. In the long run the Continental System proved costly to the French, who were increasingly overextended, and by 1810 Bonaparte was forced to alter the system drastically.

Corday d'Armont, Charlotte (1768–1793) Of a poor but noble Norman family, she remained after 1789 a royalist. Probably mentally unbalanced, Charlotte Corday was deeply affected by the fall of the Girondins, royalist propaganda and the rise of the Jacobins (qv). On 13 July 1793 she stabbed Marat (qv), who was taking a bath at the time, and paid for this deed with her life. Marat was popular with the mobs of Paris, and his death brought a wave of discontent to the volatile city. This murder strengthened the hand of the Jacobin extremists who were demanding harsh measures in dealing with political conditions within France.

Cordeliers, Club des The *Club des Cordeliers* was under the leadership of Danton (qv) and Marat (qv). The dues were lower than for other clubs, and it attracted more members. Its rhetoric was even more vehement and violent. As an ultra-revolutionary club the Cordeliers denounced Louis XVI (qv) in April 1791 in violent terms, and after the king's escape attempt they presented petitions favouring his suspension as king. By October they were participating in violence, and often their demonstrations had to be dispersed by troops. The Committee of Public Safety (qv), sensing the potential danger of the Cordeliers, moved to arrest many of its leaders who seemed now to oppose Jacobin (qv) policies. After the Terror the Cordeliers lost power and influence.

Corps Législatif A combination of the Council of Five Hundred (qv) and the Council of Ancients (qv) served as the legislative branch during the Directory. The Board of Five Directors (qv) was responsible to the legislative corps. Under Napoléon Bonaparte (qv) the *Corps Législatif* became something quite different. Legislative powers were actually in the hands of four bodies: the tribunate, the *Corps Législatif* which made up the legislature, and the Council of State, plus a conservative Senate. The *Corps Législatif*, comprising about 300 members, heard debate and then either enacted or rejected legislation. The action taken on legislation by the corps was done by secret ballot. Certainly, even under Bonaparte, the corps did have power of legislation within limits. By the Constitution of Year XII (1804), which established the empire, the *Corps Législatif*, like the other bodies, lost power. On 21 March 1804 the corps enacted the Napoleonic Code. In 1814, however, the corps tried to show independence and Bonaparte merely ordered it to adjourn rather than see it interfere in his plans to confront the allies in Germany. Louis XVIII (qv), in 1814, promised to maintain the corps, and by the Charter of 1814 (qv) the *Corps Législatif* became the Chamber of Deputies.

Corvée Known as the Royal Corvée, this institution was for all practical purposes a tax which bound the peasants to contribute a specified number of days to work on royal highways and to assist in the transport of troops. The tax was therefore paid in manual labour rather than money. Turgot (qv) first raised the issue of reform of the *Corvée*, and Calonne (qv) proposed in 1787 to do away with it. In 1790 the *Corvée* was altered and later completely abolished.

Cot, Pierre (1895–   )   Pierre Cot was France's leading exponent of aviation development during the Third Republic. He entered the Chamber in 1928 as a radical socialist deputy from the Savoy and held that post until 1942, when he exiled himself from France. Refusing to rally to Charles de Gaulle (qv), Cot remained in the United States until the end of the war. From 1951 to 1958 he held the post of deputy for the Rhône. Under Paul-Boncour in 1932 he was undersecretary of state for foreign affairs and in 1933 Daladier (qv) gave him the new portfolio of the air ministry. Cot held this post under Albert Sarraut (qv) in 1933, Camille Chautemps (qv) in 1933, Edouard Daladier in 1934, Léon Blum (qv) in 1936 and Chautemps again in 1937. After his re-election as deputy in 1951 Cot played a major role in political debates, and often allied with the Communist Party. He was a leader of the Progressive Party, which allied with the extreme left to block legislation, and gained the reputation of an obstructionist. He opposed de Gaulle's elevation to the premiership in 1958.

Coty, François (1874–1934)   A French perfume magnate, Coty, who from 1923 to 1924 represented Corsica as a senator, founded the ultra-right-wing *Solidarité française* in the 1930s. This group recruited members from the dissaffected middle class.

Coty, René (1882–1962)   Elected deputy in 1923, Coty was re-elected in 1935 and again in 1941. In 1954 he was elected president of the Republic and served until 1958. Coty was basically a traditionalist, but still tried to come to political terms with the French communists, thereby keeping them within the traditional framework of the republic. Much of Coty's four-year term was occupied with colonial crises such as the ending of the Indo-Chinese war and the critical Algerian rebellion. It was Coty who believed as early as 1954 that France's salvation rested with the strong leadership offered by General de Gaulle (qv), and Coty helped pave the way for de Gaulle's assumption of power in 1958.

Couthon, Georges (1756–1794)   A lawyer from the

83

provinces who was known as a gentle, dedicated humanitarian. After a brief and unspectacular period in the Provincial Assembly of 1787, Couthon set his sights on a political career. During this period he began to feel the effects of meningitis which would render him, by 1793, a cripple with no use of his legs. The affliction affected him, as he became a vehement revolutionary. In 1793 Deputy Couthon was elected to the Committee of Public Safety (qv). He sided with Saint-Just (qv) and Robespierre (qv) and participated in the Terror. While on the committee Couthon displayed a fanatic's zeal, and in 1793 he led the units which brought terrible destruction to the city of Lyon. Couthon fell with Robespierre and Saint-Just on 9 Thermidor (qv) and went with them to the guillotine on 10 Thermidor.

Couve de Murville, Maurice (1907–   ) A well-educated man, Couve de Murville holds degrees in literature and law. By profession he was a civil servant specialising in finance. In 1943, disgusted with Vichy policies, he rallied to the Gaullist resistance and served as a key member of the French National Liberation Committee. From 1945 to 1950 he served in the Quai d'Orsay, proving himself to be a capable diplomat. In 1954 Couve de Murville became France's permanent delegate to the North Atlantic Treaty Organisation. From 1946 to 1958 he remained close to General de Gaulle (qv), and used his position to enhance Gaullism. In 1945 he was appointed ambassador to Italy, in 1950 he held the post of ambassador to Egypt, and in 1955 he served a year as ambassador to the United States. From 1956 to 1958 he was ambassador to Germany. After June 1958 Couve de Murville held the post of foreign minister until he retired from public life.

Crampel, Paul (1864–1891) A noted French explorer, Crampel was known for his explorations around Lake Chad. From 1887 to 1889 he served as secretary for de Brazza (qv) and won the respect of the famed explorer of the Congo. In 1890 Crampel was chosen by the colonial undersecretariat and the Paris colonialists to head an expedition into Central Africa, but in 1891 he was slain while mapping that area. Known as a brutal man, Crampel nevertheless stands as an excellent explorer and was a major contributor to the founding of French Africa.

Crédit Lyonnais   Established in 1863 by Henri Germain in Lyon, the *Crédit Lyonnais* first acted as a purely local bank. In 1864 it established a branch in Paris which later became its headquarters. By the 1880s it had over seventy branch banks in every major French city. Playing a large role in French finance, the *Crédit Lyonnais* cosigned government loans for France in America during World War I. In the 1930s the bank was one of the major financial powers in France and was subjected to attacks from the left, which demanded that it be nationalised. The bank was brought under some control in the 1940s when the government attempted to centralise banking. However, this process was soon altered.

Crédit Mobilier   Created in 1852, the *Société générale de Crédit Mobilier* provided capital for industrialisation and railway building. The *Crédit Mobilier* had the support of Napoléon III (qv) and the Duc de Persigny (qv), which gave it a prime position among French financial institutions. It floated loans and issued bonds, quickly becoming one of the most important economic ventures in France. From 1852 to 1870 the *Crédit Mobilier* was responsible for building up to 18,000km of railway. By the late 1850s the *Crédit Mobilier* extended its influence outside France into Spain, Italy, and elsewhere. However, by 1856 the directors were fighting the influence of the Bank of France (qv) and other financial establishments which threatened to reduce its influence. In 1867, after a bitter confrontation with the Bank of France, the *Crédit Mobilier* fell and was dissolved as a company. A new company, the *Société de Crédit Mobilier Français*, was created and, while never reaching the peaks of financial glory attained by the old *Crédit Mobilier*, retained a strong position until it too fell during the depression of the 1930s.

Crémieux, Isaac Moise (Adolphe) (1796–1880)   Born

to a noted Jewish family from the Languedoc, Crémieux became a lawyer in Nîmes in 1817. In 1830 he went to the *Cour de Cassation* and made a reputation by 1835 as a defender of liberal causes. He was elected deputy in 1842, and in February 1848 became a member of the provisional government until April. Later, on 9 May 1848, he became a member of the Executive Commission (qv). As a minister of justice, Crémieux argued against the death penalty for political crimes. After the coup d'état of December 1851, Crémieux announced his opposition to Napoléon III and the empire and returned to law. Elected to the *Corps législatif* (qv) in 1869, Crémieux was active in the Government of National Defence of 1870 under Léon Gambetta, who had once been Crémieux's secretary. In 1870, Crémieux issued his famous decree which enfranchised the Jews of Algeria and gave them citizenship. In 1871 Crémieux was elected deputy from the Algerian Department of Algiers, and in 1875 he was elected senator.

Croix de Feu The Cross of Fire, a paramilitary, rightwing organisation of veterans, was founded by Colonel François de la Rocque (qv) in 1931. Devoted to extremist violence, this organisation was tinged with fascist ideology and was openly anti-parliamentary. Quite probably the government under André Tardieu (qv) gave some funds to the *Croix de Feu*, and in 1934 the organisation participated in the violent riots of 6 February 1934 (qv) in Paris. After 1936 the *Croix de Feu* moved more to the right and was openly in support of Mussolini. In 1936 Colonel de la Rocque renamed the group the *Parti social français*, and this party moved even more to the right.

Daladier, Edouard (1884–   ) A professional historian, Daladier left a teaching post to seek a career in politics. Elected deputy in 1919, he became known for an analytical mind and calmness in the face of adversity. A staunch defender of internal order, Daladier was the Chamber's choice for premier in February 1934 and was stern in dealing with the riots of 6 February 1934 (qv), earning the title *le fusilleur*. However,

Daladier's popularity waned when he imposed a drastic 6 per cent reduction in state salaries to save France's economic structure. Ousted because of the deteriorating financial situation, he was recalled to the premiership on 10 April 1938. In September Daladier and his foreign minister visited London in order to present a united front against Hitler's demands on Czechoslovakia, but in late September Daladier went to Munich to agree to the first dismemberment of Czechoslovakia. Arrested after the fall of France, he was tried at Riom (qv) and was incarcerated. He defended his pre-war actions successfully before a French inquiry after World War II. From 1946 to 1958 he sat as a deputy who opposed a Franco-German rapprochement in the post-war world. However, Daladier was never fully able to live down his role in the Munich crisis and the fall of France in 1940.

Danton, Georges Jacques (1759–1794)　Born at Arcis sur Aube on 28 October 1759, Danton was in 1790 named elector of the department of Paris, where he enjoyed great popularity with the mobs. Fearing the rise of the Jacobins (qv), he helped found the *Club des Cordeliers* (qv). After Louis XVI's escape attempt he voted to depose the king. After the massacre of the Champs de Mars he fled to Britain, but returned in 1792. Danton gathered about him a group of men who became known as the Dantonists or Indulgents. In 1793 Danton, who sat with the Montagnards (qv), entered briefly into the Committee of Public Safety where, for a while, he cooperated with Robespierre (qv). He assisted in the purge of the Girondins, but later argued with Robespierre over the policies of the Terror. Danton's Indulgents formed an opposition to Robespierre's government, and for this opposition Robespierre plotted the downfall of Danton. He was arrested on the orders of Robespierre and executed. Danton's death on the guillotine on 5 April 1794 sparked fear among France's political leaders and set in motion a reaction against Robespierre and the Terror.

Darlan, François (1881–1942)　A career naval officer who saw service in China and during World War I, Darlan entered the ministry of the navy in a minor post in 1926. From 1929 to 1934 he held the same post, and made the reputation of being a conservative and a nationalist. In 1939 he became commander in chief of the navy and a close confidant of Marshal Henri Pétain (qv). After the fall of France, he advocated collaborationism and replaced Pierre Laval (qv) as Vichy prime minister. In November 1942 he tried to join the allies. Darlan went to Algiers as a senior Vichy official, and he alone had the force to stop the fighting in North Africa, but his close connections with the Vichy government made him suspect in the eyes of the allies. He was murdered by a fanatic in Algiers.

Daudet, Léon (1867–1942) An extreme right-wing journalist and politician, Daudet edited and wrote for the journal of the *Action Française* (qv) from 1908 to 1928. From 1919 to 1924 he represented the Seine as a deputy. In 1927 he was arrested because of his virulent anti-semitism and his attacks on the government. He fled to Belgium and remained in exile until pardoned in 1929. During the 1930s Daudet continued to support rightist causes and defend the concepts of French fascism. He was also an early staunch supporter of the Vichy government.

Davout, Louis, Prince d'Eckmuhl (1770–1823) A noble supporter of the revolution, Davout fought on the Rhine in 1797. In Egypt he attached himself to the fortunes of Napoléon Bonaparte (qv). In 1804 he became a marshal of France. At the battle of Jena (qv) on 14 October 1806, Davout carried the day for Napoléon by defeating a superior force at Auerstadt. For this great victory Napoléon gave Davout's corps the right to be the first French troops to enter Berlin on 25 October. After Tilsit he was made governor general of the Grand Duchy of Varsovie. At the battle of Wagram, Davout distinguished himself, and later Napoléon gave him the task of preparing the invasion of Russia. He served in Russia but rallied to Louis XVIII in May 1814, surrendering to the allies the German port-city of Hamburg which he had been ordered to defend. During the Hundred Days he joined Bonaparte briefly as

88

minister of war and was retired in semi-disgrace until 1819, when he was allowed to re-enter public life as a member of the Chamber.

Déat, Marcel (1894–1955)   Marcel Déat was a vocal rightist politician who played a vital role in politics prior to World War II. In 1926 he entered the Chamber as a deputy from the Marne, but two years later lost his position. From 1932 to 1942 he represented the district of Charente and served as minister for air in the Albert Sarraut (qv) cabinet of 1936. After 1936 he turned to the right, proposing cooperation with Germany. He helped form and head the *Rassemblement National Populaire*, a rightist, pro-German organisation. During the Vichy period Déat was a leading advocate of collaboration with Nazi Germany.

Debré, Michel (1912–   )   A career civil servant, Debré in 1934 entered the government serving on the Council of State. In 1940 Debré fought against the German invasion, but was taken prisoner. After a daring escape, he joined the resistance, becoming one of its leaders. In 1945 de Gaulle (qv) asked him to join his personal staff. In 1947 he served as the French administrator for German and Austrian affairs, and from 1948 to 1958 as a senator. During that ten-year period Michel Debré became known as an advocate of European cooperation. When de Gaulle became the last premier of the Fourth Republic in May and June 1958, he asked Debré to serve as minister of justice. In this ministry, Debré was responsible for the drafting of the constitution of the Fifth Republic. He helped found the *Union pour la Nouvelle République* (UNR) (qv) in 1958, and from 1959 to 1962 he served as premier. In 1966 Debré served as minister of economy and finances and in 1968 he held the post of foreign minister.

Decazes, Elie, Duc de (1780–1860)   The Duc de Decazes was born at Saint Martin de Laye on 28 October 1780. He served Louis XVIII (qv) in 1815 as minister of police and later assumed the portfolio of the interior ministry. Louis XVIII doted on Decazes and placed a great deal of reliance on him.

A moderate, Decazes was looked upon by the ultra-royalists as a traitor to the restoration when he demanded that press restrictions be lifted in France. Decazes was toppled from power in 1820 after the murder of the Duc de Berry (qv). From 1820 to 1821 he served as ambassador to Britain, and in 1830 he rallied to Louis-Philippe, but soon retired to private life to attend to his business interests. He died at Decazeville on 24 October 1860.

Decree of 3 January 1946 (economic planning) On 3 January 1946 the French government prepared the basis for long-range economic planning by issuing the decree which called for the drafting of comprehensive economic plans. In the wake of the destruction wrought by World War II, sensible planning was an absolute necessity. The decree called for a council of planning and productivity, with members from management, industry and agriculture. This council was charged with the responsibility of reporting back to the government economic planning proposals. A general commission for planning and productivity was also set up. This commission had the duty of preparing proposals to be submitted to the government. Out of this decree, set of councils and subsequent actions grew the Four-Year Plans of the Fourth and Fifth Republics (1946–52, 1954–7, 1958–61, 1962–5). In May 1961 President Charles de Gaulle (qv) reaffirmed France's determination to continue the plans because it was 'on [its] continued progress that [France's] whole destiny now depends'.

de Gaulle, Charles (1890–1970) Charles de Gaulle, born in Lille on 22 November 1890, was obsessed with history and the past glories of France. In 1913 he entered the army, and while serving in World War I was wounded and taken prisoner by the Germans. After the war, de Gaulle remained in the army, but became distressed at the decaying condition of the French military. He wrote a number of books advocating a drastic revaluation of the French armed forces. When World War II broke out, de Gaulle, a colonel, was in command of a tank unit. Promoted to general, he entered the government as an undersecretary of state for war. In June 1940 he fled to England to encourage a continued fight against the Germans' occupation of France. Condemned by the Vichy government as a traitor and distrusted by American President Franklin D. Roosevelt, de Gaulle laboured to win for France a position of respect. By keeping most of the resistance forces under his command, he was able to control the direction of French anti-German and anti-Vichy policies. Returning to France in 1944, de Gaulle established himself as provisional president, but in 1946, after a losing campaign for a strong constitution, he resigned from power and went into retirement. Believing that the weak, parliament-dominated Fourth Republic would collapse, de Gaulle simply waited for a call by the nation for his return to power. In 1958, as a result of the Algerian war and a revolt of the military in Algiers, the Chamber and the Government ceased to function. Premier Pflimlin (qv) stood aside for de Gaulle to become the last premier of the Fourth Republic. The Fifth Republic, established by de Gaulle, was basically a strong, centralised government which reflected his own attitudes towards government. Following a nationalistic policy, de Gaulle reduced France's role in NATO, ended the Algerian war in 1962 and revitalised France's economy. Vain and imperious, de Gaulle resigned in 1969 when his plan for a decentralisation of authority in France was rejected. He retired to his country estate near the village of Colombey les Deux Eglises and died on 9 November 1970. De Gaulle left behind, however, a strong republic with a dynamic executive and a lasting, viable Gaullist political party.

Hauteclocque, Jacques Philippe de See: Leclerc, General.

Delcassé, Théophile (1852–1923) Born to a modest but respectable family at Pamiers on 1 March 1852, Delcassé drifted into journalism. He turned his attention toward politics after his marriage to a well-to-do widow, and in 1889 he was elected a deputy, standing for the radical party. In 1893 he became undersecretary of state for the colonies and in 1894 took the portfolio of the newly created colonial ministry. A friend of Eugène Etienne (qv) and a member of the *Comité de l'Afrique française* (qv), Delcassé earned the reputation of being an aggressive expansionist. Under his guidance, the French moved deeper into Africa, challenging the British presence in both East and West Africa. After the Fashoda Crisis of 1898 (qv), Delcassé became foreign minister and turned his attention towards bettering relations with Britain and towards annexing Morocco. In 1900 he concluded an agreement with Italy over Tripoli and Morocco. In 1902 and 1904 Delcassé secured agreements with Spain over Morocco. His greatest diplomatic achievement came on 8 April 1904 when England and France signed the Entente Cordiale (qv) in London. Delcassé, who was regarded by Berlin as an anti-German, was toppled from power in June 1905 as a result of the First Moroccan Crisis (qv). From 1905 to 1911 he advocated a sweeping modernisation of France's navy, and from 1911 to 1913 he served as the minister of the marine. From August 1914 to October 1915 he was foreign minister, but fell from power when Bulgaria joined the war on the side of the central powers. He remained active in politics until he died from a heart attack while in Nice on 22 February 1923.

Délégation des Gauches This leftist group in the Chamber was formed in 1902 and existed until the founding of the *Section Française de l'Internationale Ouvrière* (SFIO) (qv) in 1905. The delegation was founded by Premier Emile Combes (qv) to gain support for his policies in the Chamber and Senate. Jean Jaurès (qv) cooperated with the group, but forced a meeting in Paris (April 1905) to discuss the issue of cooperation with government, which he opposed. Growing out of this meeting was the formation of the SFIO.

Denfert-Rochereau, Pierre Marie (1823–1878) Born at Saint-Maixent on 11 January 1823, a career officer, Denfert-Rochereau graduated from the *Ecole Polytechnique* in 1843 and was sent to Italy in 1849. After a period of service in the Crimea in 1855, he was dispatched to Algeria where he served from

1860 to 1864. While military commandant of Belfort, he was rapidly promoted because of his brilliant record. In 1870 he defended Belfort with heroism and brilliance. After the defeat of France in 1870 Denfert was deeply moved and turned his attention to politics, and in 1871 he was elected to the Assembly as an opponent of peace with Germany. A vehement republican, he was elected as a revanchard and follower of Léon Gambetta (qv). Through his speeches from 1871 to 1878 he became known as an articulate advocate of the Revanche. Denfert-Rochereau died at Versailles on 11 May 1878.

Déroulède, Paul (1846–1914)   A vehement advocate of revenge against Germany, Déroulède founded the *Ligue des patriotes*, a revanchist organisation which included such members as Léon Gambetta (qv). Déroulède, who was born in Paris, became known as a poet who dealt with patriotic themes. In 1872 he published *Chants du soldat,* and three years later he wrote *Nouveaux chants du soldat.* From 1889 to 1893 Déroulède served as a deputy for Charente. However, in 1887 he supported Boulanger and in 1889 plotted against the state. During the Dreyfus affair (qv), Déroulède became known as a vehement opponent of the wrongly accused Jewish officer. Growing out of his strong rightist convictions, Déroulède tried to overthrow the government by a coup d'état in February 1899. It failed and he was exiled in 1900 and lost his following. Allowed to return to France in 1905, he retired from public life.

Desaix, Louis Antoine des Aix (1768–1800)   General Louis Desaix was born to a noble family near Riom on 17 August 1768, and he chose a career in the military. When the revolution broke out in 1789 he offered his sword to revolutionary France. He served with the army of the Rhine in May 1792, and in 1793 he was wounded. For his courage he was promoted to general on the field of battle in 1793. Desaix commanded the first troops in Egypt, and his administration there earned him the title of the 'just sultan'. Napoléon ordered him to France to assist in the Italian campaign, and at the battle of Marengo on 14 June 1800 Desaix was killed.

Deschanel, Paul (1855–1922)   Paul Deschanel, a firm republican, entered the Chamber in 1885 as a deputy for the Eure-et-Loir, and he held that post until 1920. A moderate, Deschanel opposed radicalism, socialism and Boulangism, and this opposition won for him the reputation of a conciliator. From June 1898 to May 1902 he served as president of the Chamber and held the position again from June 1914 to February 1920. Interestingly enough, Deschanel never held a cabinet position during his long career as a deputy. In February 1920, he was elected to the presidency of the republic. However, he had begun to show tendencies towards mental instability, and in 1920 suffered a total mental collapse. Forced to resign from the presidency, Deschanel lived in seclusion until his death in 1922.

Desmoulins, Camille (1760–1794)   Camille Desmoulins was born to an affluent family at Guise on 2 March 1760. While at the College of Louis le Grand, he became friends with Robespierre (qv). By 1785 Desmoulins was a lawyer in Paris. Pursuing a career in journalism, in 1789 he was partly responsible for the agitation which led to riots in Paris after the dismissal of Necker (qv) on 11 July 1789. A republican, he helped found the *Club des Cordeliers*, and he edited *Les Révolutions de France et de Brabant*. He violently attacked the Girondins (qv) in 1792 in a widely circulated tract entitled *Brissot démasqué*, and later that year became a secretary to Danton (qv). Desmoulins served in the Convention sitting with the Montagnards (qv) and again attacked the Girondins. Desmoulins used the pen again in attacking the Girondins by publishing *Histoire des Brissotins* in April 1793. He served the Terror but came to fear the rising power of Robespierre. Desmoulins, a popular orator and republican, was arrested and sent to the guillotine with Danton in Paris on 5 April 1794 during the Reign of Terror.

Desmoulins, Lucile (1771–1794)   Anne Louise Duplessis-Laridon was the wife of Camille Desmoulins (qv). She fell in love with the brilliant author and revolutionary at the age of twelve, and in 1790 she married him. Her influence on her husband was great as she constantly encouraged his political and revolutionary work. Lucile Desmoulins was arrested after Camille's execution and was herself sent to the guillotine.

Directory; The Directors   The Directory was a board of five directors chosen by the Council of Five Hundred (qv) and approved by the Council of Ancients (qv). Authorised by the Constitution of 1795, the Directory was comprised of five men. They had to be at least forty years of age and had to have served as a deputy or minister. They appointed governmental ministers, ambassadors, generals, tax collectors, as well as other lesser officials. Every year a new director was chosen, and one director presided over the executive body for a three-month period. Unfortunately for the government of France, the various councils had undue influence on the directors, despite the fact that the Directory was supposed to have some independence. The Directory was an experiment in weak executive powers; it was created because of the fear of dictatorship such as the one which had existed under the Terror of 1793-4, and to prevent the tyranny of the executive apparatus which had been so severe under Robespierre (qv).

Doriot, Jacques (1898–1945)   Doriot, an extremist member of the right, represented the Seine as a deputy from 1924 to 1937. He founded the *Parti Populaire Français*, an extreme rightist party. Doriot was a fanatical exponent of collaboration in 1940, and helped raise troops for the German cause during the period when most of France was under German occupation.

Doumergue, Gaston (1863–1937)   Doumergue began his official service as an administrator in Indo-China from 1890 to 1892 and in Algeria in 1893. He was elected deputy in 1893 for Gard and served as minister of colonies 1902–5, minister of commerce 1906–8, minister of public instruction 1908–10. Elected senator in 1910, he was foreign minister from 1913–14. Doumergue held his senatorial position from the Gard until 1924. From 1924 to 1931 he served as president of the republic and briefly held the post of president of the council of ministers in 1934. After the bloody Riots of 6 February 1934 (qv), Doumergue was called from his retirement to form some sort of government that might pull France together and he formed the Government of National Union on 7 February 1934. He tried to bring in all political factions, such as André Tardieu (qv) and Marshal Pétain (qv) of the right, a few radicals, and a number of moderates. This so-called Doumergue Experiment seemed to calm the situation, but Doumergue tried to reform the Chamber by raising the power of the premier. He alienated many supporters, and in November 1934, his Government of National Union was ousted.

Dreyfus, Alfred (1859–1935)   Captain Alfred Dreyfus was a staff officer of Jewish origin, who was accused of selling military secrets to the Germans in 1894. After an investigation it was determined that there was too little evidence to bring Dreyfus to trial, but the story fell into the hands of Edouard Drumont, who was a professional anti-Jewish writer. During Dreyfus's court martial, which was promoted by Drumont's hysterical ultra-patriotic, anti-semitic ravings, evidence, which was forged, was introduced and Dreyfus was convicted and sentenced to life imprisonment on Devil's Island. By 1898 France had divided into two camps—one supporting Dreyfus and one vehemently opposed to him. Emile Zola's (qv) *J'Accuse* aroused the Dreyfusards, and Jean Jaurès (qv) rallied the left to Dreyfus's cause. In 1899 Dreyfus was retried and found guilty again, but was pardoned by the president of the Republic. By 1900 most informed people believed the culprit to be a Major Esterhazy, who was known to be constantly in debt, and in 1906, after a civilian trial, the minister of war restored Dreyfus to rank and to army command. His health broken, he retired from active service to nurse the illnesses brought on by the rigours of Devil's Island. However, he was recalled to the colours in 1914 and served as major of artillery. The Dreyfus affair had brought to the surface the bitter anti-semitism of the nineteenth century which would plague France up to World War II. The case helped the cause of the Radical Party since many of its leaders supported Dreyfus. The exposé also helped bring about a definite check on the army and the Catholic church.

Droite Constitutionnelle   On 12 March 1890 a number of conservative Catholic deputies founded the Constitutional Right. Led by Jacques Piou (qv), the constitutionalists reluctantly believed that there had to be reconciliation between the Catholic conservatives and the secular republic. These men were mainly wealthy and knew that they needed to adjust their political positions to meet economic need. Many of their efforts were bolstered by the *Fédération electorale* (qv) and Cardinal Lavigerie's (qv) attempt to support the Ralliement (qv). In 1893 the *Droite constitutionnelle* failed, however, to cooperate with conservative republicans and lost a chance for political influence. The opportunists in the late 1890s allied with this group, but men like Louis Barthou (qv) and Raymond Poincaré (qv) refused to cooperate. This doomed the movement in the late 1890s, but it did deal a serious blow to the antirepublican right by openly urging conservative Catholics to support republican principles.

Drouyn de Lhuys, Edouard (1805–1881)   French foreign minister under Napoléon III, de Lhuys assumed that post in 1862 and fought against the anti-clerical policies of the Duc de Persigny (qv). Basically, de Lhuys supported some sort of Italian occupation of Rome which ran counter to Napoléon III's basic Italian-Roman policies. However, contrary to his own feelings, de Lhuys did conclude a convention with the Italians over Rome. This agreement of 15 September 1864 effectively kept the Italians from occupying the city of Rome, while French troops withdrew from the city. During the Austro-Prussian War of 1866 de Lhuys argued that France should make some military demonstration on the Rhine to show Bismarck that French might was real. He was overruled by Napoléon III. The year 1866 was a disaster for de Lhuys. As French troops left Rome according to the 1864 agreement, the Italian patriot Garibaldi marched on the city. French troops were forced to fight alongside papal troops, and Garibaldi's forces were defeated at the battle of Mentana. As a result, Napoléon III's Italian policy collapsed and Franco-Prussian relations were never worse. For these failures Napoléon III dismissed Drouyn de Lhuys in 1866. He retired from public life and remained aloof from foreign affairs.

Drumont, Edouard (1844–1917)   Edouard Drumont, one of France's most violent anti-semitic writers, was born in Paris on 3 May 1844. Choosing a career in journalism, he wrote *La France Juive* in 1866. This was a polemical work of a violent anti-semitic nature. In 1892 Drumont founded *La Libre Parole* which was known as France's most vehemently anti-Jewish newspaper. Spurred on by the Panama Scandal (qv) and the Dreyfus Affair (qv), Drumont continued to hammer away at his favourite theme. In 1899 he published *Les Juifs et l'Affaire Dreyfus*. His *Le Testament d'un Antisémite* (1891) summarised his philosophy. He had a direct impact on the rise of anti-Jewish feelings in France and in Germany. He died in Paris on 3 February 1917.

Dubois de Grancé, Edmond-Louis (1747–1814)   Born at Charleville on 18 October 1747, a deputy in 1789, Dubois helped found the *Club des Jacobins* (qv). He was elected member of the Convention in 1792 and sat as a Montagnard (qv). Dubois de Grancé was a primary figure in the overthrow of Robespierre (qv) at Thermidor. From 1795 to 1799 he served in the Five Hundred (qv) and in 1797 became minister of war. He opposed Napoléon Bonaparte's (qv) coup d'état of 18 Brumaire (qv) and retired from public life. Dubois de Grancé died at Rethel on 29 June 1814.

Ducos, Pierre Roger (1747–1816)   A deputy in 1792, Ducos, born at Montfort (Landes) on 23 July 1747, served with distinction and in 1795 entered the Council of Ancients (qv). He became a member of the Directory (qv) in 1799 and assisted in Napoléon Bonaparte's (qv) coup d'état of 18 Brumaire (qv). For his efforts Ducos became third provisional consul, and in 1808 Bonaparte made him senator and count and in 1815 a peer. He was exiled after 1815 because of his vote for the death of Louis XVI. He died at Ulm on 16 March 1816.

Dumouriez, Charles François (1739–1823) A career officer born at Cambrai, Dumouriez, a general of France, commanded the National Guard in 1789. In 1790 he joined the Jacobin Club (qv), but later sided with the Girondins (qv). In 1792 he was, as foreign minister, a key figure in the declaration of war against Austria. Commanding the army of the north, he fought at Valmy (qv) and in Belgium, but in 1793 began negotiations, in secret, with the Austrians. On 5 April 1793 he defected to the Austrians because of his disgust with the drift toward extremism in France. Louis Philippe (qv), the future Orléanist king of France, defected with him. His official affiliation with the Girondins seriously hurt the political fortunes of that group. The scandal caused by Dumouriez's actions aided the more vocal Jacobins (qv) in France, who demanded a purge of the Girondins. After travelling, Dumouriez assisted the Duke of Wellington in fighting against French forces in Spain in 1808, and after the end of the Spanish campaign he retired to a small estate in England.

Dupin, Amadine Aurore Lucie See: Sand, George.

Dupont de l'Etang, Pierre (1765–1840) A brilliant career soldier, Dupont was made a count in 1807 by Napoléon Bonaparte (qv). However, because of his military failures in Spain he was imprisoned on the orders of Bonaparte. Because of this incarceration, he was welcomed by Louis XVIII as a loyal supporter and in 1814 became minister of war under the restored Bourbon monarchy. From 1815 to 1830 he served as a deputy, but retired after the downfall of Charles X in 1830.

Dupont de l'Eure, Jacques Charles (1767–1855) A lawyer and member of the Parlement of Normandy in 1789, Dupont went to Paris as a member of the Council of Five Hundred (qv) in 1798. His career was not spectacular, his most important post being vicepresident of the Chamber in 1814 and during the Hundred Days (qv). Ousted in 1815 by the

Bourbon restoration, he was re-elected in 1817 and until 1848 sat with the extreme left. Known for his patriotism and integrity, he became a member of the Provisional Government in February 1848. After 1849, because of age, he retired from the Chamber and from public life.

Dupuy, Charles Alexandre (1851–1924)   One of the most prominent republicans in the Chamber, Dupuy became a deputy in 1885 as a representative of the Haute Loire. He held that post until 1900 when he was elected senator. Dupuy was president of the Council of Ministers in 1893, 1894 and 1895, and during these periods he was instrumental in supporting the Franco-Russian Alliance of 1894 (qv). He held the portfolio of the agriculture ministry in 1892 and the portfolio of the public instruction ministry in 1893. In 1894 and 1895 he served as president of the Chamber. After 1895 Dupuy remained strictly in the legislative branch of government concerning himself with laws and strengthening France in the face of German might.

Duruy, Victor (1811–1894)   A historian and liberal educationalist, Duruy became minister of education in 1863. Given a free hand by Napoléon III (qv), he expanded popular education, and in 1865 proposed a system of free public education in France. A noted liberal and fearless innovator, Duruy introduced vocational training, more emphasis on science, and the study of modern history. Over the opposition of the clergy, he advocated and established secondary education for women, and primary schools for all French children. In 1866 an education law took a great step toward free public schools. Removed by Napoléon III in 1869 after a dispute, Duruy continued to be a great influence on French public education during the Third Republic, and on the provisions of the great Ferry Education Bill of 1881 (qv). During the Third Republic, Duruy was honoured by being inducted into the *Académie des Inscriptions* in 1873, *Académie des Sciences morales* in 1879, and the *Académie Française* in 1884.

Eblé, Jean Baptiste (1758–1812)   Of humble origin,

d'Eblé became a general in 1793, and by 1808 was made a baron by Napoléon Bonaparte. From 1808 to 1812 he served Jérôme Bonaparte (qv) as the minister of war of the kingdom of Westphalia (qv). He commanded the supply units in Russia in 1812 and did a great deal to bring the remnants of the Grand Army out of Russia. He died of disease contracted during the bitter cold of the Russian campaign.

Economic Legislation   See: Decree of 3 January 1946 (economic planning).

Education Bill of 1833   See: Guizot, François.

Elizabeth of France (1764–1794)   The very pious sister of Louis XVI (qv), Elizabeth of France tried to interject a high moral tone at the royal court. In 1789 she faithfully supported her brother. She participated in the 1791 escape attempt at Varennes and followed Marie Antoinette (qv) to the Temple in 1792. Tried in 1794, Elizabeth was executed on the guillotine the same year as Marie Antoinette.

Ems Dispatch   This dispatch was the final spark which ignited the Franco-Prussian War of 1870. The French were opposed to Leopold von Hohenzollern's candidacy for the vacant Spanish throne. French Ambassador Benedetti sought an interview with Prussia's King William I at Ems in Germany. While William I stated that the Hohenzollern name would be withdrawn, the French wanted more specific guarantees that the candidacy issue would not be raised again. William I refused to agree to this, since he and Otto von Bismarck considered the first pledge of withdrawal to be satisfactory. When William I reported the Ems interview to Bismarck, the chancellor knew that he could twist it to suit his purposes. He would make it appear that Benedetti made an insulting demand and that William I made an equally offensive reply. The edited communiqué was published in a German newspaper on 14 July 1870, and news of it reached Paris the same day. The French war party around the empress and the war minister La Boeuf (qv) demanded and got a declaration of war on Prussia. This was what Bismarck wanted, since he believed that the total German unification rested on a victorious war with France.

Enfantin, Prosper (1796–1864) A socialist and one of the chief followers of Comte Saint-Simon (qv), Enfantin totally accepted the religious strain in Saint-Simonianism. He advocated female equality and a breakdown and equalisation of the social classes in France. In 1832 Enfantin tried to set up a libertine commune, but it was disbanded by a shocked government. Arrested and condemned by the government, Enfantin was pardoned, but exiled. After the revolution of 1848 he was named chief of a scientific mission in Algeria. From 1848 to 1864 he held a high post with the Paris to Lyon railroad.

Enghien Affair Prince Louis Henri de Bourbon Condé, Duc d'Enghien (1772–1804), was a royalist vehemently opposed to Napoléon Bonaparte (qv). In the early months of 1804 Enghien possibly entered into a conspiracy against Bonaparte. The police under Joseph Fouché (qv) discovered the royalist plot and arrested the conspirators, including the Duc d'Enghien. Enghien was kidnapped from his home in Baden, and on 19 March 1804 he was tried on flimsy evidence and shot; Napoléon wanted to use the act as a warning to the Bourbons. The affair was a blot on the reputation of Bonaparte, and clearly showed the undying hatred between him and the Bourbons.

Enragés After the defeats and desertion of General Dumouriez (qv) to the Austrians the political situation in France changed. There were riots in some major cities in France. In February 1792 Paris experienced severe bread riots and the *enragés* looted bakeries and stores. Their violence frightened many of the members of the Convention while others, more revolutionary in nature, recognised their value. The *enragés* called for radical reforms which the Montagnards (qv) realised were needed to save the republic. They demanded unity in the Convention, the expulsion of the Girondins (qv), heavy taxes upon the wealthy, government regulation of food prices and the creation of a revolutionary military force which would use the urban unemployed in the ranks. The 9 and 10 March 1792 insurrection against the Convention convinced deputies that a national government was needed as well as emergency measures such as the regulation of food prices and rents. Danton (qv) and the Montagnards adopted many of the *enragé* demands. The *enragés* then turned their paramilitary forces over to the Montagnards. In March and April 1793 a series of decrees which embodied *enragé* ideals were issued. The most important decree established the *Comité de Salut Public* (qv).

Entente Cordiale On 8 April 1904 Paul Cambon (qv), representing France, and Lord Lansdowne, representing Great Britain, signed in London a treaty which became known as the Entente Cordiale. The entente, which became the basis for the Anglo-French alliance, recognised England's sphere of influence in Egypt and France's predominance in Morocco. This trade, which had originally been proposed by Lord Salisbury of Britain, was hotly debated in both England and France after the British-French clash at Fashoda (qv) in 1898. It took Théophile Delcassé (qv) six years to reach a point where French interests would be served by the agreement. The French expansionists, led by Eugène Etienne (qv), had demanded such a move, but Delcassé moved towards it slowly. Besides the all important agreement over Egypt and Morocco, France and Britain also settled several other outstanding overseas issues such as Siam, the New Hebrides, Madagascar, and fishing rights in North American waters. The French gained the right to use Newfoundland beaches during fishing seasons, and the border disputes between France and Siam were acted upon. But all of this was of minor importance when compared to the major portion of the Entente Cordiale. Primarily, the April 1904 accords were important because the long-standing Egyptian question was settled and France got her free hand in Morocco. Once the Anglo-French accord was consummated, both states moved toward military cooperation. The Entente Cordiale was tested by Germany during both the First and

Second Moroccan Crises (qv) but held firm throughout World War I.

Erfurt, Conference of Between 27 September and 14 October 1808 Napoléon (qv) and Tsar Alexander I of Russia held a conference at Erfurt to discuss Franco-Russian relations. Alexander I had decided to end the French alliance and to conclude some sort of treaty with Austria. The meeting ended with a secret renewal of the Tilsit treaties (qv), but the tsar exacted promises from Bonaparte over Turkey. Despite the official communiqués, Alexander never intended to honour the Erfurt renewal of their Tilsit treaties.

Etat Français See: Pétain, Henri Philippe.

Etienne, Eugène (1842–1921) Etienne was born in Oran, Algeria, to a military-pioneer French family. After being educated in France, he returned to Algeria in 1881 and was elected deputy from Oran. In 1887 he was made undersecretary of state for colonies. Serving in that position until 1892, he became known as a militant annexationist. In 1890 he helped form the *Comité de l'Afrique française* (qv), and in 1892, after his return to the Chamber, he founded the *Parti colonial* (qv). Etienne is best known for his influence in extending French imperial interests in West Africa, Madagascar and Morocco. He served as war minister in 1905–6 and again in 1913 when he led the fight for the Three Year Law (qv) of 1913. The French element of Algeria elected him senator in 1919, and in May 1921 he died in Paris of a heart attack.

Etoile Nord Africaine (ENA) The ENA was founded in Paris in 1923 to push for an alteration in Algeria's colonial status. There was a tendency among the leadership of the ENA to seek unification of sorts among the French states of North Africa. In 1936 the ENA was replaced by the *Parti Populaire Algérien* (PPA) (qv), but the ENA played a vital role in the early movements toward Algerian independence.

Eugénie de Montijo de Guzman (1826–1920) In 1853 this daughter of an impoverished but noble family of Grenada, reputed to be one of the most beautiful women in Europe, but with a cold personality, married Napoléon III. She delivered the prince imperial in 1856, and then promptly rejected her husband. In the following decade the Empress Eugénie made Paris and the imperial court the social and style leader of the world. In 1870, with war minister La Boeuf (qv), she led the so-called war party into forcing an antagonistic policy vis-à-vis Bismarck's Prussia. After the collapse of the empire she fled to England, and after the death of the prince imperial in 1876 she retired from public life and died in Madrid.

European Defence Community   See: Communauté Européene de Défense.

Evian Accords   The Evian Accords, signed on 18 March 1962, ended the Franco-Algerian war which had raged since November 1954. Completed by representatives of France and the Algerian National Liberation Front, the accords brought a ceasefire to Algeria. An Algeria-wide referendum was held in six months to decide whether Algerians wanted total independence or a special relationship vis-à-vis France. For a one-year period all French rights and property would be respected, and no *colon* would be discriminated against by Algerian law. France would continue to provide technical and cultural assistance to Algeria, and the Algerian currency would be equal with the French franc in areas of Franco-Algerian trade. The oil-rich Sahara would be developed by both Algeria and France. All French military personnel would leave Algeria over a specific period of time, but the port of Mers-el-Kébir would be leased to France for fifteen years. Algeria would, by accepting nationhood, have total sovereignty over her territory, foreign affairs and economy. By the signing of the accords, France ended an eight-year war which had been extremely costly and which had altered France's entire political structure in 1958.

Executive Commission of 1848   On 9 May 1848 the National Assembly decided to abolish the Provisional Government of 1848 (qv) and established an executive Commission consisting of five members. On the next day François Arago (qv), Louis Antoine Garnier-Pagès (qv), Charles Maris, Alphonse de Lamartine (qv) and Alexandre Ledru-Rollin (qv) were chosen as commissioners. Under the Commission there was a cabinet of ministers which did not include the commissioners. In the wake of the June Days of 1848, the Assembly abolished the Executive Commission and placed all executive powers in the hands of General Cavaignac (qv). On 24 June 1848 the Executive Commission came to an end.

Faidherbe, Louis César (1818–1889) Born on 3 June 1818 Faidherbe became one of France's greatest explorers and advocates of imperial expansion. Faidherbe, a native of Lille, was known as the 'genius of Senegal'. After service in Africa and Algeria, he went to Senegal in 1863. His reforms brought administrative stability and prosperity to the region. Elected deputy in 1871 for the Somme, he resigned his post to return to Africa. In 1879 he returned to Paris as a senator for the Nord, but suffered a stroke in 1883 which limited his participation in debates and in active political life. Faidherbe resigned his senatorial seat in 1888 and devoted the remainder of his life to popularising the imperialist cause. He died in Paris on 29 September 1889.

Faillières, Armand (1841–1931) Armand Fallières entered the Chamber as a deputy in 1876 for the Lot et Garonne and held that post until 1890. From 1890 to 1906 he served as senator for the same district. In March 1899 he was elected president of the Senate and served until his election as president of the Republic in 1906. A firm republican, Fallières rose quickly in the Chamber, becoming undersecretary in the interior ministry in 1879. In 1882 he served as interior minister and in 1883 formed his own ministry. Under Jules Ferry (qv) in 1883 he served as minister of public education. In 1887 he held the portfolio of the justice ministry, and under Charles de Freycinet (qv) in 1890 he held the same post. In February 1906 Faillières was chosen as president, and he served until 1913. After 1913 he retired from public and political life.

Falloux, Frédéric de (1811–1886) A native of Angers, he was born on 11 May 1811. He was elected deputy in 1846 as a liberal – Falloux sat in opposition to Orléanist policies. He espoused the republican ideal in 1848, but rallied to Louis Napoléon and was made minister of public instruction in that year. In 1850 he advocated the school law known as the Falloux Law (qv), a clericalisation of French education. In the late 1850s Falloux assumed leadership of the liberal Catholics, and in 1873, as a deputy, supported Marshal MacMahon's (qv) policies. Falloux died in Paris on 6 January 1886.

Falloux Law   A law proposed by Frédéric Falloux (qv) in March 1850 to counter leftist and republican sentiments in regard to education. The Falloux law gave to members of religious orders the right to open schools with few restrictions. Councils with strong clerical representation were established to control the universities.

Fashoda Crisis   In 1898 a French force of about 200 men established a small post on the Nile near a native village called Fashoda. Commanded by Captain Jean Baptiste Marchand (qv), the French expedition was ordered to maintain a French presence on the Nile in order to challenge British colonial authority in the region. The French had never forgotten that they had lost an opportunity in 1882 to join in the occupation of Egypt. To balance their loss, from 1894 to 1898, they tried to send missions to the Nile, but most failed. Marchand, given the task, reached the river at Fashoda in July 1898. Quickly discovered by the British, the French post at Fashoda caused an international crisis. Gabriel Hanotaux (qv), the French foreign minister, was toppled from power, his place being taken by Théophile Delcassé (qv). Lord Salisbury, British prime minister and foreign secretary, wanted to calm the situation by offering France a trade of French interests in Egypt for British interests in Morocco. This Egypt-Morocco barter became the foundation for the Entente Cordiale (qv) of 1904. Supported by Eugène Etienne (qv) and the *Comité de l'Afrique française* (qv), Delcassé was able to extract Marchand from Fashoda on 3 November 1898. The Fashoda crisis marked a turning point in Anglo-French relations, and directed the course of their diplomacy toward substantive talks and final agreement in 1904.

Faure, Edgar (1908–   ) Edgar Faure was elected deputy after World War II. A radical and a member of the party leadership, he formed two governments during the Fourth Republic. From January to February 1952 and again from February 1955 to January 1956, he served as premier. He also held the portfolios for the defence, finance, justice and foreign ministries. During his first ministry he tried to arrest France's economic decline by higher taxes, but was toppled. Known as an ally of Mendès-France (qv), Faure during his second ministry floundered over North African policy. Mendès-France worked against him over financial and imperial policies, bringing about the collapse of his government. Faure continued to remain active in politics and has held posts in the Fifth Republic.

Faure, Félix (1841–1899) Born in Paris on 30 January 1841 Faure was elected deputy in 1881 for the Seine-Inférieure as a moderate republican. In 1882, 1885 and 1888 he served as undersecretary of state for colonies and as minister of the marine. An active colonialist, he won the respect of the powerful imperialists who supported his policies in the colonies. Elected president of the Republic he maintained an active interest in imperial and foreign affairs. In 1897 he travelled to St Petersburg to cement the Franco-Russian alliance of 1894 (qv). He died suddenly from a heart attack in Paris on 5 February 1899.

Favre, Jules (1809–1880) A noted liberal lawyer, Favre, who was born in Lyon on 21 March 1809, worked with Ledru-Rollin (qv) at the interior ministry in 1848. In 1858 this moderate republican opposed Napoléon III (qv) and defended Orsini (qv), the Italian bomb-thrower. He was elected deputy from Paris and sat in the opposition to Napoléon III. In the Government of National Defence Favre was minister of foreign affairs and negotiated the armistice with the Germans on

28 January 1871. He then served as a deputy and in 1876 was elected senator. Favre remained faithful to his liberal but vehemently anti-socialist views until his death at Versailles on 28 January 1880.

Fayolle, Marie-Emile (1852–1925)   A brilliant soldier, he commanded the French sixth army on the Somme River in 1916 and 1917, and after the Italian disaster at Caporetto, he was sent to shore up the military effort there. Fayolle commanded the French army group which pushed the Germans to the Rhine in 1918.

Fédération des Associations Viticoles   The association of wine producers in France was formed in 1913. This federation aided the producers in learning more about wine production, marketing and exportation which helped the producer and in turn greatly assisted the French economy.

Fédération Electorale   Etienne Lamy (qv) was called to Rome by Pope Leo XIII in 1895 to be given the task of organising French Catholics. Leo XIII believed that the political aspects of the Ralliement had to have one leader. Lamy in January 1896 returned from Rome but found that many conservative Roman Catholics refused to cooperate with the republic. In 1896 he founded the *Fédération electorale* to promote unity among Catholics, but in 1898 the federation failed to win many seats in the Chamber. This was due mainly to Lamy's attempts to give to French Catholicism a liberal tone.

Fédérés   The Fédérés had their origins in the hectic days of June–July 1789 when, in the provinces, groups of people formed patriotic organisations known as *fédérations*. Many of these Fédérés were anti-Paris, distrusting the influence that the city might have on the course of the revolution. Members of the various National Guards joined these regional federations, and on 14 July 1790, one year after the fall of the Bastille, the Fédérés gathered in Paris on the Champs-de-Mars to celebrate the *Fête de la Fédération*. They took an oath to king, law, and state. Lafayette (qv) administered the oath. When war was declared in April 1792 the Fédérés were called upon to go to the front to repulse the autocratic invaders. As the war went badly, the Fédérés' temper began to change, and under the influence of propagandists from the radical elements, this group, once loyal to king, state, and law, began to murmur against traitors in the assembly. Many Fédérés groups argued in 1792–3 that France needed a wholesale participation of the population in the war—a *levée en masse*, and on 10 August 1793 a deputation of Fédérés argued before the convention for such a move. When Lazare Carnot (qv) issued the call, the Fédérés enforced the *levée en masse* in the rural areas. After the escape attempt by Louis XIV (qv) and the royal family in 1791, the Fédérés manifested more a tendency toward radicalism, and by 1792–3 they were used by various factions in the convention for their own purposes.

Ferry Education Bill of 1881 (Law of 16 June 1881) In 1880 Jules Ferry (qv) proposed sweeping reforms for French education. He believed that education in the modern state had to be free from costs, compulsory and strictly secular. In the Chamber these principles were adopted by the republicans, but were opposed by royalists and staunch Catholics. Instruction was to be given to both girls and boys and was to be quite modern, utilitarian, and patriotic. Primary schools could be closed one extra day per week besides Sunday so that children could be given religious instruction in the church or in the home. Ferry relied on Paul Bert (qv), the brilliant anti-cleric deputy, to lead the fight in the Chamber. The Chamber passed the Ferry Education Bill in December 1880; it was agreed to in the Senate in the spring of 1881; and it went into effect in June 1881. The Law of 16 June 1881 provided for free, secular and compulsory schools for France. Jules Ferry considered this law and the Law of 28 May 1882, which firmly prohibited religious instruction in the public schools and which removed all religious objects from the schools, to be one of the most important pieces of republican legislation passed during his tenure as president of the Council of Ministers.

Ferry, Jules (1832–1893) One of the most vocal opponents of Napoléon III (qv) and an austere Protestant, Ferry, who was born at Saint Dié on 5 April 1832, served in the Chamber prior to the Franco-Prussian War and held a post in the Government of National Defence. Adolphe Thiers (qv) made him minister to Greece. Ferry entered the Chamber as a deputy in 1876 and served until 1889 when he became a senator. He was openly opposed to clerical control of schools and proposed numerous laws to negate the Falloux Law (qv) and to secularise French public education. As minister of public instruction and as president of the Council of Ministers (1880–1 and 1883–5), Ferry pushed through the Chamber the Ferry Education Bill (the Law of 16 June 1881) (qv) and the Law of 28 May 1882, which were designed to diminish church control of schools. Later known as the master imperialist, Ferry, during his 1880–1 ministry, first opposed colonial expansion. However, by 1883 he had changed his opinion and took France into Tunisia, Tonkin, West Africa and Madagascar. Ferry's concept of colonialism for national and economic rather than for cultural and humanitarian reasons was adopted by Eugène Etienne (qv) and other imperialists. As a result of the crisis following the Wilson affair (qv), Ferry tried to win the presidency of the Republic in 1887 but failed simply because he was not able to inspire public confidence in his policies. He was elected president of the Senate only a few weeks prior to his death in Paris on 17 March 1893.

Feuillant Club   Founded after the Massacre of the Champs de Mars (qv), the Feuillant Club was formed by less radical, less extreme Jacobins (qv) who deserted their club in disgust over what they saw as immoderate policies. Lafayette (qv), Sièyes (qv) and Barnave (qv) all associated with the Feuillants, but eventually the club lost members as men drifted back to the Jacobins. Very few provincial Jacobin clubs became associates of the Paris-based Feuillants. After the escape attempt of Louis XVI in June 1791, the remaining Feuillants divided over the issue of the future of the royal institution. Many now adhered to the policies of Robespierre (qv) in the Assembly. In 1792 there was a brief attempt to form a Feuillant ministry under Lafayette, but it failed and this marked the end of their influence.

Fez, Treaty of   Signed on 30 March 1912, this agreement marked the final step in the French acquisition of Morocco. The French, by treaty with Sultan Moulay Abd el Hafid, established a protectorate over Morocco. General Hubert Lyautey (qv) was named the first resident general of the protectorate.

Five Hundred, Council of   Created by the Thermidorian constitution of 1795, the Council of Five Hundred served as a type of lower house in the *Corps Législatif* (qv) with the Council of Ancients (qv). The council accepted men who were over thirty years of age and who already had some legislative experience. The Five Hundred nominated lists of candidates to fill the Directorship, and the Council of Ancients held veto power over their proposals for legislation.

Flandin, Pierre Etienne (1889–1958)   Flandin formed a government in November 1934 after Doumergue's (qv) Government of National Union had been ousted. Basically he was as unable to control events as Doumergue had been. Seeing himself as the saviour of the Republic from the fascist threat, Flandin was faced with economic deterioration at home and growing fascist-military aggressiveness in Italy and in Germany. His stubborn refusal to devalue the franc caused the downfall of his government. In 1936 he served as foreign minister but failed to deal effectively with either Mussolini or Hitler. His inability to cope with the growing fascism at home and abroad seriously damaged his political career. As foreign minister Flandin travelled to London to try to rally British support for united action against Germany when Hitler decided to occupy the Rhineland in 1936. Britain's cabinet refused Flandin's appeals, and he returned to Paris disgusted with this lack of Franco-British cooperation against Hitler. In fact, Flandin appeared to lose any hope of ever halting German actions in Europe. During the Vichy period, Marshal Pétain (qv) replaced Pierre Laval (qv) with Flandin in December 1940, and he served until February 1941 when he was replaced by Admiral François Darlan (qv). Again, Flandin left public life a discouraged, defeated man.

Floquet, Charles (1828–1896)   A member of the National Assembly in 1871, Floquet tried without success to reconcile the Paris Commune (qv) with the government. From 1876 to 1882 he represented the Seine as a deputy, from 1882 to 1889 the Pyrénées-Orientales and from 1889 to 1893 the Seine again. In 1894 he was named senator from the Seine. President of the Chamber from 1885 to 1888 and again from 1889 to 1892, he was an avowed enemy of General Georges Boulanger (qv) and also a political foe of Jules Ferry (qv). In April 1888 Floquet formed his own cabinet which excluded many of Ferry's followers.

Floréal, Coup of 22   The years 1797–8 were serious ones for the Directory (qv) government. The military setbacks and the deepening financial crisis which resulted in the 25 September 1797 decree that two-thirds of the public debt would be paid off by government-issued bonds irritated the electorate. By 1798 the issued bonds were worth only from 3 to 5 per cent of face value. The wives of the Directors, even Joséphine (qv), wife of Napoléon Bonaparte (qv), scandalised the public with their behaviour. All in all, the Directory faced grave problems in the elections of 1798. These elections saw a dramatic rise in Jacobinism. The old Jacobins (qv), much to the horror of the conservative Directors and Council, claimed a great victory at the polls. The Directory, totally ignoring the constitutionality of such a move, simply declared the election results annulled. This occurred on 11 May 1798 and is called the Coup of 22 Floréal, Year VI. This open flaunting of the constitution and dictatorial power politics paved the way for the Coup of 30 Prairial (qv) by Abbé Sieyès (qv), and it later served as a basis for Napoléon's Coup of 18 Brumaire (qv). Constitutional rule in France was therefore doomed by the actions of 22 Floréal.

Foch, Ferdinand (1851–1929)   Foch fought as a student at Metz and entered the regular army in 1874. Promoted to general in 1907, he was an open advocate of Anglo-French military cooperation and created a study centre which became known as the *Ecole des Marchaux*. From 1914 to 1916 his reputation grew, and in 1916 he was given command of the French armies. In March 1918 he took command of all allied forces. He retired from active service in 1918 and wrote against a harsh peace with Germany. Foch opposed the occupation of the Ruhr and warned that France's actions were driving a wedge between her and England thus weakening the Entente Cordiale (qv).

Fontainebleau, Conference of   The Fontainebleau Conference of September 1946 followed the Franco-Vietnamese Accords of 6 March 1946 (qv), and the Fontainebleau Accords attempted to cement relations between Vietnam and France. The number of French technicians to help in the establishment of Vietnamese industry was enumerated, and a unity of coinage and customs duties was established between France and Vietnam. Vietnam was given the right to establish a limited number of consular offices in other capitals. These accords lasted as a basis for Franco-Vietnamese cooperation until the Auriol-Bao Daï Accords of 1949 (qv).

Fontainebleau, Treaty of   This treaty signed on 12 April 1814 between Napoléon and the allies marked the first fall of Napoléon. While very favourable to him, it did force him to surrender, for all time, for himself and his descendants, all rights to the French and Italian thrones. His wife, Marie Louise (qv), was allowed to retain the title of empress, and his family could retain most of their royal titles. He was given Elba as a principality and pensions were paid to all members of his family as well as to him, a clause which Louis XVIII (qv) tried to evade. He received a ship and a bodyguard as part of his personal retinue. The treaty, drawn up on 11 April 1814, was signed by the allies and ratified by Napoléon at Fontainebleau. On the evening of 12 April he tried to commit suicide but the attempt failed. On the morning of 16 April 1814 he began his journey to Elba.

Foucauld, Charles de (1858–1916) Explorer, soldier, missionary, Charles de Foucauld entered the army intending to follow a military career. He served in Algeria and helped explore Morocco. His trips to Morocco were not dangerous, but daring. His memoirs and reports for the French government were filled with valuable social, political and geographical information, and they marked him as an expert in North African affairs. De Foucauld, who had lived the life of a rakish playboy, became interested in religion and underwent a deep spiritual conversion. He became a Trappist monk in 1901 and retired to the Sahara as a missionary, where he studied the ways of the Tourges. He resisted attempts by Colonel Marie Laperrine (qv) to do espionage work for the French military in the Sahara. De Foucauld was murdered by the militant muslim Senussi Brotherhood in 1916.

Fouché, Joseph (1754–1820) Born in Nantes on 19 September 1754, Fouché was elected deputy in 1792. He was known as one of the bloodiest terrorists in France, and his excessive actions in repressing anti-revolutionary sentiment in Lyon pointed this out with great clarity. However, he was able to live down this reputation by playing on his opposition to Robespierre (qv) and the Terror. Fearing Robespierre, he sided with the Thermidorians, but was briefly arrested in 1795. He denounced Paul Barras (qv), and for his efforts he was named ambassador to Milan in 1798. In 1799 Fouché became chief of police and served Napoléon Bonaparte (qv) during the coup d'état of 18 Brumaire (qv). In 1809 he was made the Duc d'Otrante, but despite his open support for Bonaparte, he secretly tried to negotiate a peace treaty with England. He was discovered and disgraced, but after 1810 was able to curry favour with Louis XVIII. Despite the fact that he rallied to Bonaparte during the Hundred Days, Fouché became head of the Provisional Government in 1815 and again offered his service to Louis XVIII. He served the second restoration as minister of police for a brief period, but was exiled in 1816 as a regicide. Fouché became an Austrian citizen and died in Trieste on 25 December 1820.

Fouchet, Christian (1911–) A career diplomat, Fouchet joined the Free French in early 1940 and was used by General Charles de Gaulle (qv) as a diplomat. After World War II he served as one of the founders of the *Rassemblement du Peuple Français* (RPF) (qv) and in 1951 was elected as a deputy for the RPF. From 1954 to 1955 he served as minister to Tunisia and to Morocco, where he had to deal with the difficult questions of independence for those North African states. In 1958 he was appointed ambassador to Denmark. De Gaulle called on Fouchet to serve in 1961 on the committee which dealt with political unity for the member states of the European Common Market. In 1962 Fouchet was the last high commissioner for Algeria, and after leaving Algeria he served in the Pompidou cabinet until his resignation in late 1962.

Fould, Achille (1800–1867) A financier and a member of the House of Fould-Oppenheim, he was elected deputy in 1842 and sat with the anti-Orléanist opposition. From 1849 to 1851 Fould served as minister of finance, and for his efforts he was elected a senator. In 1860 he entered private business, but was recalled to assume the portfolio of finance minister from 1861 to 1867. He died at Tarbes on 5 October 1867.

Fouquier-Tinville, Antoine Quentin (1746–1795) Born to an affluent family at Herouel on 12 June 1746, a prosecutor and member of the police, Fouquier joined the revolution in 1789. In 1793 he was named accuser of the revolutionary tribunal, where he earned a reputation as a bloodthirsty extremist. He faithfully served the Terror and Robespierre, and became one of the most feared and hated men in France. After purging the Girondins, Fouquier-Tinville turned against Robespierre and worked to send him to his death. But he himself was arrested in Paris and executed on 7 May 1795 because of his actions while serving the Terror.

Fourcroy, Antoine François de (1755–1809) A famed

116

chemist, Fourcroy was elected deputy in 1793 and was named to the committee of public instruction. He was a member of the Council of Ancients and Bonaparte later placed him in charge of public instruction in France.

Fourier, Charles (1772–1835) Fourier was born in affluence in Besançon on 7 April 1772. Fourier's family was reduced to poverty in 1793. He served in the army and in 1808 published *La Théorie des quatres mouvements et des destinées générales*, in which he explored the issue of poverty. In 1822, leaning more towards the utopian left, he published *Le Traité de l'association domestique et agricole*. Following this he published *Théorie de l'unité universelle*. Basically Fourier rejected economic liberalism as oppressive and espoused a form of communalism. He envisioned the creation of *phalansteries* of utopian socialist fighters which would struggle against class oppression, and he looked towards a day of decline for capitalism and liberalism. He believed that the evil within civilisation and the government's unwillingness or inability to correct those evils were based on the idea of private property. To remedy this situation, Fourier proposed a new order in society called *Phalanges* which would be self-contained communities holding all property in common and producing exactly what society needed for its members. The struggle against property and capitalism would then be in the form of utopian communalism and not by barricades or blood in the streets. Fourier died in poverty in Paris on 9 November 1835, but his influence was great.

Francists An extreme right-wing movement founded by Marcel Bucard in the early 1930s, the Francists were openly pro-fascist. In 1934 Bucard sent Mussolini and Hitler telegrams expressing the Francists' solidarity with Fascist Italy and Nazi Germany. During the riots of 6 February 1934 (qv) Bucard's organisation played a prominent, violent role.

Franco-Austrian Alliance of 1812 Bonaparte forced the Austrians to sign an alliance which pledged 30,000 troops to the French army. Once these troops were mustered for service the Austrians were to give up control over them, and the troops fell under French command.

Franco-Austrian-British Treaty of 1815 This secret agreement was the invention of Talleyrand (qv), who represented France at the Congress of Vienna. Signed on 3 January 1815 the three powers of France, Austria and England pledged mutual assistance to each other if they were attacked. This treaty, which Talleyrand believed superseded the four-power coalition, provided for troops from the three countries and provisions for inviting other smaller states to join. Aimed directly at Prussia and Russia, the treaty was actually unenforceable owing to political and military conditions in Europe at the time. Actually, the treaty was a gigantic bluff aimed at stopping Russian actions in Poland and curbing Prussian designs on Saxony.

Franco-Cambodian Accords On 8 November 1949 representatives of the French and Cambodian governments met in Paris to sign an accord which was similar in text to the the Auriol-Bao Daï Accords (qv) of March 1949 and the Franco-Laotian Accords of July 1949 (qv).

Franco-Congolese Accords In 1894 the British and Belgians reached an accord known as the Anglo-Congolese treaty. By this agreement Belgium leased from Britain the Bar el Ghazal area near the Nile, which effectively blocked any French effort to obtain a foothold on the Nile. The outcry in France was severe, and the colonialists, especially the *Comité de l'Afrique française* (qv) and foreign minister Gabriel Hanotaux (qv), demanded that Belgium renounce the agreement. On 14 August 1894 France and Belgium signed the accords which abrogated the 1894 Anglo-Congolese treaty. This opened the way for the French to make an effort at establishing a post on the Nile, which culminated in the Fashoda crisis (qv) of 1898.

Franco-Czechoslovakian Treaty This treaty, signed on 25 June 1924, was a part of France's alliance system in eastern Europe. The alliance provided for mutual aid in the event of German aggression. This pact reflected a serious concern by

France for the new states of eastern Europe and for the possibility of German aggressiveness. The treaty with Czechoslovakia and the Franco-Polish Alliance of 1921 (qv) aimed at reducing the threat of any German attack and were, in the long run, a substitute for the old Franco-Russian Alliance of 1894 (qv). However, by 1936 there were serious doubts as to the practicability of these treaties and more emphasis on Maginot Line type defences. Czechoslovakia tried to shore up the alliance and even signed a pact of mutual aid and assistance with the Soviet Union on 16 May 1935. However, during the Munich crisis over the Sudetenland area of Czechoslovakia, these pacts were of very little value. In 1938 France and Britain bowed to Adolf Hitler and allowed the first partition of Czechoslovakia, despite the existence of the pact.

Franco-German Accords of 1911   After the Germans sent a gunboat to the port of Agadir in Morocco on 1 July 1911, Europe was plunged into the Second Moroccan Crisis (qv). After a period of tension and hectic diplomacy, France and Germany signed the Franco-German Accords of 4 November 1911 which ended the crisis. These accords called for the ceding of a portion of the French Congo to Germany in exchange for a portion of the German Cameroons known as the 'duck's bill'. Germany promised to recognise the ultimate annexation of Morocco into the French empire. The accords were a basic diplomatic defeat for Germany, and the whole crisis opened a new era of intense European distrust and hatred between France and Germany.

Franco-Indian Accords   On 18 October 1954 the Indian Congress voted to incorporate the five French-Indian enclaves into the Indian national union. At New Delhi on 24 October 1954 representatives of India and France signed the Franco-Indian Accords which ended the French imperial presence in India. Two years later these accords were finalised in the Franco-Indian Treaty of New Delhi on 28 May 1956.

Franco-Italian Agreement of 1900   Théophile Delcassé (qv), French foreign minister, had a definite plan for the

French acquisition of Morocco. One stage of his plan called for an agreement with Italy over Tripoli and Morocco. In 1899 Delcassé sought an agreement with Italy, but he failed primarily because Italy desired an open public declaration in regard to Tripoli. However, in January 1900 official talks began over the Morocco-Tripoli question. By 4 January 1901 the two states formally exchanged notes on the matter; the matter was not decided by formal treaty, but by formal diplomatic notes. The effect of the agreement was twofold. Firstly, the trade was a step toward France's acquisition of Morocco and Italy's takeover of Tripoli. Secondly, Italy moved further from the German-dominated Triple Alliance toward the French.

Franco-Italian Armistice of 1940   On 10 June 1940 Mussolini of Italy announced a declaration of war against France and Britain, and Italian troops attacked French military units in south-eastern France. The French, while losing the war against the Germans, did make gains against the Italians. However, on 22 June 1940 a Franco-German armistice was signed near Paris, the Armistice of Compiègne (qv), which necessitated a similar move with Italy, Germany's ally. On 24 June 1940 General Hutzinger and Marshal Badoglio signed a Franco-Italian armistice which ended the fighting between the two states.

Franco-Laotian Accords   On 19 July 1949 Vincent Auriol (qv) signed an accord with representatives of the Laotian government which was similar in content to the Auriol-Bao Daï Accords (qv) of 9 March 1949.

Franco-Moroccan Accords of 1956   By the Treaty of Fez (qv) of 1912 France occupied Morocco, but by 1954 the imperial situation in North Africa had altered. There was a violent rebellion in Algeria, and the Tunisians were demanding at least internal autonomy. In August 1953 the French government had exiled the popular Sultan Muhummud V to Madagascar, but the experiment ended in dismal failure. On 5 November 1955 Muhummud V returned in triumph to Morocco, and

France recognised him as the legitimate ruler. By the next day, the French government announced a willingness to discuss fully Moroccan independence. The Franco-Moroccan Accords entailed a treaty which recognised the unity and the independence of the kingdom. With war raging in Algeria and talks between France and Tunisia, there was little France could do but recognise the end to her imperial presence in western North Africa.

Franco-Polish Alliance Signed on 19 February 1921, this alliance was part of France's search for security after World War I. The agreement made in Paris set the tone for the French treaties in eastern Europe, since the five-point treaty was a binding military alliance and was aimed at the possibility of German aggression toward Poland.

Franco-Prussian Alliance of 1812 On 24 February 1812 Napoléon Bonaparte (qv) forced the king of Prussia to sign a military alliance to furnish 20,000 soldiers to the French army. The French gained the right to move troops through Prussia at will, and supplies could be taken within Prussia with virtually no guarantee of repayment.

Franco-Rumanian Treaty On 10 June 1926 France and Rumania signed a military alliance. This treaty, like the Franco-Czechoslovakian Treaty (qv), was another block in France's security treaties in eastern Europe.

Franco-Russian Alliance of 1894 The Franco-Russian Alliance of 1892 had its roots in the collapse of the Bismarckian diplomatic system and the ousting of the Iron Chancellor by William II in 1890 over the issue of a German-Russian reinsurance treaty. After a series of negotiations a Franco-Russian military convention was signed on 18 August 1892. Aimed specifically at the Triple Alliance, which was enumerated in the agreement, the treaty called for aid to France by Russia if she were attacked by Germany or Italy. If Russia were attacked by Germany or Italy, France pledged to attack Germany. In the case of mobilisation it would occur 'immediately and simultaneously'. In January 1894, by an exchange of diplomatic notes originated by France, the military protocols of 18 August 1892 attained the full force of a binding treaty. In 1913 this was reconfirmed by a military protocol. This treaty, the subsequent talks and the 1913 reconfirmation, were victories for French diplomacy. France was no longer isolated. The ring of isolation which Bismarck had imposed on France after the Franco-Prussian War of 1870 was broken, and Germany had to contend with France on one border and Russia on the other.

Franco-Russian Reinforcement Accords of 1899 Fearing moves by England and Germany toward an alliance, France and Russia decided to reinforce their alliance of 1894 (qv) with several new clauses. There were two important additions to the alliance. The first promised a mutual increase of military forces in order to maintain a balance among all European armies. Secondly, the reinforcement accords of 1899 reconfirmed the original 1894 Franco-Russian Alliance. In 1900 a third clause was added to the 1899 agreement in a military protocol citing numbers of troops available for use. By this reinforcement accord the alliance of 1894 became a continual fixed alliance.

Franco-Russian Treaty of 1859 This secret treaty, signed on 3 March 1859 by French foreign minister Léon Walewski (qv) and a Russian negotiator, was aimed mainly at helping Italy. Russia would by her presence on the Russo-Austrian border keep Austrian troops tied down. Russia did not pledge military action, but did state that she had a favourable attitude toward expansion in Italy by the House of Savoy.

Franco-Saar Convention of 1950 A good example of the lingering antagonisms between France and Germany after World War II was the situation over the Saar. In 1947 France proposed a liberal constitution for the Saar, and in October 1947 a French-sponsored referendum showed overwhelming support for an autonomous Saar. France in early January 1948 recognised the Saar as independent, and on 3 March 1950 France and the Saar signed a convention which limited the controls of the French high commissioner. The accords also recognised a Saar nationality and allowed Saarian diplomatic representation in Paris. The last part of the accord called for economic integration between the two states, against which Germany vehemently protested. The Saar question continued to fester between France and Germany until the fall of 1956 when the Saar returned to Germany.

Franco-Siamese Frontier Accords of 1902 The Franco-Siamese Accords signed on 7 October 1902 fixed borders between French Indo-China and Siam.

Franco-Soviet Pact of 1935 On 2 May 1935 France and the Soviet Union signed a pact which provided aid by one power to the other if the other were attacked, provided that power did not provoke the attack. Pierre Laval (qv), who held the post of foreign minister after the assassination of Louis Barthou (qv), wanted this agreement as a part of his search for French security. He reversed a policy of friendship with Germany, which was a part of the diplomacy of the 1920s, for a policy of security. Stalin, due to Nazi hostility, felt the need to expand Russia's system of alliances in case Adolf Hitler did indeed intend to carry out some of his anti-Soviet threats. Looking back to the Franco-Russian Alliance of 1894 (qv), one French politician proclaimed that France 'had returned to a traditional equilibrium in [her] diplomacy'. Maxim Litvinov, foreign minister under Stalin, felt that with this pact Russia joined into an 'anti-aggressor front', a front which might be aimed at a militantly anti-Soviet Russia posture and, fearing the rising aggressiveness of Nazi Germany, he concluded this pact for definite security purposes. The French government did not pursue the pact with any great vigour, and Russia was not consulted during the Munich crisis of 1938.

Franco-Spanish Moroccan Accord of 1900 French foreign minister Théophile Delcassé (qv) knew that once he had reached an agreement with Italy over Morocco and Tripoli he must seek an accord with Spain over Morocco, since Spanish claims on Morocco were strong. As a preliminary to substantive talks on Morocco, Spain and France signed an accord on 27 June 1900 which settled the borders between French Africa and Spain's Rio de Oro and Rio Muni. Delcassé believed (and he was correct) that the accord of 1900 was a key step toward the settlement of French and Spanish spheres of influence in Morocco.

Franco-Spanish Moroccan Accord of 1902   In the summer of 1902 Spain decided to begin talks with Théophile Delcassé (qv), the French foreign minister, over the fate of Morocco. It appeared clear that France was moving toward the acquisition of Morocco. On 8 November 1902 France and Spain concluded an agreement which delimited spheres of influence. This accord was replaced by the Franco-Spanish Moroccan Accord of 1904 (qv).

Franco-Spanish Moroccan Accord of 1904   After the signing of the Franco-Spanish Moroccan Accord of 1900 (qv) and the Franco-Italian Agreement of 1900 (qv), Théophile Delcassé (qv) turned toward a full-scale agreement with Spain over the future of Morocco. After the signing of the Entente Cordiale (qv) in 1904, Spain had almost no alternative but to come to terms with France over that area of western North Africa. By May 1904 the preliminary arrangements for a partition which favoured France were concluded. On 3 October 1904 the full treaty was announced. This treaty enlarged Spain's total area and superseded the Franco-Spanish Moroccan Accord of 1902 (qv).

Franco-Spanish Moroccan Accord of 1912   On 27 November 1912 France and Spain signed an accord which finally delineated the spheres of influence given to France and to Spain. This agreement confirmed Spain's control of northern Morocco and the territory of Ifni. Spain had little choice in the matter since France had already signed the Treaty of Fez of 1912 and was taking steps to finalise the territorial acquisition.

Franco-Tunisian Convention of 1956   Pierre Mendès-France (qv), premier of France, on 31 July 1954 announced a policy of moving toward some form of internal autonomy for Tunisia. He stated that he wanted discussions to begin as soon as possible, and on 1 June 1955 Habib Bourguiba, chief of the Tunisian Neo-Destour (New Constitutionalist) Party, returned to Tunis. On 5 June 1955 premier Edgar Faure (qv) signed an agreement with Tunisian leaders which gave administrative independence to Tunisia. Bourguiba, the strongest of the Tunisian leaders, rejected the June agreement because it fell short of full independence. Discussions continued and on 20 March 1956 France and Tunisia signed the Franco-Tunisian Convention of 1956 which recognised the independence of Tunisia and the close cooperation of the two states. Pressed by a critical war in Algeria, France could do little but end her presence in Tunisia in order to concentrate on repressing the growing violence in Algeria.

Franco-Turkish Treaty of 1921 In 1921 the French were deeply engaged in a struggle to maintain territorial claims on Turkey. These claims were a result of agreements made during World War I, and the French intervention, carried on in concert with Britain and Greece, was highly unpopular in France. In 1921 Henri Franklin-Bouillon (qv) journeyed to Ankara, Turkey, to discuss terms for ending the situation. In discussion with Mustafa Kemal it was decided that the French action would end. On 20 October 1921 Franklin-Bouillon and Kemal signed a treaty which was almost a separate Franco-Turkish peace. Basically the French withdrew from Turkey and received concessions on the Turko-Syrian border. The Ankara agreement ended a very unpopular and unprofitable French intervention in Turkish affairs.

Franco-Vietnamese Accords of 1946 In the early months of 1946 the French republic attempted to deal with the difficult question of her colonial empire in Indo-China. Pressures were building in south-eastern Asia for some semblance of independence. To pay court to Indo-Chinese sentiment and to counter growing anti-imperial sentiments in France, the representatives of France, Tonkin and Annam signed an accord on 6 March 1946. Tonkin and Annam were recognised as independent and were given admittance to the French Union. French troops, however, were kept in Indo-China and a referendum for Cochin-China was scheduled to gauge opinion in that area in regard to union with Tonkin and Annam. The 1946 accords were followed by the Conference of Fontainebleau (qv) and the Auriol-Bao Daï (qv) Accords which tied France to Indo-China until 1954.

Franco-Yugoslav Treaty of Friendship This treaty, a part of France's efforts in eastern Europe, was signed on 11 November 1927 between Aristide Briand (qv) and Yugoslav representatives. The treaty bound France and Yugoslavia in a defensive alliance, and was another step in the formation of the Little Entente in eastern Europe.

François-Poncet, André (1887–   ) A career diplomat, André François-Poncet served as a leftist deputy in 1924, but in 1928 entered the diplomatic service. He was ambassador to Germany from 1931 to 1938, and his role in the 1938 Munich crisis which dismembered Czechoslovakia is still questioned. After 1938 he served in Italy, but was interned after 1940. After 1945 he devoted his life to scholarly endeavours.

Frankfurt, Treaty of This treaty, signed on 10 May 1871, ended the Franco-Prussian War. An indemnity of 5 thousand million francs was imposed on France, and the province of Alsace and a third of the province of Lorraine were separated from the French state despite Bismarck's objection to such a move. German troops were to be stationed on French soil until the indemnity was paid. While the terms were, in French eyes, draconian, the treaty gave rise to an underlying hatred for Germany, the Revanche. The desire to regain the lost provinces and avenge the Frankfurt disgrace remained a constant if somewhat muted factor in French political life until 1914.

Franklin-Bouillon, Henri (1870–1939) A radical leader, Franklin-Bouillon served in the Senate as chairman of the powerful foreign relations committee. From 1910 to 1919 he served as deputy from the Seine et Oise. From 1919 to 1923 he was out of power, but returned in 1923 as a deputy from the same district and was deputy until his retirement from politics in 1936. In September 1917 he held the post of minister of state under Paul Painlevé (qv). He violently attacked Clemenceau's policy in the Middle East and supported a friendly stance in regard to Kemalist Turkey. During the 1930s he tried to gain the premiership, but failed.

Frayssinous, Denis-Luc (1765–1841) A cleric who opposed Bonaparte and was suspended in 1808, Frayssinous, who was born at Curières on 9 May 1765, zealously supported restoration ultra policies. For his support he served from 1823 to 1828 as grand master of the university and in 1825 as minister of religions. He was exiled after 1830 because of his opposition to the July monarchy. He returned to France in 1838 and died at Saint-Geniez on 12 December 1841.

French League for Women's Rights In 1876 the French League for Women's Rights was founded to secure for all French women the basic civil and political rights accorded to French men. The concept of women's rights was met with open hostility in the Chamber of Deputies, and only a few laws were passed to integrate French women into the mainstream of France's political life. The major aim of the league was to secure for them the right to vote. This did not, however, come about until the Ordinance of 21 April 1944 (qv). The feminist agitation brought about the Law of April 1881 which allowed a married female who was part of the labouring force to open a bank account and to maintain that account without the male's consent. This law only applied to women working in factories, but in 1907 all married working women gained the same right. In 1938 French women were no longer considered minors, and in 1942 they gained the right to sell their own property and land. The agitation continued after World War II to keep up the movement toward improvement of the role of women in French life.

Freppel, Charles-Emile (1827–1891) A brilliant theologian, Freppel held a chair in theology at the Sorbonne. In

1862 he preached Lenten services at the Tuileries. He wrote for the *Correspondant*, upholding traditional Catholic principles, and in 1870 he was named Bishop of Angers. In 1870 Freppel was deeply moved by the annexation of Alsace, the province of his birth, and from his pulpit he preached a doctrine of ardent patriotism. Five years later he created the Free University of Angers. Being a firm monarchist, he was convinced that he should stand for election to the assembly. Once in the chamber, as a deputy from Brest, he sat with the right and fought against the secularisation of schools. However, he departed from his ideological alignment and defended the colonial policies of Jules Ferry (qv).

Frey, Roger (1913–   ) Born on the island of New Caledonia, Frey rallied to General de Gaulle (qv) in 1940. He served in the Italian and French campaigns and saw service in Germany. As part of de Gaulle's entourage, Frey from 1947 to 1952 was a key member of the *Rassemblement du Peuple Français* (RPF) (qv). In 1958 he immediately sided with de Gaulle and helped form the Gaullist *Union pour la Nouvelle République* (UNR) (qv). From 1958 to 1959 he held the post of secretary general of the UNR. He helped draft the constitution of the Fifth Republic, and in 1959 served as minister of information. Known as a brilliant administrator with a flair for reformism, Frey has continued to play a vital role in the Fifth Republic.

Freycinet, Charles de (1828–1923) A friend of Léon Gambetta (qv), de Freycinet helped organise the Government of National Defence in 1870. From 1877 to 1879 he served as minister of public works, and from 1879 to 1880 and again in 1882 he held the presidency of the Council of Ministers. He was minister of foreign affairs in 1885, and from 1888 to 1893, minister of war. From 1890 to 1892 he was premier. De Freycinet continued to fight for a normalisation of relations between the church and the state, and he supported the Ralliement (qv). He continued to advocate and to vote for extended military service such as the Three Year Law of 1913. In 1882 de Freycinet was elected to the *Académie des Sciences*, and in 1890 he was elected to the *Académie française*. His service to the Republic was great, and his major contribution was of mature cabinet stability and serious public administration. He served France during World War I from 1915 to 1916 as minister of state and continued in the Senate until 1920.

Friedland, Battle of   On 14 June 1807 Napoléon inflicted a stinging defeat on the Russians at Friedland in East Prussia. The defeat was not total since the Russian armies retired in good order, keeping their combat ability intact. This defeat brought about the discussions between France and Russia which led to the Treaties of Tilsit of 1807 (qv).

Fructidor, Coup of 18   The Directory (qv), fearing internal difficulties, decided to purge the Assemblies of ultraconservative deputies. Napoléon Bonaparte (qv) was called upon to send a general to take command of the troops which guarded the Assembly at the Tuileries. On 4 September 1799, or 18 Fructidor, Year V, General Augereau (qv) commanding the troops purged over 130 royalist and conservative members of the Assembly. The directors hailed this as a step to avoid a royalist coup d'état. Two notable directors were forced to resign from that body in fear for their lives. François Barthélemy (qv) at first refused to resign, but he was forced out and sent to prison. Lazare Carnot (qv), one of the most famous of the directors, had to flee from France. The Fructidor action had two very positive effects. First, the coup strengthened the Directory, at least temporarily, and secondly, it enhanced the prestige of Napoléon Bonaparte, who supported the use of Augereau's troops to aid in the coup d'état.

Gaillard, Félix (1919–   )   A deputy in 1946 and president of the Radical Party from 1958 to 1961, Gaillard formed a government which lasted from November 1957 to April 1958. Gaillard inherited the problems of *immobilisme* (qv) and the Algerian War. These two problems, one internal, the other external, made actual government in France impossible. Criticised for his concessions to Tunisia in 1958, Gaillard faced bitter opposition from the army and the right. After 1958 he tried to salvage the Radical Party and make it a vital force in the Fifth Republic.

Galliéni, Joseph-Simon (1849–1916)   A professional soldier, Galliéni served in Tonkin, the French Sudan and Madagascar. His *tache d'huile* concept was used to pacify these areas for France. Basically, he believed that strong governmental French authority had to be established. This authority would slowly extend French control over native tribes, exploiting differences and antagonisms, thereby making French control more sure. A friend of Eugène Etienne (qv) and Hubert Lyautey (qv), Galliéni was a hero to the imperialists. In 1914 Galliéni, an ill man, was named military governor of Paris and second in command to General Joffre (qv). His famed 'Taxi Cab Army' turned the tide of battle on the Marne River in 1914. From 1914 to 1916, the dying Galliéni served as minister of war.

Gallifet, Gaston (1830–1909)   An explorer and colonial soldier, Gallifet was named minister of war in 1899. Serving under René Waldeck-Rousseau (qv), he was not interested in colonial affairs, and tried as a conservative to end the Dreyfus (qv) affair. In 1900 he was violently attacked by both ends of the political spectrum as being too soft in dealing with ultra-Catholics and Dreyfusards, and was forced to resign from the war ministry.

Gambetta, Léon (1838–1882)   A burly, one-eyed republican of Italian origin, Léon Gambetta became a lawyer in 1860. In 1869 he was elected deputy for Marseilles. At the same time Gambetta campaigned for a seat for the volatile Paris working-class district of Belleville, where he issued his famous Belleville Manifesto (qv). Once in the assembly, he joined the opposition to the empire and to Napoléon III's (qv) policies. As a member of the Government of National Defence, Gambetta proclaimed the republic at the Hôtel de Ville on 4 September 1870. Named minister of the interior, he escaped from Paris in a balloon to organise, in October, an army to relieve Paris. Believing in the possibility of another Valmy (qv), he soon became discouraged. Opposing an armistice with the Germans, he resigned from the government. He was elected a deputy for Bas-Rhin in February 1871, and he protested against the German annexation of Alsace-Lorraine. In July 1871 he resigned his seat for Bas-Rhin to stand as a deputy for Paris, where he was elected. From 1871 to 1873 he fought against the return of the Comte de Chambord (qv) and the re-establishment of the French monarchy. When President MacMahon (qv) dissolved the Chamber on 16 May 1877, Gambetta, who was fully dedicated to republicanism, along with Adolphe Thiers (qv) fought together to defeat the monarchist threat posed by the actions of MacMahon. The electoral triumph sustained by the republicans elevated Gambetta to their leadership. From 1876 to 1879 Gambetta was president of the Budget Commission, and from 1879 to 1881 he held the post of president of the Chamber. However, it was not until 1881 that he became president of the Council of Ministers. His 'Grand Ministry', short-lived as it was, turned out to be something of a dismal footnote to his career. Opposed by President Jules Grévy (qv), deserted by those allies who feared his dictatorial nature, and failing to include any first-rank republicans in his cabinet, he was unable to accomplish much. The Gambetta ministry lasted from November 1881 to February 1882, and after his fall, he became very embittered. Weakened by a bullet wound, Gambetta died on 31 December 1882 at Ville d'Avray. However, he did much to sustain the fragile, young Third Republic, and he left behind a number of dedicated republicans who would continue to keep alive the republic which he had proclaimed in September 1870.

Gamelin, Georges (1879–1958) Seeing service in World War I with Joffre (qv), Gamelin rose in rank and in 1930 joined the general staff under Maxime Weygand (qv). One of the main commanders in 1940, he was disgraced because of the fall of France in 1940 and was removed from command by Paul Reynaud (qv).

Garnier, Marie-Joseph (1839–1873) A famous colonial explorer, Garnier, from 1860 to 1862, led an expedition to Cochin-China which prepared French claims to that area of south-eastern Asia. After 1870 he returned to explore and pacify Tonkin, but was killed in an ambush.

Garnier-Pagès, Etienne Louis (1801–1841) Garnier-Pagès was born in Marseilles on 27 December 1801. A liberal lawyer, he was one of the major leaders in the opposition to Orléanist policy. He helped found the liberal society *Aide-Toi, le Ciel t'aidera*, and was one of its chiefs from 1831 to 1835. He died in Paris on 23 June 1841.

Garnier-Pagès, Louis-Antoine (1803–1878) Brother of Etienne Louis Garnier-Pagès (qv), Louis was also born in Marseilles, on 16 February 1803. Elected deputy in 1842, he allied himself with the ultra-liberal opposition to Louis Philippe. In 1848 Garnier-Pagès became a member of the Provisional Government of 1848 (qv) as the minister of finance. He also held the post of commissioner in 1848. However, in June 1848 he was removed by General Cavaignac (qv). Garnier-Pagès opposed the rule of Napoléon III and later played a minor role in the Government of National Defence in 1871. In 1871 he stood for election to the Chamber, lost, and retired from public life. He died in Paris on 31 October 1878.

Geneva Accords of 1954 On 26 April 1954 a meeting of the great powers was convened in Geneva to discuss the future of Indo-China and to decide the course of the French presence in south-east Asia. On 7 May 1954 word reached Geneva of the fall of Dien Bien Phu garrison. This news moved the powers, divided along ideological lines, toward a final accord, and representatives of the Vietminh, the communist Vietnamese insurgents, were invited to send a delegation to the Geneva meeting. On 4 June 1956 the treaties of independence for Vietnam were initialled, and on 20 July the full text of the Geneva Accords was ready for signature. The accords imposed an immediate ceasefire on Vietnam, Laos and Cambodia. The Vietminh were to evacuate Laos and Cambodia. After two years, free elections were scheduled for Vietnam. The United States would guarantee the armistice and accords. On 29 December 1954 France and the states of Indo-China signed full treaties of independence in Paris. By 30 March 1956 all French troops had departed from Vietnam, but Vietnam was divided into two states separated along the seventeenth parallel.

Girondins   The Girondins were primarily deputies of fairly moderate persuasion, many of whom came from the Gironde. Young lawyers who were basically idealists, the Girondins soon attracted a large following in the Assembly and were supported by businessmen, merchants, industrialists and financiers. The Girondins, originally known as the Brissotins (qv), followed a policy of *laissez-faire* and advocated a federal system for France. They controlled the Assembly from 1791 to 1792, moved against the *émigrés* and declared war against the autocratic powers. With military reverses in 1792, the Girondins came under attack by the radical Jacobins (qv), and, after the attacks on the king by mobs on 10 August 1792, their popularity fell rapidly. In January 1793 they vainly attempted to save the king's life, but failed. With the establishment of the Committee of Public Safety the fate of the Girondins was sealed, and Maximilien de Robespierre (qv) moved against them, arresting and executing many Girondin leaders including Brissot (qv) and Roland (qv). After the massive revolt of 31 May 1793 the Girondins were proscribed, but after Thermidor the official ban against them was lifted in March 1795, and many returned to the Assembly. Most Girondins joined with the Thermidorians to effect a moderate-conservative republican revolution. However, the Girondins were weakened and would never again dominate French politics.

Goblet, René (1828–1905)   A follower of Léon Gambetta (qv), Goblet served as minister of the interior in 1882. He then joined the radical opposition to the second Ferry (qv) government. After a period of service as minister of education, he became premier from 1886 to 1887 and in 1887 served as chief of the Quai d'Orsay. By 1893 Goblet began to move closer to the socialists, and his own political power was seriously weakened.

Gouvernement Provisoire de la République Française (GPRF) General Charles de Gaulle (qv) gave this title to the *Comité Français de la Libération Nationale* (CFLN) (qv) as he became determined to re-establish civil government in France during and after the liberation. The allies—Britain, Russia and the US—finally recognised the GPRF as the legitimate government of France in June 1944. Basically the provisional government lasted until the October 1945 elections to a Constituent Assembly. The Constituent Assembly was given seven months in which to draft a constitution for the Fourth Republic. In January 1946 de Gaulle stepped down and his place taken by Félix Gouin, and in 1946 the provisional government was replaced by the ineffective Fourth Republic.

Gouvion Saint-Cyr, Laurent (1764–1830)   Artist and soldier, Gouvion, in 1792, became a member of the *Chasseurs Républicains*, and, after service in the army of the Rhine (1792–7), he was named a general in June 1794. From 1799 to 1800 he took part in campaigns in Italy and Germany, and in 1800 he became a *conseiller d'état* charged with a number of diplomatic missions to Naples and to Spain. Napoléon Bonaparte (qv) named him a Marshal of France during the Russian campaign of 1812, and in 1813 he helped defend Dresden. With the return of Louis XVIII (qv) to France, Gouvion Saint-Cyr rallied to their cause and was made a peer of France. Loyal to the Bourbons, he became minister of war in 1815 and later minister of the marine in 1817. Louis XVIII made him a marquis in 1817, and from 1817 to 1819 he held the post of minister of war. After charges were levelled against him, accusing him of favouring the old imperial army, Saint-Cyr retired to his estate and lived the remainder of his life away from public view.

Gramont, Antoine (1819–1880)   From 1863 to 1870 Gramont, Prince de Bidache, served as minister to Austria, and he was responsible in large part for hostile French attitudes towards Prussia. It was Gramont, as minister of foreign affairs in 1870, who instructed the French minister to Prussia to force a response from Prussia's William I in regard to the Spanish Hohenzollern candidacy. This action resulted in the Ems Dispatch (qv) and the disastrous Franco-Prussian War.

Grande Armée Catholique Royale In the spring of 1792 the royalists in the Vendée and in Brittany formed the Royal Catholic Grand Army to fight against the revolution. Comprised of individual peasants who resented actions against the church, priests deprived of their parishes, and local nobility, the Grand Army was anything but large, but it was effective and caused a menace to the government in Paris. Fighting from ambush and encouraged by England and by *émigrés*, the army fought on for several years, causing great concern in Paris. Eventually, by 1793, due to the death of many noble leaders and the violent countermeasures taken by Jean Carrier (qv), the army dwindled and the peasants returned to their farms. The army was an attempt by nobles, non-juring priests, and confused peasants to counter the revolution, and it was symptomatic of the type of royalist activity against Paris and the revolution.

Great Act of 1892 (working conditions) The rising calls for reforms along the lines of the famous English Factory Acts were to lead to the minor reform bills of 1848, 1874 and 1885. By the last decade of the century the demands for humanitarian reforms culminated in what many parliamentary leaders called the Great Act of 1892. This regulated female labour and stopped the employment of children under thirteen years of age; working days were limited to ten hours per day, almost all manual labour was forbidden on Sunday, and if a worker did attend his job on Sunday he would be compensated on another day. This act motivated another law of 1893 which ensured adequate hygiene and safety of workers and required that free medical care at factories be available. This law was followed by the more comprehensive law of 15 July 1893 (qv) which dealt with national medical care. The Great Act of 1892 was

135

hailed as a step forward as far as progressive social legislation was concerned. The Great Act of 1892 and the Law of 15 July 1893 set the tone for the legislation of the next century.

Great Fear The Great Fear occurred in late July 1789 and lasted for several weeks in the rural areas of France. After a period of desperate hunger and worry over events at Versailles, the rural peasantry were electrified by the news of the Bastille's fall. As starving peasants rifled the fields, the owners of the farms felt that this despoilation was an aristocratic plot or even, some speculated, a liberal plot. Rumours of troops or brigands pillaging and raping sent the countryside into a state of panic. Suddenly the peasantry attacked symbols of the old regime, burning feudal rolls and often attacking châteaux. The fear spread to major population centres such as Nîmes, Tours and Bordeaux. The impact of fear and violence in these provincial but major cities was dramatic. Bordeaux was France's third largest town, and Nîmes ranked ninth. Order was finally restored by the forces available to provincial city and small-town magistrates, but the fear left a legacy of distrust in the provinces against the revolution.

Grégoire, Henri (1750–1831) Born near Lunéville in a small village called Vého on 4 December 1750, Grégoire's youth was spent in very modest circumstances. Educated by Jesuits, he entered the priesthood and in 1789 was elected a deputy for the Clergy. A liberal, Gregoire helped draft the Civil Constitution of the Clergy, and in 1791 he was elected Bishop of Blois. During the Convention of 1792 he represented the Loir-et-Cher and fought for the abolition of slavery. He refused to accept the French Concordat with the church. In 1801 he became a member of the Senate and served with a rare independence of convictions. Elected deputy from Isère in 1819, Grégoire's election was declared invalid. Until his death in Paris on 28 May 1831 Grégoire consistently refused to retract any statement or action he had made during the revolution.

Grévy, Jules (1807–1891) Grévy was born to a well-to-do family at Mont-sous-Vaudrey in the Jura on 15 August

1807. He was a lawyer and a liberal in the tradition of 1848, and from 1871 to 1873 served as president of the National Assembly. From 1876 to 1879 he was president of the Chamber, and in 1879 was elected as the first true republican president of the French Republic. Re-elected in 1885, he was ousted as president as a result of the Wilson affair (qv) in 1887. He retired to his home in the Jura and died there on 9 November 1891.

Group Coloniale The Colonial Group, led by Eugène Etienne (qv) and other militant colonialist deputies, was also known as the *Parti colonial* (qv). It was instrumental in popularising the cause of imperialism in the Chamber.

Guesde, Mathieu Jules (1845–1922) A liberal adversary of the Second Empire, Guesde was imprisoned as a pacifist in 1870. Condemned as a communard in 1871, he was exiled to Italy but was pardoned in 1876 and returned to France to begin a career in left-wing journalism. In 1879 he founded the *Parti ouvrier* (qv), a marxist workers' party; but basically he opposed the doctrinaire marxists and refused to cooperate with them. He thought of the *Parti ouvrier* as a revolutionary not a reformist party. From 1893 to 1906 he served as a deputy for Lille and gained a reputation as an enemy of Jean Jaurès (qv). Guesde brought the *Parti ouvrier* into the *Section française de l'Internationale ouvrière* (qv) in 1905, and he gave the new party a revolutionary tinge. He believed that cooperation with bourgeois governments was impossible. The followers of Guesde accepted his idea that socialists remained in opposition until they controlled the government and could reform it according to marxist principles. However, when World War I broke out in August 1914, René Viviani, president of the Council, formed the *Union Sacrée* (qv), and he asked Jules Guesde to become a member, and although he had once preached against cooperation with anything but a true socialist government, he joined this union. Guèsde accepted the title of minister of state, which carried no departmental duties. However, Guesde's presence in the government was a symbolic gesture of unity in the face of the threat of defeat at the hands of the Germans, and the old socialist saw this as more of a danger to French socialism than cooperation with a mixed, non-socialist government.

Guizot, François (1787–1874)   A protestant intellectual, Guizot was born in Nîmes on 4 October 1787 and studied in Geneva and Paris. He became a professor of history at the Sorbonne in 1812 and rallied to the restoration and served Louis XVIII. In 1822 he was suspended from his duties at the university. In 1828, after the publication of his *History of the English Revolution*, he was restored to his position, but in 1830 he played a role in the downfall of Charles X. In August 1830 he became minister of the interior and in 1832 entered into a cabinet with Adolphe Thiers (qv) and the Duc de Broglie (qv). As minister of education he organised primary education in 1833. Guizot's Education Bill of 1833 established a primary school in every commune in France, and the bill also provided for expanded facilities to train teachers. The concept of widespread free, compulsory education was not a part of the bill, and indeed, general education was not highly thought of nor an accepted premise. The Guizot law was, despite its shortcomings, properly called the Charter of Primary Education. In 1840 Guizot served as minister to Britain, but was recalled because of his rather irritating personality which did not help Anglo-French relations. In 1840 he formed a ministry which was conservative and suspicious of parliamentary reforms and public opinion. His conservative attitudes, which tended to be uncompromising, antagonised liberal public opinion. When French liberals scheduled a mass meeting in Paris on 22 February 1848 Guizot cancelled it, and this inflamed opinion even more. He fell because of his opposition to the liberal Banquet Movement (qv) and during the revolution of 1848 he was forced to flee France. After 1849 he devoted himself to the writing of history and the advancement of conservative government in France. He died at Val-Riches (Calvados) on 12 October 1874.

Hague, Treaty of the   On 16 May 1795 the treaty of the Hague was signed between France and Holland, which was occupied by French troops. The treaty gave France the areas of Flanders, Maestricht and Venlou. A huge indemnity was levied on the Dutch, who were also bound to France by an alliance.

Halévy, Daniel (1872–1962)   An historian, critic and sociologist, Halévy described in detail living and working conditions in rural France. His observations had a dramatic impact on legislation pertaining to agricultural France. He was responsible for promoting vast amounts of social legislation during the Third Republic. In 1937 he wrote *La République des ducs*, which described the crisis of 1876–7 in France. In 1938 he edited, with a collaborator, *Lettres de Gambetta, 1868–1882*. His visits to a rural village on the edge of the Massif Central, over a twenty-five-year period, formed the basis for his famous *Visites aux paysans du Centre* (1907–34), which was first published in Paris in 1935.

Hanotaux, Gabriel (1853–1944)   Hanotaux was born at Beaurevoir in the Aisne on 19 November 1853. A professional historian of high reputation, he served in the Chamber from 1886 to 1889 as a follower of Gambetta (qv) and Ferry (qv). A close ally of the colonialists, he was known as an imperialist militant. In 1892 he took a post in the Quai d'Orsay, and from 1894 to 1895 and from 1896 to 1898 he was chief of the foreign ministry. Hanotaux reinforced the Franco-Russian Alliance of 1894 (qv) and confronted the British in Africa. It was as an expansionist that he gained his fame. He pushed French claims in East and West Africa almost to the point of a diplomatic rupture between England and France. He was toppled from power as a result of the Fashoda Crisis (qv) in 1898 and never returned to the government. His *Histoire du Cardinal Richelieu* and *Histoire de la nation française* stand as classics of French history. After 1898 he devoted his life to history and popularising the colonial cause. Continually called upon as a speaker and lecturer, Hanotaux remained a popular figure in political and colonial circles. He died in Paris on 11 April 1944.

Harmand, François-Jules (1845–1921)   A leading imperial theorist, Harmand began his career as an administrator in Indo-China in the 1880s. Through his many books and articles he helped popularise colonialism. His main interest was to win the French away from the concept of assimilation (qv) to the newer concept of associationism (qv).

Haussman, Georges Eugène (1809–1891) A native of Paris, Haussman was born on 27 March 1809. An administrator under Louis-Philippe (qv), Haussman rallied to Napoléon III, and in 1852 went to Paris as prefect of the Seine. He helped rebuild Paris by enlarging boulevards, constructing parks and squares and raising buildings. He was ousted from his post in 1869. He fell from public view and died in his native city on 11 January 1891.

Hébert, Joseph René (1757–1794) A writer turned revolutionary Hébert was born at Alençon on 15 November 1757. Hébert was a prominent member of the *Club des Cordeliers* (qv) and served in the insurrection of 10 August 1792 (qv). In the Assembly he sat with the Montagnards (qv) and struggled against the Girondins (qv). Arrested on 24 May 1793, he was freed by a Paris mob four days later. His victory marks a decline in Girondist fortunes. Hébert was an extreme anti-Christian who wished to wipe out the faith in France, and his overt hostility to the Jacobins (qv) earned him the hatred of Robespierre (qv), Couthon (qv) and Saint-Just (qv). Hébert was arrested during the Terror and executed on 24 March 1794. After his death the Hébertists (qv) continued their hatred of the traditional church.

Hébertists The Hébertists followed Hébert (qv) who had been a leader during the violence of 10 August 1792 (qv). Extremists who demanded a far-reaching alteration in France's religious life, they had the cathedral of Notre Dame converted into a temple dedicated to Reason and in the space of thirty days over 2,000 churches were converted to the worship of Reason. The Hébertists followed an economic policy which was quite close to socialism. The Committee of Public Safety (qv) decided to crush the Hébertists, and Maximilien de Robespierre (qv) undertook a campaign against them. Hébert went to the guillotine as did many prominent Hébertists, but the movement survived as Hébert's followers continued to urge a drastic alteration in France's religious life.

Helvetian Republic   Switzerland, named the Helvetian or Helvetic Republic, played a major strategic role in French campaigns in northern Italy in 1800. In early 1798 France had taken Switzerland by force and created the Helvetian Republic. Recognised as a critical geographical factor as far as campaigns in Italy or southern Germany were concerned, the French government was determined to keep it attached to France. By the Treaty of Lunéville (qv) in early 1801 between France and Austria, the existence of the Helvetian Republic was recognised. In theory it was organised with a republican system, nominally independent from France. However, in 1802, due to severe internal disagreement, delegates from the republic called on Bonaparte to mediate between the factions. Bonaparte, while opposed to federalism, did allow a redrawing of the Swiss political system into the Swiss Confederation by the Act of Mediation of 1803. Bonaparte remembered the military importance of Switzerland and kept it tied to France by military alliance.

Hérault de Séchelles, Marie-Jean (1759–1794)   A noble and a liberal, Hérault was a devotee of Rousseau. He sat with the Montagnards (qv) and was elected to sit on the Committee of Public Safety in 1793. While not on friendly terms with Robespierre (qv), he did endeavour to serve the Terror, but he earned the hatred of Robespierre who accused him of plotting with foreigners against France and the Terror. Hérault was denounced, tried and guillotined.

Herriot, Edouard (1872–1957)   A major leftist politician and mayor of Lyon from 1905 to 1912, Herriot headed the *Cartel des Gauches* (qv) government in 1924. During his tenure as president of the Council of Ministers, he met with the British prime minister Ramsay MacDonald in England. He also urged and got France to recognise the Soviet Union on 28 October 1924. Basically Herriot opposed Raymond Poincaré's (qv) harsh policies against Germany, and during his premiership he sought to reverse this policy. In 1932 he served as premier again for a brief period and held a post in the Pierre Laval (qv) government which he resigned in protest over the Hoare-Laval Pact (qv). Herriot had hoped to maintain a solid allied front against Italian aggression in Ethiopia, but failed. Between his resignation from the Laval government and 1939 he called for French resistance against the Germans. After the fall of France and the collapse of the Third Republic he opposed the Vichy government in 1940 and during the war years 1940-4 he was persecuted by the Vichy administration.

Hoare-Laval Pact   This pact signed between Sir Samuel Hoare, England's foreign secretary, and Premier Pierre Laval (qv) on 8 December 1935 was a futile attempt to settle the Ethiopian crisis on terms very favourable to fascist Italy. This abortive pact marks one of the first attempts to reverse France's search for security in Central Europe and a turn to Mussolini's Italy.

Hoche, Louis-Lazare (1768–1797)   Hoche began his career in the army in 1784 and entered the National Guard. As a sergeant in 1789 he rallied to the revolution and in 1792 was given the rank of lieutenant in the 58th Infantry Regiment. In September 1793, after a brilliant performance against the British at Dunkerque, Hoche was promoted to a brigade general. A month later he was given command of the army of the Moselle. While serving in the army of Italy, he was arrested in April 1794. However, after Thermidor he was released and returned to active military duty. He commanded the troops in the Brest-Cherbourg area and in July 1795 Hoche defeated a royalist force. Also in 1795 he took part in operations in the Vendée. In 1797 he was given command of the army of the Sambre-et-Meuse and fought against the Austrians. He fell in battle at Wetzlar on 18 September 1797.

Hubert, Lucien (1868–1936)   A deputy and senator, Hubert served in the Algerian administration under Charles Jonnart (qv). He advocated social reforms in Algeria in respect to Muslims and wrote articles and books supporting reformism.

Hugo, Victor (1802–1885) The son of a soldier, Victor Hugo, who was born at Besançon on 26 February 1802, became a famous writer and commentator on France's social and political life. Imprisoned in 1814 because of his father's connection with Napoléon Bonaparte (qv), he learned to dislike political oppression of any sort. By 1819 his first works appeared and by 1825 he was honoured as a major writer. During the Orléanist period (1830–48) Hugo's fame grew as works were published and presented in the theatres of Paris. A liberal in 1848, he sat in the Assembly as a deputy and espoused moderate republicanism. In 1852, after Napoléon's coup d'état of 1851, he fled France and resided in Belgium. In 1856 he refused an amnesty from Napoléon III and exiled himself to England. In 1861 Hugo finished his classic work *Les Misérables* in Belgium. In 1870 he returned to France and was elected deputy in 1871. In 1872 he retired from politics to continue writing. He died in Paris on 22 May 1885.

Hundred Days, The While Napoléon was in exile on Elba, political and social conditions in France grew worse. Louis XVIII's (qv) Charter of 1814 (qv) was far from being fulfilled, and the public debt was mounting. The downgrading of Napoleonic generals in favour of royalists, many of whom fought against France during the Napoleonic Wars, carried discontent into the military. Bonaparte himself was restless and decided to attempt a return to France. On 1 March 1815 he landed in southern France, and he entered Paris in triumph on 20 March 1815. The allies, assembled in Vienna, heard of Napoléon's return and Louis XVIII's flight and branded Napoléon an international outlaw. While he maintained the façade of a liberal ruler, all his measures were temporary and depended on the military outcome of a clash with the allies. On 18 June 1815 he lost the Battle of Waterloo (qv) and retreated to Paris. By 8 July 1815 Louis XVIII had again entered Paris, and seven days later Napoléon surrendered to the British. The allies' anger over the Hundred Days was, as can be imagined, severe. Louis XVIII was urged by the Duke of Wellington to hasten to France to keep the allies from dismembering the state. On 3 July 1815 Paris capitulated to an allied army, and on 8 July Louis XVIII again entered Paris. Tallyrand (qv) began to negotiate with the allies who were determined to be less lenient than they had been in 1814. France was reduced to the borders of 1790, and the fortresses of Saarlouis and Landau were ceded to the allies along with some eastern border areas. A large war indemnity was imposed in the sum of 700 million francs. A five-year military occupation was imposed on France as punishment. The new terms were signed by all parties on 20 November 1815 in Paris.

Immobilisme; immobiliste *Immobilisme* was primarily a malady of the Fourth Republic's political system. On the whole, *immobilisme* was simply a standstill policy. It meant neither a retreat backward nor any great reformist moves forward. Some conservatives saw this as a means to combat communism and the *Parti Communiste Français* (PCF) (qv). Pierre Mendès-France (qv) was one of the premiers who attempted to move out of the lethargy of *immobilisme*, but he had little success. Many pro-colonial deputies tried the tactics of *immobilisme*, in regard to the issue of independence for Morocco and Tunisia, but the Fourth Republic had enough strength to come to terms with the feelings of separatism in North Africa. It was clear by 1958 that *immobilisme* and its advocates had created a chaotic governmental situation in France which could only be remedied by strong leadership.

Imperial Recess of 1803 After two years of hard work from 1801 to 1802 Napoléon had outlined to the German rulers, to the Russian tsar and to Emperor Francis I of Austria a scheme for the redrawing of the map of Germany to France's benefit. The Imperial Recess reduced the free cities from fifty-two to six, and the small ecclesiastical states of southern Germany were abolished, save one. Bavaria, Württemberg, and Baden also gained a good deal of territory as a result of the suppression of the free cities. Napoléon had extended France's frontiers to the Rhine and had weakened Austrian and Prussian influence in the German states.

Indispensable Freedoms Adolphe Thiers (qv) made a speech on 11 January 1864 in the legislative body as a deputy for Paris. In it he outlined the centre-opposition programme. The five Indispensable Freedoms were: the freedom of safety for the citizen, the freedom to exchange ideas, the freedom of national representation, the freedom of the electors and freedom for the Assembly to represent the will of the majority.

Indo-China See: Auriol-Bao Daï Accords; Fontainebleau, Conference of; Franco-Cambodian Accords; Franco-Laotian Accords; Franco-Vietnamese Accords of 1946; Geneva Accords of 1954.

Interpellations The Right of Interpellation was a procedure whereby a minister could be called before the Chamber to explain his actions to that body. If the Assembly was not satisfied, a vote of no confidence could be registered against the government. Actually the practice had begun during the revolution in 1791, but Napoléon III suspended the right from 1852 to 1869. The Third Republic reconfirmed the right in the Law of 13 March 1873 (qv).

Italy, Kingdom of Napoléon Bonaparte had paid court to the goals of Italian nationalism when he created the Cisalpine Republic (qv). However, he converted the Italian states into the Italian republic. In March 1805, as a result of imperial ambitions, the republican concept was abandoned and the Italian republic was changed into the Italian kingdom; in Milan Napoléon took the crown of Italy for himself.

Jacobins; Jacobin Club Officially the Society of the Friends of the Constitution, the Club originated in 1789 and in 1790 admitted non-deputies as members. By 1791 there were over 400 Jacobin clubs in all of France. A club of the left, it grew more radical from 1789 to 1791 and at the same time it became the strongest of all clubs. It imposed a 'party' discipline which meant a united block of votes in the Assembly. Slowly, the Jacobins became associated with extreme equalitarianism and violence. After the crises of August and September 1792, the Jacobins, headed by Maximilien de Robespierre (qv), became supreme in the Assembly. Leading the attack on the Girondins (qv) in 1793, they played on the patriotism and the fears of the people. They had an important role in the government during 1793 and 1794. They tended to support a centralisation of the state, strict economic controls and a patriotic war against the autocratic powers of Europe. Jacobins were prominent in their support of the purge of the Girondins, and the Jacobin leadership supported the Terror. After Thermidor, the Jacobin Club was in disrepute, and in 1794 it was ordered to purge its ranks of Robespierrists. On 12 November 1794 the club was formally suppressed. Jacobin sentiment continued in France and there were several Jacobin revolts after 1794.

Jaurès, Jean (1859–1914) Jean Jaurès was born at Castres on 3 September 1859. The father of French evolutionary socialism, Jaurès entered the Chamber in 1885 as a devout republican. In 1889 he won fame in an attack on General Georges Boulanger (qv), and for his defence of the Republic he lost his position in the Chamber. He turned to journalism and in his articles showed a definite move toward socialism. By 1892 his socialism, idealistic and humanitarian with a dash of militancy, was formed. Jaurès returned to the Chamber in 1893, and there defended the workers' right to strike. A champion of Captain Dreyfus (qv), in 1898 he lost his seat in the Chamber because of his outspoken support for him. From 1898 to 1902 he wrote his *L'Histoire socialiste de la révolution française*. In 1902 he returned to the Chamber, and associated with the *Parti socialiste français*, supporting Emile Combes's (qv) efforts to separate church and state. In 1905 Jaurès helped form the *Section Française d'Internationale Ouvrière* (SFIO) (qv). After 1905 he opposed socialist entry into governments as being against working-class interests. As a result of the Second Moroccan Crisis (qv) of 1911, he devoted more time to the world peace movement and on 31 July 1914 was murdered by a rightist fanatic. Jaurès's work for peace had marked him in the eyes of the ultra-patriotic as a traitor, and as war clouds in Europe gathered many rightists believed that Jaurès had to be silenced if France was to enter the war as a united nation.

Jena, Battle of   The battle of Jena, fought on 14 October 1806, was a complete defeat for the Prussian armies. The French armies under the general command of Napoléon Bonaparte (qv) and General Davout (qv) won a brilliant victory at Jena and at Auerstadt. On 25 October 1807 French troops under General Davout marched into Berlin. Panic gripped the Prussian army, and they surrendered to the French in vast numbers, but a portion of it continued its resistance. At the battle of Eylau on 7 February 1807 a combined Russian-Prussian army engaged the French armies with no actual victory for either side. By late June 1807 French troops had occupied most of Prussia. The battle of Jena, one of Napoléon's greatest victories, marked the disgrace, surrender and occupation of Prussia.

Jeunesses Patriotes   The young patriots was a right-wing organisation in France during the 1930s. Often violent, they espoused a form of French fascism. Founded by Pierre Taittinger in 1924, they participated in the riots of 6 February 1934 (qv).

Joffre, Joseph (1852–1931)   Joffre, born at Rivesalles on 12 January 1852 was a soldier who saw extensive colonial service, and was a friend of General Joseph Galliéni (qv), who helped his career. Promoted to general in 1902, Joffre was marked for supreme command, and in 1911 he was elevated to chief of the French general staff. In 1914 he was instrumental in winning the battle of the Marne, but by 1915 and 1916 his offensives had failed with tragic losses. Joffre was known as a man with an unshakeable confidence in France and in France's armies. One of his main contributions to the war effort in 1914 was his calmness and his inspiring faith in France's ultimate victory. He was replaced by General Nivelle after the costly battle of Verdun in 1916, but was given a marshal's baton. Dispatched to America on a diplomatic mission in 1917, Joffre was hailed as a hero, but in 1918 he retired to write. He died in Paris on 3 January 1931.

Jonnart, Charles Célestin (1857–1927) One of the most famous of Algerian governors, Jonnart entered the Chamber in 1889. He allied himself with the moderate republicans and in 1893 held the post of minister of public works in the Casimir Périer (qv) government. During the 1894 debates on the creation of a colonial ministry he was prominent in the defence of the new ministry. His speeches attracted the attention of Eugène Etienne (qv) and the imperialists, who welcomed Jonnart's appointment as governor general of Algeria in 1901. Appointed by René Waldeck-Rousseau (qv), Jonnart served two years in Algeria before returning to France. From 1903 to 1911 he again served as governor general of Algeria, and in 1919 proposed the Jonnart Laws (qv) which gave some reforms to Algerian Muslims. From 1921 to 1924 he served as French ambassador to the Vatican.

Jonnart Laws In 1919 the French Chamber passed a series of laws which were sponsored by Charles Jonnart (qv), an ex-governor general of Algeria. These laws enfranchised a limited number of Algerian Muslims. Basically, a small number of Muslims were given the vote under a special status which did not force a Muslim to renounce Islamic law in order to obtain French citizenship. There would be a larger electorate for Algerian assemblies. The right to vote for mayor was extended to almost a million Muslims who could qualify, and certain civil service posts were open to Algerians. The Jonnart Laws, passed in 1919 after fierce debate, came as too little too late for the Muslims, who were already embittered by years of ethnic discrimination.

Joséphine, Marie Joséphine Rose Tasche de la Pagerie (1763–1814) Born in Martinique on 23 June 1763, she arrived in France in 1779 and married the Viscount de Beauharnais (qv). She bore two children, Hortense (qv) and Eugène (qv). Arrested by the Jacobins in 1794, she was released after Thermidor. For a period of time, the impoverished Joséphine was Paul

Barras's (qv) mistress, and in 1796 she married Napoléon Bonaparte. In 1809, after she had failed to give Napoléon any children, she was divorced by him. She was, however, maintained in grand style, and she received the allied conquerors in 1814 at Malmaison as the empress of France. Joséphine died at Malmaison on 29 May 1814.

Joxe, Louis (1901–   )   Joxe, an historian by profession, organised the Gaullist resistance in Algeria from 1940 to 1943 and served as the secretary general to the French National Liberation Committee in Algiers from 1943 to 1944. During the period of the provisional government, under General Charles de Gaulle (qv), Joxe remained in Paris as the chief of the resistance in Algeria. From 1946 to 1952 he held a post at the Quai d'Orsay, and in 1952 he was named ambassador to Russia, where he served for three years. In 1956 he was named ambassador to West Germany. After de Gaulle's return to power in May 1958, Joxe returned to France to serve as an advisor to the general until July 1959. Because of his knowledge of Algeria, he was given the task of negotiating an end to the Algerian War in March 1962.

Junot, Andoche (1771–1813)   Entering the army in 1791, Junot attached himself to Napoléon at Toulon. He served in Italy and in Egypt, and in 1805 he was named ambassador to Portugal. In 1806 he was given command of the Portuguese armies and fought in Spain. In 1813 Junot became governor of Venice, but killed himself the same year.

Kellermann, François Etienne (1735–1820)   Born in Strasbourg, Kellermann entered the army as a cadet in 1752. In 1756 he became a lieutenant and during the Seven Years War he fought in Poland. In 1789 he rallied to the revolution, and in March 1792 he was nominated a lieutenant general. Subordinated to General Dumouriez (qv), Kellermann still maintained an independence of spirit and command. On 20 September 1792 he won the battle of Valmy, defeating the Austrians. A hero, Kellermann was given command of the army of the Alpes, and he conquered the Savoy in 1793. In

October 1793 he was imprisoned in Paris by the Convention but was liberated in January 1795. He was not to play an important military role again. In 1799 he became a senator, a Marshal in 1804, and in 1808 he was named Duc de Valmy. He rallied to the Bourbons and survived the restoration.

Kerillis, Henri de (1889–1959) A right-wing journalist, de Kerillis attacked the government and defended the rioters who took part in the Riots of February 1934 (qv). An early supporter of a new approach to Germany, he changed his mind and wrote against the Munich agreement. De Kerillis remained in France during the war years, and after liberation retired from public life.

Kléber, Jean-Baptiste (1753–1800) Born in Strasbourg, Kléber entered a military school in Bavaria, and from 1776 to 1785 he served in the Austrian army. He returned to his native Alsace and became the inspector of fortifications at Belfast. In July 1789 Kléber enlisted in the national guard of Belfast. After service in the army he was made a brigadier general and served in the Vendée, and in 1794 he served in the army of Ardennes. In 1796 he retired from the service but was recalled for the Egyptian campaign in 1798. After Napoléon Bonaparte (qv) left Egypt, Kléber, discontented with his position, commanded the armies of the Orient. He was murdered by a muslim fanatic on 14 June 1800 in Cairo as he was preparing a new campaign in Egypt.

Labédoyère, Charles Huchet (1786–1815) Born in Paris on 17 April 1786, Labédoyère was a career army officer who saw service in Poland from 1806 to 1807 and in Spain in 1808. Labédoyère rallied to Louis XVIII (qv) in 1814. During the first restoration he was awarded the Cross of Saint Louis by the Bourbons. He was given command of the 7th Regiment of the Line, but in March 1815, during the Hundred Days (qv), he joined Napoléon Bonaparte (qv) at Vizille near Paris. Napoléon named him a brigadier general and made him an aide de camp to the emperor. After the fall of Napoléon, Labédoyère, who had been elevated to general of a division, was seized by the restoration forces, tried, and shot on 19 August 1815 in Paris.

La Boeuf, Edmond (1809–1888)   In 1869 La Boeuf served as minister of war in the Ollivier (qv) cabinet, holding the post from 1869 to 1870 during the very critical period surrounding the Franco-Prussian War. La Boeuf was a confidant of Empress Eugénie (qv) and a leader of the anti-Prussian war faction in the French court. During the war of 1870 he continually opposed peace and was dismissed from his post as a result of France's many defeats and humiliations.

Labour Relations   See: Social Legislation.

Laclos, Pierre Ambroise de (1741–1803)   Born in Amiens on 18 October 1741, Laclos became an artillery officer and served until 1788. In 1782 he wrote his first novel, *Les Liaisons dangereuses*, a classic tale of a libertine. From 1788 to 1792 Laclos served the Duc d'Orléans (qv), and he became more infatuated with the republican cause. In 1792 he re-entered the army, but was imprisoned because of his association with Philippe-Egalité (qv). However, in 1799 Laclos was reinstated as a general and fought in Germany and Italy. He fell in battle at Tarente on 5 September 1803. A hundred years after his death two other works, *De l'Education des femmes* (1903) and *Lettres* (1904) were published.

Lafayette, Marie Joseph (1757–1834)   An army officer born to great wealth at the Château de Chavaniac (Haute-Loire) on 6 September 1757, Lafayette served in the American revolution and returned to France to lead the liberal pro-American faction at court prior to 1789. As a liberal he advocated reforms at the first meeting of the *Etats généraux* in 1789 and served the National Guard, commanding them during the Massacre of the Champs de Mars in 1791 (qv). During the hectic period of 1789 Lafayette tried to rally the king and the nobility to the revolution. He saw himself as a powerful force with a large following, but this was later proved to be a very false assumption. His popularity diminished, he fled France and was interned by the Austrians. After the Treaty of Campo

Formio (qv) he was released and took up residence in Germany. Lafayette was allowed to return to France in 1800 but refused to serve Napoléon Bonaparte (qv). During the Hundred Days (qv) he entered the Chamber and opposed Bonaparte, but he was also vocal in demanding moderation by the restored Bourbon Louis XVIII (qv). In 1818 he formally associated with the ultra-liberal left in the Assembly, and he criticised the policies of the ultras. Disgusted with the repressive policies of King Charles X (qv), Lafayette in 1824 undertook an extensive tour of America, and returned to France even more determined to oppose the ultra-conservative policies of the Bourbons. In 1830 he was instrumental in bringing Louis Philippe (qv) to the throne of France. In fact, it was Lafayette who convinced the populace to accept the Orléanist as king of the French. In 1831 Lafayette returned to the Chamber as an open advocate of liberal reformism, and he did not hesitate to criticise Louis Philippe and his administration, if necessary. He died in Paris on 20 May 1834.

Laffitte, Jacques (1767–1844)   Born on 24 October 1767 at Bayonne, Laffitte, one of France's leading financiers, became regent of the Bank of France in 1809. After 1815 he served as deputy and sat in the liberal opposition. Because of his liberalism he was removed from the directorship of the bank. Laffitte was one of the prime movers in bringing Louis Philippe to the throne in 1830, and he served as minister of finance from 1830 to 1831 and as president of the Council of Ministers from 1831 to 1832. Playing a vital role in the industrialisation of France, Laffitte continued from 1831 to his death in Paris on 26 May 1844 to support liberal reforms.

Lainé, Etienne (1767–1835)   Born in Bordeaux on 11 March 1767, Lainé practised law there until he was elected to the *Corps législatif* in 1808. He served in that body until 1813. Lainé was made *Préfet* of the Gironde in 1814, and from 1814 to 1815 he served as president of the Chamber of Deputies under Louis XVIII (qv). A royalist, Lainé served from 1816 to 1817 as minister of the interior. In 1817 he pushed for a modification of the election laws to serve Bourbon purposes. He served as minister of state from 1820 to 1821, but he opposed the extreme policies of Charles X (qv). After the 1830 revolution, Lainé retired from public life.

Lakanal, Joseph (1762–1845)   Joseph Lakanal was born to a good family at Serres (Ariège) on 14 July 1762. An excellent student, he pursued a career in teaching. As a member of the clergy, Lakanal held a high post in the office of the Bishop of Pamiers in 1791. In 1792 he was elected deputy for Ariège to the Convention, and once in the Convention he earned a place on the Committee for Public Instruction. Under his guidance the committee enlarged and modernised the system of schools in France. He became a member of the Five Hundred (qv) in 1795, but two years later he retired from politics. Under Napoléon Bonaparte (qv), Lakanal returned to government service as inspector of weights and measures (1807), and he guided France's acceptance of the metric system. In 1816 he fled France and took up a post as president of the University of New Orleans, Louisiana. He returned to France in 1836 and died in Paris on 14 February 1845.

Lamartine, Alphonse de (1790–1869)   Born in Mâcon on 21 October 1790, Lamartine was a member of a minor noble family. As a schoolboy, Lamartine admired Chateaubriand and Rousseau, and he showed an ability for writing poetry. However, in 1809 he began to study law, but because of family financial difficulties he had to quit. In 1811, after a trip to Italy, Lamartine wrote a tragic play. After the abdication of Napoléon Bonaparte (qv) in 1814, Lamartine entered into the service of Louis XVIII. He remained loyal to the king during the Hundred Days (qv), and after the second restoration of Louis XVIII, tried to obtain a diplomatic post but was turned down by the king. In 1817 he again began to write, and in 1820 he published *Les méditations poétiques*. His poetry attracted the attention of the royal court, and in 1819 he was named an attaché to the embassy at Naples, Italy. In 1823 he published

La mort de Socrate and *Les Nouvelles méditations*. A year later, inspired by Byron's death in Greece, he wrote *Le Dernier chant du pèlerinage d'Harold*. To show his royalist resentment, he wrote *Le chant du sacre* in honour of Charles X in 1825. In 1825 he was dispatched to Florence as the secretary to the ambassador, and in 1829 he was elected to the *Académie Française*. In 1830, Lamartine left the diplomatic service and went into politics as a liberal. In 1835, deeply depressed by the death of Julia, his ten-year-old daughter, Lamartine drifted away from his Catholic faith. As a deputy he championed liberal and democratic concepts, fighting against slavery and against the policies of Louis-Philippe. Lamartine continued to write, and in 1836 he published *Jocelyn*, followed by *Les Recueillements poétiques* in 1839. By 1843 he was acknowledged as the leader of the liberal opposition, and as such he warned against the revival of Bonapartism in France. In 1847 he published his famous *Histoire des Girondins*, an apologia of the revolution. Lamartine joined the Banquet Movement (qv) and was instrumental in the downfall of the Orléanist monarchy in February 1848. As minister of foreign affairs in the provisional government, Lamartine saw himself as the soul of the liberal movement, but in the presidential elections of 1848 he obtained a mere 17,910 votes against the 5½ million won by Louis Napoléon (qv). His political career ruined, Lamartine found himself in dire poverty. He continued to write, publishing *Les Confidences* and *Les Nouvelles Confidences* to raise money. After the coup d'état of 2 December 1851, Lamartine retired from public view. Struck by tragedy after tragedy, Lamartine sunk deeper into poverty, finally selling his family home in 1861. He died an embittered, discouraged man in February 1869 in a small house lent to him as a charitable gesture.

Lamoricière, Louis-Christophe de (1806–1865)   A famous colonial soldier, Lamoricière was born in Nantes on 5 February 1806. In 1828 he entered the army as an officer and was sent to Algeria in 1830. While in Algeria, Lamoricière organised the first Arab Bureau and the first regiment of

Zouaves. In 1840 he served as second-in-command to Bugeaud (qv) and fought against Abdel Kader in 1843–4. He received Abdel Kader's surrender in 1847. Elected deputy for Sarthe in 1846, he served that district during the critical days of the revolution of 1848. After Louis Napoléon's (qv) coup d'état of 2 December 1852 Lamoricière was expelled from France. Allowed to return in 1857, he took command of the army of the Papal States in Italy in 1860. He soon retired from active military service, returned to France, and died at Prouzel on 11 September 1865.

Lamy, Etienne Marie (1845–1919)   A noted liberal Catholic deputy, Lamy helped to establish in 1896 the *Fédération électorale* (qv). This liberal group was organised, with Pope Leo XIII's blessings, to reconcile French Catholicism with the republic.

Laniel, Joseph (1889–   )   Laniel became a deputy in 1932, and from 1945 to 1958 he represented the anti-radicals in the Chamber. He served as president of the Council of Ministers from June 1953 to June 1954, and his premiership was marked by the entry of Gaullists into the government. Laniel's government was typical of the Fourth Republic in that it appeared unable to accomplish much. In May 1954 the French-held Vietnamese fortress of Dien Bien Phu fell to the Vietminh, the communist rebels, and, during the agony of the siege, veterans and soldiers had physically assaulted Laniel. In June 1954 after the Indo-China base had fallen, Laniel was ousted from power by the Chamber.

Lannes, Jean (1769–1809)   Born on 11 April 1769 at Lectoure, Lannes in 1792 joined the volunteers of Gers, his home district. This son of a grocer won an officer's commission in 1793 and followed Napoléon Bonaparte (qv) to Egypt. By 1799 he was a general and commandant of the Guard for the First Consul. He fought in Italy and in 1804 was made a marshal. In 1808 he was granted the title of Duc de Montebello for his great victory over the Austrians at that place. Napoléon had a very high regard for Lannes's military ability.

However, his career was cut short when he fell mortally wounded at Essling. He died in Vienna, Austria, on 31 May 1809.

Laperrine, Marie Joseph (1860–1920) Laperrine was a career officer who won fame during the pacification of Algeria's Sahara when he commanded the Oasis Territories from 1902 to 1910. A close confidant of Eugène Etienne (qv) and a member of the *Comité de l'Afrique française* (qv), Laperrine forcefully controlled the Sahara and considerably reduced the incidence of violence and rebellion. From 1914 to 1919 he commanded the Saharan Territory. In 1920 he died in an aircrash.

Lattre de Tassigny, Jean Joseph de (1889–1952) Lattre de Tassigny was born in the Vendée at Mouilleron-en-Pareds on 2 February 1889, and he saw service in World War I, and in Morocco from 1921 to 1926. In 1939 he was promoted to general, but was interned by the Germans. Tried at Riom (qv) in January 1943, he escaped and joined the Fighting French. In 1945 he became chief of staff. During the Indo-Chinese war he began to build a Vietnamese national army, but returned to France in 1952 because of ill health and died at Neuilly-sur-Seine on 11 January 1952.

Laval, Pierre (1883–1945) Pierre Laval was born at Chateldon (Puy-de-Dôme) on 28 June 1883, the son of an innkeeper. He was elected deputy in 1914, but manifested pacifist views and was ousted soon after from the Chamber. In 1924, with the victory of the *Cartel des Gauches* (qv), he returned to the Chamber. Elected senator in 1927, he began to shift to the right and in November 1934 became foreign minister. From 1935 to 1936 he was premier of France. During his period as chief of the Quai d'Orsay Laval negotiated the Hoare-Laval Pact (qv) of 1935 with Sir Samuel Hoare of Great Britain which tried to settle the Ethiopian crisis on terms favourable to Italy. After the fall of France in 1940, Laval was instrumental in seeking an armistice with the Germans. He served as minister of state and as vicepresident of the Council of Ministers until July 1940 when he supported Maréchal Pétain's (qv) bid for power. Convinced of an ultimate German victory, Laval was a leader of the collaborationist element in the Vichy government. This stance caused him to make many enemies, and in December 1940 he was ousted. However, by 1942 he was able to return to the government as minister of foreign affairs, the interior and information. In 1943 Laval had lost confidence in a German victory and sought to bring about a reconciliation with the allies. The Germans took him to Germany in 1943, and after the fall of Nazi Germany he fled to Spain, but was extradited. Finally arrested in Austria, Laval returned to France, stood trial for treason and was executed at Fresnes on 15 October 1945.

Lavigerie, Charles Martel (1825–1892) A dedicated churchman, Cardinal Lavigerie founded the Society of Missionaries to Algiers, or the White Fathers. His pro-imperialist position earned for him and the White Fathers the respect and support of Etienne (qv) and the colonists. In 1884 Lavigerie was made primate of Africa, and he was a firm supporter of the Ralliement (qv).

Law of 5 April 1928 (social security) The law of 5 April 1928, passed during the premiership of Raymond Poincaré (qv), was a landmark in French social legislation. It set in motion the French social security system which went into effect in 1930. The thrust of the law was aimed at all people in France, but in actual practice only employed persons were covered. The self-employed were not forced to contribute to the system. There were also definite problems in covering agricultural workers and their employers. Old age pensions, disability compensation, workmen's compensation and family allowances had been partly in effect since the Law of 14 July 1913 (qv). The basic law of 1928 was superseded by the Decree of 4 October 1945 which affected the general organisation of the programmes. The ordinance of 19 October 1945 extended social insurance to all non-agricultural workers, and the Act of 11 March 1932 provided for the *allocations familiales* (qv). After World War II the social security system increased benefits up to 80 per cent for the cost of medical care. The basic law of 5 April 1928 was instrumental in altering the whole course of French social awareness, and it stands as a landmark in social legislation.

Law of 9 December 1905 By this bitterly debated law the French republic declared that no religion was recognised by the state. The church retained its possessions, and 'associations' were set up to safeguard its interests. Many church buildings and other properties were taken over by the state, but reverted back to the associations for religious use if the associations could qualify under the law. Under no circumstances would the associations receive any payment from the state. This law called for a very strict inventory of church property, but when the process of cataloguing began, riots developed. The government of Georges Clemenceau (qv) backed down after a death occurred and troops called to help in the inventory protested at their role in the cataloguing process. This December 1905 law officially separated church and state and assured liberty of religious belief.

Law of 11 February 1950 (labour-management contracts) From 11 to 18 June 1936 the Chamber, under the guidance of Léon Blum (qv) and the Popular Front (qv), passed a series of social laws. One called for the *conventions collectives* (or *contrat collectif*) which allowed an employee's agent to negotiate a contract with his employer concerning working conditions, salaries, etc. This agent represented the mass of the labourers. The law recognised collective bargaining. The constitution of 1946 recognised this right as well as the right to strike. However, collective bargaining had been suspended after World War II, and the demands for its return contributed to a severe cabinet crisis in late 1949. Once the right was reaffirmed the government sought to extend it. By the Law of 11 February 1950 the government of the Fourth Republic got the right to extend certain collective agreements to an entire industry or whole region, which would go beyond the original scope as envisioned by the signatories. The major problem with this legislation was simple. Industry complained that government was interfering too much. Labour argued that it frankly did not go far enough. But the law stood as a major attempt by the Fourth Republic to bring order to its economic house.

Law of 14 July 1913 (family assistance) In the summer of 1913 the Chamber recognised the demands by Jean Jaurès (qv) and other leftists for a major alteration in French social legislation. In the Chamber many of the centrist and all of the leftist parties combined to pass the Law of 14 July 1913 which set aside allowances for large families. All levels of government were, according to the law, responsible for helping large families. Each head of a household who had his legitimate or acknowledged children under his responsibility received a sum for each child. The local council approved the sum which was then authorised by higher authorities including the minister of the interior. This vital piece of social legislation set the tone for family assistance, but should not be confused with the *Code de la famille*. The Law of 14 July 1913 did foreshadow the *allocations familiales* (qv) of post-World-War-II France.

Law of 15 July 1893 (medical care) On 15 July 1893 the French Chamber passed a law which dealt with the concept of free medical care in France. Every French citizen, without funds, could receive medical care which would be paid for by the local government, departmental government or the state. This law provided for home care or hospital treatment. Foreigners who became ill were accorded the same treatment only if France had a reciprocal agreement with the foreigner's government. The governmental agencies which paid for the medical care could put in a claim against relatives of the poor individual or against any society of cooperation which had any responsibility for medical care at all. Each small town, according to the law, had a link with a town having a hospital. This law marked the beginning of the French medical service system, which grew into a comprehensive system of health care by the time of the Fourth Republic.

Law of 13 March 1873 This critical law regulated the

powers of the National Assembly and the responsibility of ministers, and reconfirmed the Right of Interpellations (qv). Consisting of five articles, the law was one in a series of *ad hoc* measures to give form to the government of the Third Republic. Article one dealt with the relationships of the president of the Republic and Assembly. Article four defined the Right of Interpellation (qv), and article five stated that the Assembly would not be dissolved before it passed laws pertaining to the powers of the legislative and presidential branches. According to article five the Assembly had to decide on the form of the second chamber which would follow basically the type of organisation in use in the Assembly. This article also stated that the Assembly was charged with the duties of passing electoral laws. Conservative in nature, this law gave specific powers to the legislative and presidential branches of government in the hope that their powers, thus delegated, would preserve the conservative character of the government.

Law of 28 May 1882 (education reform)   See: Ferry Education Bill of 1881.

Law of Suspects   See: Revolutionary Tribunal.

Lebon, André (1859–1938)   Deputy and author, Lebon held the post of minister of colonies during the Fashoda (qv) crisis. From 1893 to 1898 he was deputy from Deux-Sèvres, and in 1895 he held the portfolio of minister of commerce under Alexandre Ribot (qv). In 1896 Jules Méline (qv) picked him to be minister of commerce, and by 1898 he held the post of minister of colonies. Although toppled from power in 1898 and politically weakened by his role in the Fashoda crisis, André Lebon wrote many articles and books on Fashoda, Madagascar, and West Africa.

Lebrun, Albert (1871–1950)   Lebrun was born in Mercy le Haut on 29 August 1871. He became an inspector of mines and was a deputy (1900) and a senator (1920) from Meurthe-et-Moselle. A member of the moderate *Union Républicaine*, Lebrun won a reputation for seeking the middle ground. Lebrun served as minister of colonies under Joseph Caillaux (qv) in 1911, Raymond Poincaré (qv) in 1912 and Gaston Doumergue (qv) from 1913 to 1914, and he also served in the Clemenceau (qv) war cabinet. Lebrun was elected president of the Republic in 1932 and was re-elected in 1939. After the fall of France he was deposed by the Germans. He played a very minor role in politics during the Vichy period and retired from politics in July 1940. Arrested by the Germans in 1943, he was released in 1944 from his incarceration in the Tyrol by the allied military forces. He retired from public life soon after, because of ill health. He died in Paris on 6 March 1950.

Lebrun, Charles François (1739–1824) Charles François Lebrun was born at Saint Sarveur-Lendelin in the Manche district on 19 March 1739. He became a lawyer in 1762 and in 1768 proposed a drastic reform of the Parlements. A reformist noble, Lebrun, Duc de Plaisance, was elected to the *Etats Généraux* in 1789. He was arrested during the Terror, survived and was elected to the Council of Ancients (qv) in 1795. In 1799 he was chosen to be third consul and was given the task of reorganising French finances, which he did well. He rallied to Louis XVIII (qv) and was made a peer of France in 1815 but retired from public life soon after. He was recalled to the Chamber in 1819. Lebrun died at Sainte Mesme on 6 June 1824.

Leclerc, General Jacques Philippe de Hauteclocque (1902–1947) De Hauteclocque, better known as General Leclerc, was born to an excellent family at Belloy Saint Léonard in the Somme on 28 November 1902. He attended St Cyr and graduated in 1924. After service in Morocco, he entered the French War College and manifested brilliance in his studies. De Hauteclocque, the professional soldier, assumed the name Leclerc after he fled to England in 1940 to protect his family. He organised a very successful campaign in the Cameroons in August 1940 and staged a spectacular march from the Chad to Libya to join the British. On 28 August 1944 Leclerc's second French armoured division marched into Paris and liberated it from the Germans. His popularity was never higher, and many political groups sought him as a candidate for high office, but he preferred to remain in the army. After the war he served in Indo-China and was killed in an aircrash in Algeria near Colomb Béchar in the Oranais on 28 November 1947.

Ledru-Rollin, Alexandre Auguste (1807–1874)   Born in Paris on 2 February 1807, Ledru-Rollin chose a career in law, joining the Bar in 1830. He made a name as a liberal because of his articles which appeared in the *Journal du Palais* in 1838 and *Le Droit* in 1841. Elected deputy for Mans in 1841, he sat with the opposition and was a leader in the revolution of 1848. He founded the liberal newspaper *La Réforme*, which echoed his liberal views. From April to June 1848 he served on the executive committee of the Republic and held the post of minister of the interior. He failed to support the more violent element and was branded a traitor by the left. He was exiled in 1849 and remained abroad until 1869. He returned to France and in 1874 was elected deputy, but on 31 December 1874, soon after his election, he died in Fontenay aux Roses.

Lefebvre, François Joseph (1755–1820)   Lefebvre was born at Rouffach on 20 October 1755, the son of a miller. He served in the French Guards at the age of fifteen, and in 1783, while a sergeant, he married Catherine Hubscher, the regimental washerwoman. She was known as *Madame Sans-Gêne*. He enlisted in the National Guard in 1789 and served in the army of the Moselle. In 1794 he was elevated to general of division. After the coup d'état of 18 Brumaire (qv), Lefebvre rose higher because of his support for Napoléon Bonaparte (qv). He became a senator in 1800 and was elevated to marshal of the empire in 1804. In 1808 he was named Duc de Danzig, and Lefebvre saw service in Spain in 1808, Austria in 1809 and Russia in 1813. His relationship with the restored Bourbons was not good, and he was dismissed from service until 1819, when he was recalled to duty. He died, however, a year later in Paris on 14 September 1820. Lefebvre was known for his total dedication to the simple life.

Lesseps, Ferdinand Marie de (1805–1894)   Born at Versailles on 19 November 1805, the genius who created the Suez Canal and the Panama Canal, de Lesseps began his career as a diplomat with posts in Lisbon, Tunis and Cairo, where he met Muhummed Ali of Egypt. Because of his friendship with Ali, de Lesseps undertook the building of the Suez Canal for Napoléon III. However, after an honoured career, in 1889 he was ruined when it was discovered that bribery and graft abounded in the administration of the Panama Canal company. De Lesseps and his son were sentenced to prison in 1893, but the elder de Lesseps, a tragic figure, was released immediately because of old age. Vicomte de Lesseps died in near poverty at Chênaie près de Guilly (Indre) on 7 December 1894.

Levée en Masse   On 23 August 1793 the Committee of Public Safety under the guidance of Lazare Carnot (qv) issued a decree that all unmarried Frenchmen were 'in permanent requisition for the service of the armies'. For the first time in history an entire nation was mobilised, in patriotic fervour, for a war. The women were to make clothes and tents, and the married men were to serve in the transportation and quartermaster corps. Children and the aged were given specific tasks. After this total levy armies and nations at war would never be the same.

Ligue Coloniale de la Jeunesse   The Colonial Youth League was founded in 1894 for the purpose of aiding imperial expansion. It helped finance special courses at the Sorbonne which were educational and propagandist. Hoping to germinate interest among the young for a colonial, administrative career, it attracted young men from the age of fifteen to thirty. Teams of lecturers visited the *lycées* and *collèges*. Supported by Joseph Chailley-Bert (qv), Eugène Etienne (qv) and members of the *Comité de l'Afrique française* (qv), the Colonial League of Youth played a vital role in imperial expansion.

Ligue de la Patrie Française   Founded in 1898 as a right-wing ultra-nationalist group by Paul Bourget (qv), Maurice Barrès (qv) and others, the league was a voice of the anti-Dreyfusards. This organisation died out when the *Action Française* was formed in 1905.

Ligue pour la Défense des Droits de l'Homme   In 1898 this league was organised to oppose the *Ligue de la Patrie française* (qv), and violently attacked the anti-Dreyfusards. Noted intellectuals such as Charles Péguy (qv), André Gide, and Marcel Proust, fearing the effect of the Dreyfus Affair (qv) on basic civil liberties in France formed the League for the Defence of the Rights of Man. This league announced as their purpose the desire to preserve the rights won for all Frenchmen by the Revolution of 1789. The members of the league pledged that they would fight against the virulent strains of anti-semitism and nationalism which caused the Dreyfus Affair and the attacks upon personal liberty.

Ligurian Republic   On 15 June 1797 Napoléon Bonaparte (qv) reorganised the city of Genoa and its immediate environs into the Ligurian Republic and tied it to France by an alliance. The governmental institutions of the city were remoulded along French Republican lines. Napoléon had begun to remake the face of Italy, creating a number of republics such as the Cisalpine Republic (qv). By the Treaty of Lunéville (qv) of February 1801 the existence of the Ligurian Republic as well as the Helvetic (qv), the Cisalpine, and the Batavian (qv) Republics was recognised. However, in 1803 as part of Bonaparte's policy of stricter French control, the Republic's constitution was altered so that Napoléon, as First Consul, could name its leader. The Ligurian Republic also became a military district to ensure France's military status in the area. In May 1805 Napoléon annexed the Ligurian Republic to the new kingdom of Italy and had himself crowned King of Italy at Milan on 26 May 1805. The Congress of Vienna in 1815 awarded Genoa as a free port to the Kingdom of Sardinia, and Genoa passed under Sardinian control. However, Napoléon Bonaparte, by his creation of the Ligurian Republic, albeit short-lived, brought Italian nationalism to a head.

Lindet, Robert (1746–1825)   A very successful lawyer,

164

Robert Lindet was a noted moderate liberal prior to 1789. On 10 July 1793 he was elected to the committee of public safety (qv), and he was placed in charge of subsistence, clothing and transportation. As these duties became more demanding in the autumn of 1793, Lindet allowed Robespierre (qv) to take over parliamentary duties. Lindet soon won the title 'food dictator' due to his energetic implementation of his job. Lindet was known as a technician rather than a theorist, and he quickly disavowed Robespierre's excesses. Because of this, he survived Thermidor, but in 1794 he retired, returning only in 1799 by invitation to assume the portfolio of the finance ministry. During the empire he devoted himself to business, and he survived the restoration despite his background.

Locarno Pacts   The years following World War I were confused ones in respect to European diplomacy. Germany remained outside the group of nations which made up western Europe. Britain did not approve of France's continual harsh treatment of Germany, and at the Cannes Conference of January 1922 she requested that Aristide Briand (qv), the foreign minister of France, should try to alter Franco-German relations for the better. Briand believed that the long-standing Entente Cordiale (qv) of 1904 was in jeopardy. After two years of international discussions, the major powers of western Europe met at Locarno in Switzerland to discuss the status of borders and the question of Germany's relationship to western Europe. On 16 October 1925 France, Great Britain, Germany, Belgium and Italy signed the Locarno Pacts which ensured the status quo for all western European borders. The pacts also renounced war as a part of international relations. Germany was recognised as part of the European community of nations, and on 8 September 1926 she joined the League of Nations with France's support. The Locarno Pacts were hailed by Briand as the start of a new era in Europe. For several years after, European diplomats pointed to the 'Spirit of Locarno' as a beneficial influence on European diplomacy.

Loménie de Brienne, Etienne Charles de (1727–1794)

A cardinal, Loménie de Brienne became general controller of finance in 1787. From 1787 to 1788 he was a virtual prime minister in France. He saw the continually deteriorating economic conditions and in 1788 issued the call for the *Etats Généraux* to convene to discuss the chaotic national economic situation. In 1791 he renounced his cardinalate and indicated his readiness to take the oath to the Civil Constitution of the Clergy (qv). Arrested in 1793, Loménie de Brienne was executed soon after. He had realised that French finances prior to 1789 needed a complete revitalisation, but his calls for a stamp tax fell on deaf ears.

Loti, Louis Viaud Pierre (1850–1923)   Born at Rochefort on 16 January 1850, Loti became a naval officer, making his first voyage in 1867. He began to write while in service, using the empire as a backdrop for his novels. In 1879 he published *Aziyadé* and a year later he wrote *Rarabu*. *Madame Chrysanthème* appeared in 1887 and *Fantôme d'Orient* in 1892. After serving in Indo-China and China, he retired from the service in 1910, only to be recalled to the colours in 1914. He died at Hendaye on 10 June 1923. Loti was a writer of exotic novels who used his imperial experiences and helped to popularise the concept of expansion in France.

Loubet, Emile (1838–1929)   Loubet was born in Marsanne in the Drôme in 1838 and became a lawyer in Montélimar. Elected deputy in 1876, Loubet was immediately singled out as a staunch defender of the Republic. In 1885 he was elected senator and served from 1887 to 1888 as minister of public works. After a brief term as minister of the interior in 1892, he set his sights on the presidency of the Republic, which he obtained in 1899. During his term, which lasted until 1906, he received Tsar Nicholas II in 1901 and travelled to Russia in 1902, London in 1903, Rome in 1904 and Madrid and Lisbon in 1905. He had a dramatic impact on France's English and Russian alliances. As president of France, Loubet pardoned the wrongly accused Captain Dreyfus (qv) and during his term as president, Dreyfus was restored to rank by the minister of war, Eugène Etienne (qv). After 1906 he retired from public life, dying at La Bégude in 1929.

Louis Philippe (1773–1850) Of liberal mind in 1789, Louis Philippe who was born in Paris on 6 October 1773, the Duc d'Orléans, joined the National Guard and the Jacobin (qv) Club in 1790. He fought at Valmy (qv) under General Dumouriez (qv), but deserted to the Austrians. However, he refused to bear arms for the allies against France. In 1796 he visited America, and from 1800 to 1815 resided in Britain where he began to build up a personal fortune. Louis Philippe returned to France in 1815, but was distrusted by the ultra-conservatives because of his activities and his father's revolutionary background. From 1815 to 1817 he returned to Britain to manage his fortune. From 1817 to 1830 he became the focal point for French liberals. In 1830, when Charles X (qv) was ousted, Adolphe Thiers (qv), Jacques Laffitte (qv) and Marquis de Lafayette (qv) conspired to bring him to power. Known as the middle-class king, Louis Philippe supported business and industrial expansion. During his eighteen years (1830–48) he used moderate leaders to guide the Chamber, but did, in 1835, restrict the press. During the early 1840s he helped to bring about a revival of Bonapartist feeling, which worked against him since there was an active claimant to the Bonapartist throne. The dullness of Louis Philippe's rule as king of the French motivated many young men to develop a definite interest in Bonapartism and republicanism. A revival of liberal and republican sentiment caught the government unawares, and on 22 February 1848 rebellion broke out against Louis Philippe. He was toppled from power, fled to England and spent his remaining days overseeing his personal fortune. He died at Claremont, England on 26 August 1850.

Louis XVI (1754–1793) Grandson of Louis XV, Louis XVI, who was born at Versailles on 23 August 1754, became dauphin in 1765 and in 1770 married Marie Antoinette (qv) of Austria. In 1774, upon the death of Louis XV, the young and very inexperienced Louis came to the throne. Louis felt lil-prepared to take the throne of France. He was shy and easily swayed by his wife and by advisers. He inherited a serious financial problem, and he attempted to arrest France's economic decline by calling Necker (qv), a protestant banker, to Versailles. From 1776 to 1781 Necker tried to bring economic stability to France, but failed owing to opposition at court. Louis engaged France in a costly war to aid America gain her independence. After using Calonne (qv) and Loménie de Brienne (qv) as finance ministers, Louis XVI recalled Necker in 1788. But it was clear that serious steps had to be taken, and in 1788 the king convened the Three Estates. After the Tennis Court Oaths (qv) of June 1789 and the dismissal of Necker which brought about rioting in Paris and the Fall of the Bastille (qv) in July 1789, Louis lost control of the situation. In October 1789 he was taken with his family to Paris, where he remained a virtual prisoner. In June 1791 he was stopped at the town of Varennes during an escape attempt. This sealed his fate. On 10 August 1792 (qv) there was a severe revolt against the king and state which marked the end of monarchism in France. On 21 September 1792 he was dethroned and France was declared a republic. After this there were demands for Louis to be brought to trial, and despite defences by the Girondins (qv) in the Assembly, Louis XVI was tried and then guillotined on 21 January 1793.

Louis XVII, Louis Charles (1785–1795) The second son of King Louis XVI (qv) and Marie Antoinette (qv), Louis Charles was born at Versailles on 27 March 1785. Named Duc de Normandy, then dauphin in 1789, he was imprisoned with his family in the Temple in Paris. After the death of his father he was kept in isolation from January 1793 to January 1794. He died on 8 June 1795 from unknown causes. The title Louis XVII was given to Louis Charles by Louis XVIII, who wished to present to the world an unbroken line of kings of France, a throne untouched by the revolution.

Louis XVIII (1755–1824) Born at Versailles on 17 November 1755, the Comte de Provence was the brother of King

Louis XVI. He became a leader in 1787 of the aristocrats in France and when he fled France in 1791 he soon became the avowed leader of the *émigrés*. In 1795 he officially assumed the title of Louis XVIII and undertook a tour of Germany in 1796 and Russia in 1798. In 1800 he tried to entice Napoléon Bonaparte (qv) to restore the monarchy but failed. After the Treaty of Tilsit (qv), Louis fled Russia and then resided in Britain. After 1813 he began seriously to consider the eventual reality of the restoration and found a supporter in the sly person of Talleyrand (qv), who had an uncanny talent for self-preservation. Upon his return to France on 4 June 1814 Louis XVIII issued a fairly liberal charter for France which showed him to be of moderate persuasion, but he refused to recognise that the kings of France had ever ceased to be on the throne. For example, he recognised the existence of King Louis XVII (qv) as a ruling sovereign by taking the numerical designation of XVIII. During the Hundred Days (qv), Louis was forced to flee from Paris to Belgium, and returned only in November. However, he still maintained his moderate political stance despite the complaints of the ultra-royalists, led by the Comte d'Artois, the future Charles X (qv). From 1820 to 1824 Louis XVIII had to contend with the extremist policies of d'Artois and the ultras. In 1815 he successfully fought against the Chambre Introuvable (qv) but won few battles for conciliation and moderation after the dissolution of the Assembly. He died in Paris on 16 September 1824.

Lunéville, Treaty of This treaty was signed on 9 February 1801 between France and Austria. Superseding the Treaty of Campo Formio (qv), the agreement gave France the Rhine as a frontier and gave Austria control over Venetia. Those states losing territory as a result of Lunéville were to be compensated at the expense of the small ecclesiastical states of Europe.

Lyautey, Hubert Gonzalve (1854–1934) A career officer and graduate of St Cyr military academy, Lyautey, who was born in Nancy on 13 November 1854, remained throughout his life a conservative and a staunch Catholic. A militant imperialist, he served in Indo-China in 1894 and in Madagascar in 1897. While in Indo-China and Madagascar he came under the influence of Joseph Galliéni (qv). It was Galliéni who taught Lyautey the techniques of colonial administration which Lyautey would use while resident general of Morocco. From 1903 to 1906 he commanded the Ain Sefra garrison in southern Algeria. While there he manifested an independent, often insubordinate turn of mind. Allied with Eugène Etienne (qv) and the *Comité du Maroc* (qv), Lyautey displayed militancy in respect to the annexation of Morocco. Promoted to general in 1907, he travelled in Morocco. After the Treaty of Fez (qv) of 1912, he became Morocco's first resident general and governed with great success, giving Morocco stability and internal security. Following a brief period as minister of war in 1916, he returned to Morocco where he governed until his retirement in 1925. Promoted to the rank of marshal of France, he returned to France to devote the last nine years of his life to publishing his letters. His family home in ruins as a result of World War I, Lyautey moved to Thorey, where he died on 21 July 1934.

MacMahon, Patrice Marie Edme Maurice de (1808–1893) A career officer of conservative monarchist persuasion, MacMahon rose rapidly in rank because of his distinguished service in the colonies. He served in the Crimean War in 1855 and won distinction when he fought well at Malakoff. In 1856 he became a senator, and in 1858 he took command of the military forces in Algeria. During Napoléon III's (qv) intervention in Italy, MacMahon served again with gallantry at Magenta (qv). For his services, Napoléon III named him a marshal of France and elevated him to the title of Duc de Magenta. From 1864 to 1870 he was governor general of Algeria. During the Franco-Prussian War of 1870 MacMahon fought at Wissembourg, and at Reichshoffen MacMahon had to retire to Châlons. However, he was outmarched by the Germans and forced to move to Sedan. During the early stages of the battle he was wounded, and in September 1870 was taken prisoner by German forces. In 1871 he commanded the Versailles army which fought against the Commune (qv). In 1873 he became president of the Republic, but viewed himself mainly as a guardian of the monarchy. Refusing to sanction a royalist coup d'état, MacMahon worked for a conservative-royalist majority in the Chamber. On 16 May 1877 he dismissed the republican prime minister Jules Simon and dissolved the republican-controlled Assembly, but lost in the elections which followed. MacMahon had tried to establish the responsibility of ministers to the president of the executive branch of government, and he wanted to make the Chamber a conservative body. But in both of these endeavours he failed, and in 1879 he resigned from the presidency and retired to private life.

Madrid, Conference of   From 1879 to 1880 the European powers met in Madrid to discuss the status of Morocco and the position of Moroccan subjects who sought the protection of the consular representatives of the European nations. France, Britain, Portugal, Spain, Germany, Sweden, Belgium, Austria and Italy attended the conference. Morocco and the United States were also present, but England and France were the two major powers in attendance. On 24 May 1880 the powers, including Morocco, signed a series of sixteen protocols, and by June had drafted an eighteen-point convention which defined Morocco's status as an independent nation basically equal with the European states. Certain abuses such as the taking of Moroccans under the protection of European consuls were, in theory, done away with. The convention on 3 July 1880 ended the conference, and for fifteen years imposed a status quo on Morocco. The convention did, however, open the question of Morocco's sovereignty, and did show that the European powers, especially Spain, France and Britain, had imperial interests there.

Magenta, Battle of   This battle, between French and Austrian forces, was fought in Italy on 4 June 1859 with an army led by Emperor Napoléon III (qv). This was part of his

Italian policy, and he was in command of a joint French-Piedmont force. While the Austrians were defeated, Napoléon III lost confidence in Piedmont's Victor Emmanuel, and the huge number of dead, dying and maimed horrified the French emperor. After Magenta, Napoleon III decided to withdraw from the war.

Maginot, André (1877–1932) Maginot began his public career as an official in Algeria and was elected deputy in 1910. From 1913 to 1914 he served in the war ministry. On the outbreak of the war of 1914 he volunteered for service and lost a leg at the battle of the Marne in 1914. In 1917 he served as minister of colonies and from 1920 to 1924 as minister of pensions. In 1931, as war minister, he advocated the building of the Maginot line, a line of defensive bunkers which were eventually built on the Franco-German border.

Maine de Biran, François Pierre (1766–1824) Born in Bergerac on 29 November 1766, de Biran, the son of a medical doctor, drifted from one profession to another. In 1785 he served in the royal army but left it after 1789. Until 1795 he studied mathematics and natural science. In 1795 he was named administrator of the Dordogne, and in 1797 he was appointed to the Five Hundred. However, the election was annulled by the coup of Fructador, and he retired to his country estate. In 1803 he published *Mémoire sur l'habitude* and in 1814, deeply grieved by his wife's death, he wrote *Mémoire sur la décomposition de la pensée*. In 1810 he received from Napoléon Bonaparte the legion of honour, and he became a member of the *Corps législatif* in 1812. He developed a dislike for the imperial government and in 1814 the restored Bourbons recalled him to Paris. After the Hundred Days (qv) de Biran returned to the Chamber as a deputy from Bergerac and served until his death in Paris on 10 July 1824.

Maistre, Joseph Marie de (1753–1821) A philosopher and man of politics, Joseph de Maistre was born at Chambéry to a family of local magistrates. He studied law under the Jesuits and in Turin, Italy. Because of his conservative and outspoken views, he was exiled, first to Switzerland then to Venice. During a stay of fourteen years in Russia, he formulated his rightist views which appeared in his work *Examen de la philosophie de Bacon*, which appeared fifteen years after his death. This work was a vehement assault against the works of Sir Francis Bacon, who seemed to Maistre to represent modern materialism at its worst. Joseph de Maistre died in Turin in 1821.

Malesherbes, Chrétien Guillaume de Lamoignon de (1721–1794)   Malesherbes was born in Paris on 6 December 1721 to a noted family. In 1751 he took his father's place as president of the *Cour des Aides*. He began to show an affinity with enlightened men. He was exiled for a brief period until recalled by Louis XVI (qv) in 1775 to assume the position of minister of the *Maison du Roi*. He became minister of state from 1787 to 1788 and emigrated at the outbreak of the revolution in 1789. In July 1793 he returned to France to serve Louis XVI and helped to defend the king during his trial. In 1792 he was arrested and died on the guillotine on 2 April 1794.

Malraux, André (1901–   )   Writer, politician, teacher, Malraux was an early supporter of Charles de Gaulle's (qv) resistance movement in 1940 and was the chief of the Gaullist resistance in south-western France until liberation in 1944. From 1945 to 1946 he served as the minister of information for General de Gaulle. During the period of de Gaulle's retirement from 1946 to 1958, Malraux served him as an adviser. During this period Malraux continued to write and to enhance his international reputation as a French author. After 1958 he held the position of minister of cultural affairs. His most famous works include *L'Espoir*, *Les Voix du Silence* and *Anti-Mémoires*.

Malvy, Jean Louis (1875–1949)   A leftist politician, Malvy served as minister of the interior in the *Union Sacrée* (qv). He caused great irritation among French politicians by refusing to use Carnet B (qv) against suspected subversives and to take action against pacifists. From 1914 to 1917 Malvy was at the centre of controversy, and after the industrial strikes and army mutinies of 1917, during which he again refused to act, Clemenceau (qv) accused him of treason. Arrested and tried with Joseph Caillaux (qv), he was pardoned in 1924. Malvy returned to the Chamber, but never again held a ministerial post.

Mandats Territoriaux   The policy of using the assignats (qv) as currency had failed, and in 1796 the Directory (qv) ordered the plates to be broken. In early 1796 the assignats were repudiated, stabilised at only 3 per cent and replaced by the *Mandats Territoriaux* which would be accepted for the sale of public lands. In 1797 the Directory decreed that all taxes would be paid in specie, thereby showing the directors' lack of faith in paper currency.

Mandel, Georges (Louis Rothschild) (1885–1944)   A journalist who began his career with Georges Clemenceau (qv), Mandel was known as a Machiavellian figure in French politics. He served Clemenceau as a personal and political adviser, and was instrumental in the arrest, trial and conviction of Joseph Caillaux (qv) and Louis Malvy (qv). In 1919 he won a seat as a deputy from the Gironde, and he held that post until 1924. For four years, from 1924 to 1928, he was out of power, but in 1928 he sought the Gironde seat again, won it, and held it until his arrest by the Vichy government in 1942. As deputy, the conservative Mandel spoke out on the issue of French military strength. In 1934 he took the portfolio of post and telegraph in the cabinet of Pierre Etienne Flandin (qv) and held the post in the cabinet of Pierre Laval (qv) in 1935. He entered the government of Albert Sarraut (qv) again as minister of post and telegraph. In 1936 Mandel openly opposed the Popular Front (qv) and urged that France militantly confront the growing Nazi German menace. In 1940 he became minister of colonies under Paul Reynaud (qv), and from this position he tried to influence French policy toward Germany. In 1940 he urged the French government to flee to North Africa to continue the fight against Germany. He was arrested, interned and murdered by a pro-axis Frenchman in 1944.

Mangin, Charles (1866–1925)   Born to a military family at Sarrebourg on 6 July 1866 he became a famous colonial soldier in Senegal and the Sudan. Mangin served with Jean Baptiste Marchand (qv) at Fashoda (qv) in 1898. He fought as a general in World War I and commanded French occupation forces on the Rhine where he openly encouraged a movement toward autonomy. He died in Paris on 12 March 1925.

Manifesto of the Intellectuals   In 1935 over 140 members of the French Chamber and Senate issued a resolution supporting the League of Nations' sanctions against Italy. The right wing in France reacted by issuing the Manifesto of the Intellectuals on 4 October 1935 in favour of Italy's position in the Italo-Ethiopian War. Charles Maurras (qv), Ferdinand de Brinon (qv) and Léon Daudet (qv) signed it, as might be expected. However, many noted authors and academicians also signed the manifesto, showing how deeply divided was intellectual opinion in France.

Mantua, Secret Agreement of   On 20 May 1791 Austria, Prussia and several German states secretly agreed to form an autocratic front and to move against revolutionary France and to aid Louis XVI, who was a virtual prisoner in Paris.

Marat, Jean Paul (1743–1793)   Born at Boudry, Switzerland on 24 May 1743 Marat became a medical doctor, but in 1789 deserted medicine for violent revolutionary journalism. He founded the *Ami du Peuple*, which was suppressed in 1792. Exiled, he fled to England and returned to join the *Club des Cordeliers* (qv). He was elected deputy in 1792. He became more violent, attacking the Girondins (qv), and was arrested. The Girondins were determined to silence Marat whom they saw as a dangerous idol of the Paris mobs. However, his trial proved to be, for the Girondins, a serious miscalculation because Robespierre claimed that the trial was an attack on the Jacobins (qv) and on the liberties of the people. Marat was acquitted by the Revolutionary Tribunal, and the riots of 31 May 1793, staged in support of him, marked the collapse of Girondin political power. On 13 July 1793 Marat was murdered in his bathtub by Charlotte Corday (qv), a demented royalist, and his murder gave Robespierre and the Jacobins the opportunity to purge all the Girondin leaders from the Convention, thereby securing radical control of that body.

Marchand, Jean Baptiste (1863–1934) A colonial soldier and imperialist militant, Marchand, who was born at Thoissey (Ain) on 22 November 1863, was allied with Eugène Etienne (qv), chief of the Paris-based colonialists and with the *Comité de l'Afrique française* (qv). In 1896 he was given the mission of crossing Africa from west to east and establishing a French post on the Nile to challenge the British presence on the river. Marchand's weak force of 200 men confronted the British at Fashoda (qv) in late September 1898. In early December 1898, Marchand was forced to evacuate Fashoda, but upon his return to France he was fêted as a hero by the imperialists. During World War I he commanded colonial troops on the western front. He retired from the military after the war and spent his remaining years writing and enjoying his position as a hero. He died in Paris on 14 January 1934.

Marie, André (1897–   ) André Marie was a radical elected deputy in 1928. After World War II he was one of the chiefs of the Radical Party who opposed the policies of Pierre Mendès-France (qv). From July to August 1948 he was premier of a lacklustre and not especially successful cabinet.

Marie Antoinette (1755–1793) Born in Vienna on 2 November 1755, daughter of Holy Roman Emperor Francis I and Maria Theresa, Marie Antoinette received only the most meagre education before her marriage to the French dauphin in 1770. Her four-year period as wife of the dauphin was most difficult as she tried to learn the rudiments of etiquette. In 1774 she became queen of France. Her activities brought a wave of shock to France, and her reckless spending earned her the title of *Madame Déficit*. She tended to act in favour of the

French alliance with Austria, which made her more unpopular in France. As France collapsed into financial chaos, Marie Antoinette led her court cliques against Louis XVI's (qv) various finance ministers, and her actions won her the title of *Madame Veto*. She never accepted the events of 1789 and continued to desire openly Austrian aid against the revolution. She followed her husband from Versailles to the Tuileries, and in 1792 she was imprisoned in the Temple. Her actions in the escape attempt at Varennes (qv) in 1791 made her the target of the rising Jacobin (qv) radicals in 1791. Separated from her children in August 1793, Marie Antoinette was imprisoned in the Conciergerie. In October 1793 she was put on trial, convicted and executed on 16 October 1793.

Marie Louise (1791–1847)   Marie Louise was the daughter of Francis I of Austria, born in Vienna on 12 December 1791, and on the advice of Prince Metternich she married Napoléon Bonaparte (qv) in 1810. In 1811 she bore Bonaparte a son, the Duc de Reichstadt (qv), and during Napoléon's major campaigns she served as regent in France. Her influence with Napoléon declined in 1813 when Austria joined the coalition against France. In 1814, with the fall of Napoléon, she returned to Austria where Metternich introduced her to Count Neipperg, a notorious seducer. Marie Louise refused to follow Bonaparte into exile at either Elba or Saint Helena, and she appeared indifferent to his death in 1821 and to the death of her son in 1832. She received in 1815 the Duchy of Parma and Guastalla which she administered with the help of Count Neipperg. She died in Vienna on 18 December 1847.

Maritain, Jacques (1882–1972)   A professor of philosophy, noted Catholic intellectual and leading exponent of Neo-Thomism, Maritain argued that the fall of France in 1940 was due to moral and religious decay. From 1945 to 1948 he served as ambassador to the Vatican.

Marmont, Auguste de (1774–1852)   Entering the army in 1792 he served in Italy with Bonaparte and in 1806 became governor of Dalmatia, where he had a liberal administration.

Made Duc de Raguse in 1808, Marmont surrendered Paris to the allies in 1814. He rallied to the restoration and followed Louis XVIII during the Hundred Days (qv). From 1821 to 1830 he served as governor of Paris, and followed Charles X (qv) into exile in 1830. Maréchal Marmont died in Venice on 22 July 1852.

Marrast, Armand (1801–1852)   Born on 5 June 1801 at Saint Gaudens, Marrast studied at the *Ecole supérieure* and took a doctorate. A liberal, he was knocked by the state for having participated in the funeral of a very liberal deputy in 1827. From 1827 until 1834 he wrote for *La Tribune* and in April 1834 he fled to England. Marrast returned to France in 1836 and joined the staff of the liberal journal *Le National*, rising to directorship by 1841. Known as a vocal opponent of the Orléanist government, he became one of the leaders of the political opposition outside of the Chamber. In February 1848, during the revolution, he helped form the *Réforme* group in the Chamber and the club of the same name. Because of his position as editor of *La National*, Marrast was asked to serve in the provisional government (qv) from February until April 1848. On 9 March 1848 he became mayor of Paris, where he set up the *Garde Mobile* to defend the government. In July 1848 Marrast became president of the Assembly, and he broke totally with the Paris insurgents. He was defeated in the elections of 1849 and retired from public life as a disappointed, disgusted man. He died in Paris on 10 March 1852.

Martignac, J. B. Gaye (1778–1832)   Martignac, a native of Bordeaux, began his career by working with Abbé Sièyes (qv) in 1798, and after colourless but solid service, he became a deputy in 1821. After serving in Spain in 1823 he returned to France to pursue a political career, and in 1828 became minister of the interior. Vicomte de Martignac, determined to capitalise on liberal political victories, abolished press censorship to a degree and promised eventual liberty of the press. He was violently attacked by the ultras and by the left. In 1829 Charles X (qv) replaced him, but by 1830 Martignac had lost all political influence, retired from public life, and died in Paris on 3 April 1832.

Marty, André (1886–1956)   Extreme leftist leader of the French Communist Party, Marty led a mutiny of the French Black Sea Fleet in World War I. Elected deputy in 1924, he opposed the leadership of Maurice Thorez (qv). After World War II Marty and Thorez clashed bitterly over the question of cooperation with socialist governments. Marty believed that Thorez's search for respectability had damaged the revolutionary image of the communists. Marty was expelled from the party two years before his death, but continued to sit as a deputy during that period of disgrace.

Masséna, André (1756–1817)   From a humble family, Masséna was born in Nice on 6 May 1756. In 1775 he served in the Royal Italian Army, and in 1789 he joined the National Guard. He was elected lieutenant colonel of volunteers from the Var in 1792. Masséna served under Napoléon (qv) in Italy and won the approval of Napoléon. Named chief of the army of the Helvetic Republic (qv) in 1799, he defeated the Austrians near Zurich in September 1799. Masséna served in the *Corps législatif* (qv) from 1803 to 1807, and in May 1804 he was named marshal of France. In 1806 he helped install Joseph Bonaparte (qv) in Naples. In 1808 Napoléon named him the Duc de Rivoli, and for his bravery in the Austrian campaign of 1809 he was elevated to the title of the Prince d'Essling. He commanded the army of Portugal and was disgraced by his defeats at the hands of the Duke of Wellington in 1811. Masséna tried to rally first to the Bourbons in 1814 and then to Napoléon during the Hundred Days (qv). During the second restoration he was broken and impoverished and died, a disgraced man, in Paris on 4 April 1817.

Matignon Accords   The Matignon Accords were negotiated by the Popular Front (qv) government of France under Léon Blum (qv), between management and labour. In May and June 1936, immediately after the victory of the Popular Front, there were massive sit-down strikes as workers occupied factories. To halt the labour strife, on 7 June 1936, delegates of the French labour movement, management and government signed the accords. Collective bargaining, freedom to join a union and pay rises were all recognised by the accords. Article six pledged employers not to take action against strikers. Labour considered the Matignon Accords an incomplete victory, while management was openly dissatisfied with them. In the long run these accords alienated management from the government and did not actually satisfy the demands of labour.

Maurras, Charles (1868–1952) Author, philosopher and prophet of integral nationalism, Maurras served as a leader of the rightist *Action Française* (qv). He opposed France's entry into World War II and supported the Vichy regime. Arrested in 1944, he was imprisoned in 1945 but released seven years later because of his advanced age.

Maury, Jean Siffrein (1746–1817) Born at Valréas on 26 June 1746, Maury, a bishop, defended traditional monarchy in 1789 and fought against anti-clerical republicanism. For his efforts he was made cardinal in 1794. He fled to Russia in 1799 and became the Pope's representative to Louis XVIII as Comte de Provence (qv). In 1806, however, Maury rallied to Bonaparte and assumed control of the Diocese of Paris. In 1814 he fled to Rome to avoid the wrath of the restored Bourbons and was incarcerated there by the church until his death on 11 May 1817.

Mediation, Act of (February 1803) The cantons of Switzerland were organised by the French into the Helvetic Republic (qv) as a method of aiding French military efforts. As part of the concepts of the spread of revolutionary ideals, the republic was given a liberal constitution and was bound to France by an alliance. However, there were severe internal conflicts between the people in the mountain and the urban areas as well as violent disagreements between the various linguistic groups. In 1802 the Swiss sent delegates to Napoléon Bonaparte (qv) to ask him to mediate in their problems. Napoléon, as First Consul, began to search for an end to the troubles, and out of this came the Act of Mediation of February 1803. Switzerland was re-organised into the Swiss Confederation with a stronger, centralised government and was bound to France by treaty. By this act Napoléon hoped to bridge the gap between the old and the new and to bring some unity to diverse Swiss factions.

Méline, Jules (1838–1925) A lawyer with republican tendencies, Méline entered the Chamber in 1872 as a deputy from the Vosges, a post which he held until 1903. He held his first cabinet position as undersecretary for justice in the cabinet of Jules Simon in 1876. He served as minister of agriculture in 1883 under Jules Ferry (qv), and he advocated strong protective tariffs to protect French agriculture and industry. In 1892 Méline proposed a highly restrictive tariff known as the Méline Tariff of 1892. Protectionism and high tariffs were gaining in popularity and Méline's own efforts represented one more step in that direction to protect home industry and agriculture which made French tariffs some of the highest in Europe. The tariff so heavily protected food producers that French farmers prospered, and France reached about a 90 per cent self-sufficiency in foodstuffs. After serving as president of the Chamber from 1888 to 1889, he assumed leadership of the opportunists in the assembly. He supported agricultural credits and after 1892 turned even more toward a policy of tariff protectionism. On 29 April 1896 he formed his own government, and as president of the Council of Ministers he pushed the protective tariff. His work was cut short when he was toppled by the Fashoda crisis (qv) in 1898. Méline then served as a senator from 1903 until his death and as minister of agriculture from 1915 to 1916, concerning himself primarily with agricultural reforms.

Mendès-France, Pierre (1907–   ) Mendès-France, one of the most important politicians of the Fourth Republic, was elected deputy in 1932, and from 1943 to 1945 allied himself with the Gaullists and the Radical Party. From June 1954 to February 1955 he was president of the Council of Ministers, and he tried to modernise radicalism by extending party organisation to every city and village in France. It fell to

Mendès-France to pull French troops back from Indo-China after the fall of Dien Bien Phu in May 1954 and the ending of the Geneva Conference on Indo-China during the summer of the same year. After this, Mendès-France had promised to bring peace to France within one month. However, he became involved in another colonial war in November 1954 in Algeria, and it was his colonial North African policies which toppled him in February 1955. Dynamic and capable, Mendès-France was able to attract young people, women and technocrats in some numbers into the party by displaying a progressive vigour. However, the right hated him and continually worked against him, especially when he proposed independence for Morocco and Tunisia. By 1956 he appeared to be in firm control of the party, but divisions over colonial questions split the party, and in 1957 Mendès-France resigned his position as its leader. The Radical Party, splintered and weakened, suffered in the great Gaullist victory of 1958.

Messimy, Adolphe (1869–1935) A career army officer, Messimy left the military for a career in politics. In 1902 he was elected deputy for the Seine, and held that position until 1912. Not certain of re-election in the Seine, he stood for election in 1912 in the Ain and represented that district as deputy until 1919. From 1923 until his death, Messimy was a senator from the Ain. In 1911 he held the portfolio of the colonial ministry, and in 1914 René Viviani (qv) asked him to be minister of war. He became deeply shaken when it appeared that the Germans would take Paris in August 1914, and Viviani, shocked by Messimy's open defeatism, was forced to remove him. Messimy returned to serve in the army, and he never again held a cabinet-level post.

Messmer, Pierre (1916–   ) A career civil servant, specialising in colonial and military affairs, Messmer joined the anti-Nazi resistance early in 1940 and participated in World War II as a Free French officer. He fought in North Africa, Italy, France and Germany. In 1945 he saw service in Indo-China, and from 1947 to 1948 served as chief of staff to the

French commissioner in Indo-China. After brilliant service in Africa, in 1958 he rallied to Charles de Gaulle (qv) who in 1960 chose him to be minister of the armed forces because he envisioned a number of sweeping military reforms which Messmer would carry out.

Meusnier de la Place, Jean Baptiste (1754–1793) Meusnier de la Place, born in Tours on 19 June 1754, belonged to a family of nobles of the Robe. As he had mathematical and engineering ability, he was sent to Cherbourg, where for a decade he worked on various tasks and public projects. He was known as a man of learning and frequent visitor to the Academy of Science, to which he was admitted in 1784. He rallied to the revolution and was sent to serve in the Army of the Rhine. An ardent defender of the revolution, he was killed in battle defending Cassel on 13 June 1793. Meusnier de la Place was a fiery supporter of liberalism and the revolution and also a brilliant man of science.

Military Organisation   See: Ordinance of 7 January 1959.

Millerand, Etienne Alexandre (1859–1943)   Born in Paris on 10 February 1859, elected deputy in 1885, Millerand served as minister of commerce from 1899 to 1902 and as minister of public works in 1909. He was one of the first socialists to co-operate with the government by taking a cabinet post. For this he incurred the wrath of Jean Jaurès (qv) and the regulars of the Socialist Party, who decided to expel him from the party. During the immediate pre-war years, from 1912 to 1913, he served as war minister and held the same post from 1914 to 1915. After World War I, Millerand served as commissioner for Alsace-Lorraine in 1919, and a year later he assumed the presidency of the Council of Ministers. When President Paul Deschanel (qv) became ill, Millerand assumed the office of president of the Republic. He bitterly opposed the *Cartel des Gauches* (qv), and after the *cartel* victory in 1924 he was forced to resign. In 1925 he was elected senator and held that post until his death at Versailles on 6 April 1943.

Mirabeau, André Boniface (1754–1792)   Born in Paris on 30 November 1754, André was the brother of the famous Gabriel-Honoré Mirabeau (qv). He joined the French army and served in the American revolution. Unlike his brother, André Mirabeau was a defender of the Bourbon regime, and in 1789 he was elected deputy to the nobility for Limousin. Like his brother, André was intemperate, and his obesity gave him the nickname of *Mirabeau-Tonneau*. Disgusted with revolutionary events in France, he left the country in 1790 to join the *émigrés* to struggle against the revolution. However, due to his irritating and overbearing personality, he fought with royalist leaders over policies and tactics. He retired to Fribourg en Brisgau and died on 15 September 1792.

Mirabeau, Gabriel-Honoré (1749–1791)   Gabriel-Honoré Riquetti de Mirabeau was born to a notable family at Bignon in the Loiret on 9 March 1749. His father, Victor (5 October 1715–13 July 1789) was a famous economist. At the age of three Mirabeau was terribly disfigured by smallpox. Later he constantly argued with his father about his tendencies to be a spendthrift and a wastrel, which his father seriously opposed. In 1769 Mirabeau left home after a final, bitter argument with his father over debts. Several times jailed because of his debts, he disliked the old regime and turned his oratorical powers against Louis XVI (qv) as an absolutist monarch. In 1776 he published *Essai sur la despotisme*, an attack upon French absolutism, which forced him to flee France for a time. In 1777 he was imprisoned for his essay. However, Mirabeau in 1782 wrote *Lettres de Cachet*, which was an erotic account of his life. His wife obtained a divorce from him, but in 1784, complete with a new mistress, he returned to Paris. From 1785 to 1789 Mirabeau made a reputation as a debator and as a critic of the Bourbon regime. In 1788 he went to Prussia and met King Frederic II. He wrote *De la Monarchie prussienne sous Frédéric le Grande* in 1788. In 1789 he was elected to the *Etats Généraux*, where he quickly rose to a position of leadership in the Third Estate. Mirabeau was prominent in the June days of

1789, when he supported the idea that the Third Estate was indeed the Assembly of France. From 1789 to 1791 he developed and advocated a parliamentary system with a strong royal executive and with ministers who would be responsible to the parliament and to the executive. Known for his debaucheries and love of pleasure, Mirabeau died in Paris on 2 April 1791 fo overwork and excess. He had tried and failed to reconcile the Assembly with the king, and for his actions he was branded as an agent of the Bourbons, a reputation he did not deserve.

Mission Civilisatrice Closely allied to the ideal of assimilation (qv), the *mission civilisatrice* was the 'white man's burden' of France. As the name implies, the civilising mission carried to the colonies the values, technology and symbols of French civilisation. The mission hoped for a rapid and lasting transmission of culture to the colonies. However, by the late nineteenth century the civilising mission as a factor in French imperial expansion was given second-rank status and was slowly replaced by the concept of association (qv). The *mission civilisatrice* continued to be an ideal which was expressed for the public, but among the imperialists it was an outdated concept.

Mitterand, François (1916–   ) Elected deputy in 1946, Mitterand served as the president of the *Union Démocratique et Socialiste de la Résistance* in 1953. In 1954, as minister of the interior, he took steps against extreme nationalists in France who were attacking the government over its policies toward Indo-China and Algeria. From 1959 to 1962 he served as a senator, and in 1962 returned to the Chamber where he planned a campaign for the presidency. In 1965 he ran against Charles de Gaulle (qv) for the presidency and lost. Mitterand had manifested his opposition to de Gaulle and the Gaullists during the Fourth Republic and this carried over into the Fifth Republic. After de Gaulle's death, Mitterand continued to be very active in anti-Gaullist politics.

Mizon, Louis Alexandre Antoine (1853–1899) Colonial explorer and soldier, Mizon worked with de Brazza (qv) in the Congo. He displayed an irritating personality and an extreme dedication to French expansion. Because of his devotion to imperialism he was chosen by Eugène Etienne (qv), the under-secretary of state for colonies, to undertake a number of important exploratory missions in 1890. He explored areas of the Niger river and Benué river in 1890 and in 1892. His actions along the Niger and Benué brought him into direct conflict with the British Royal Niger Company, and eventually the London government forced his recall. Mizon's arrival in Paris was marked by a hero's welcome. He died suddenly while holding the post of governor of Djibouti.

Mollet, Guy (1905–   ) A member of the Social Party, Guy Mollet served as mayor of Arras, a socialist deputy and secretary general of the party. In 1946 he came to Paris as a deputy. From January 1956 to May 1957 he held the position of president of the Council of Ministers. After 1951 he was a respected leader in the Chamber since he controlled the massive socialist vote which could mean the success or failure of governmental programmes. During his premiership, however, Mollet began to flounder over colonial questions, especially the Algerian morass. He attempted to impose a French settlement on Algeria and failed. In 1958 he rallied to de Gaulle (qv) and later this support cost him the leadership of the *Section Française de l'Internationale Ouvrière* (SFIO) (qv).

Montagnards The Montagnards, or the men of the mountain, sat on the left in the French Assembly and opposed the Girondins (qv). Among their number were Marat (qv), Danton (qv), Desmoulins (qv) and Robespierre (qv). While the Girondins represented the middle class and those opposed to the predominant position of Paris in the revolution, the Montagnards saw themselves as the defenders of the people. Ironically, the Montagnards were fairly affluent and held high positions in society. They were perhaps more removed from the people than were the Girondins, but through Montagnard and Jacobin oratory they maintained the fiction of being 'of the people'. More urban, the Montagnards distrusted the provincial outlook of the Girondins. Many Montagnards also belonged to the Jacobin Club (qv), and the Girondins accused the Montagnards of being against private property and against public order, but basically these charges were untrue. The Mountain made itself felt during the debates over a new constitution for France in 1793. Attacking a Girondist report in February 1793 on a new system, a committee was set up by the leadership of the Mountain to construct a new system. What emerged was the Constitution of 1793 (Year I) which was basically a compromise between the Girondin proposals and Montagnard beliefs. Completed by 24 June 1793, the document provided for universal manhood suffrage, a unicameral legislative body, a ministerial system which was responsible to the Assembly, electoral assemblies, and a bill of rights. Bold provisions suggested by Robespierre to maintain the poor were carefully left out for compromise purposes. However, in their patriotism, most Montagnards advocated laws to protect public safety which brought about the excesses of 1793. During the Themidorian Reaction many Montagnard leaders were arrested, and on 20 May 1795 (I Prairial, Year III) an insurrection broke out in Paris. A number of Montagnards were arrested and six were condemned to death for complicity in the revolt. The Prairial revolt and the arrest of Montagnards marked the ascendancy of the Girondins, eighty of whom had recovered their seats in the Convention. The restored Girondins seized this golden opportunity to purge the Assembly of Montagnards.

Montalembert, Charles Forbes René de (1810–1870) Born in London on 15 April 1810, Montalembert, son of an *émigré*, tried his hand at diplomacy under the Bourbons. However, he became close friends with Victor Hugo (qv), and after the revolution of 1830 he sided more and more with the liberals. He wrote for the journal *L'Avenir*, which was both liberal and Catholic and which was condemned by Rome in 1832. He sat with various liberal Catholic groups and struggled for a liberalisation of parochial school curriculums. Disliking the violence of 1848, Montalembert organised the 'Party of Order', which favoured Louis Napoléon (qv) in the elections of 1848. Montalembert struggled for the passage of the Falloux Law (qv) in 1850. He served as a deputy under the empire, and in 1852 was elected to the *Académie Française*. Not re-elected in 1857, he wrote for *Le Correspondant*, arguing against ultra-conservatism among Catholics. Montalembert was disapproved of by Pope Pius IX for his defence of Polish Catholics. He died in Paris on 13 March 1870.

Montoire, Meeting at On 24 October 1940 Maréchal Pétain (qv) and Adolf Hitler met in a railway car at Montoire in France to discuss the future of Franco-German relations. While the principle of collaboration was established, Pétain refused to yield the French fleet to the Germans and Hitler did not press the point. Pétain, unfortunately, publicly accepted the concept of collaboration with the Germans and this in the long run seriously tarnished his reputation.

Moreau, Jean Victor (1763–1813) Moreau was born on 14 February 1763. A Breton and son of a lawyer, he studied law and defended the Parlement of Rennes against Royalist policies in 1788. In 1789 Moreau formed an artillery company in the national guard. He rose to the rank of colonel, and in December 1793 he was made a brigadier general and served in the army of the North. Promoted again in 1794, he took command of the army of the North in 1795. In September 1798 he was made inspector general of the army of Italy, which he finally commanded for a brief period. Moreau participated in Napoléon Bonaparte's (qv) coup d'état of 18 Brumaire (qv), and in November 1799 he was named to the command of the armies of the Rhine and the Helvetic Republic. However, Moreau became more opposed to Bonaparte, and he participated in plots hatched by General Pichegru (qv). Dismissed from the army in 1804, Moreau emigrated to the United States, but he was recalled to service by Tsar Alexander in 1873. Moreau served the allied cause in Germany, but he was mortally wounded in battle at Dresden and died at Lahn in Bohemia on 2 September 1813.

Morellet, André, Abbé (1727–1819) Morellet was born

in Lyon on 7 March 1727 and entered the church, but he preferred intellectual rather than clerical pursuits. He was an independent cleric who was quite close to the *encyclopédistes*. His major works include *Théorie du paradoxe* (1775), *Les si et les pourquoi* (1760), *Lettre sur la police des grains* (1764), and his important *Pensées libres sur la liberté de la presse*, which appeared in 1795. He fought against revolutionary excesses. Elected to the *Académie Française* in 1785, he lived to see the Bourbons finally restored in 1815. He died at Versailles on 12 January 1819.

Morny, Auguste Charles Joseph de (1811–1865)   De Morny, who was born illegitimate in Paris on 21 October 1811, joined the army in 1830 and served for eight years in Algeria. He entered industry in 1838 and did not do much in politics until the revolution of 1848. After the return to France of Louis Napoléon (qv), his half-brother, de Morny rallied to the Bonapartist cause and participated in the coup d'état of 2 December 1851. As minister of the interior, he controlled the police, and this control ensured the success of the coup d'état. After a period of inactivity de Morny returned to the *Corps Législatif*, over which he presided in 1854. An exponent of liberalism, he helped form the liberal empire by the decrees of 1860. After 1860 he served until 1862 as ambassador to Russia. In 1862 he retired, was made a duke and spent the remaining three years of his life attending to his business investments.

Moroccan Crisis of 1905, First   After the Fashoda crisis of 1898 (qv), the French imperialists led by Eugène Etienne (qv) and the *Parti colonial* (qv) mounted a campaign to annex Morocco into the French empire. Abd el Aziz (qv), the ruling sultan of Morocco, was weakened by French colonial efforts and his state became mired in anarchy. Because of long-standing claims on Morocco, the French foreign office under Théophile Delcassé (qv) began to work out a series of diplomatic accords with Spain and Italy concerning the future of Morocco. In April 1904 the signing of the Entente Cordiale (qv) appeared to seal the doom of Moroccan independence.

The militant actions of Colonel Hubert Lyautey (qv) in Algeria and the aggressiveness of the *Comité du Maroc* (qv) in Paris seemed to indicate that France would in 1904 or 1905 move against Morocco. But William II and his advisors decided to attempt to halt France's movement there. Trying to weaken the Anglo-French entente of 1904 and to halt French expansion in the western Maghreb, William II landed at Tangier in March 1905. He made a militant speech calling for the independence of Morocco, and by his actions he interposed German strength between Morocco and France. The First Moroccan Crisis was the first real test of the British-French Accords, and the entente held firm despite German threats. The crisis was resolved in 1906 at the Algeciras Conference (qv), but France was denied the right to annex Morocco.

Moroccan Crisis of 1911, Second In 1905 William II, Kaiser of Germany, tried to test the strength of the Anglo-French Entente Cordiale of 1904 (qv) and block French colonial efforts in Morocco by precipitating the first Moroccan Crisis (qv). These attempts failed when Germany faced defeat at the Algeciras Conference of 1906 (qv). In 1909 Germany and France signed an accord recognising French privileges in Morocco. In 1911 rioting broke out in many Moroccan cities, and the French sent troops into Fez on 21 May 1911 to help the sultan and to save European lives. On 1 July 1911 the Germans sent the gunboat *Panther* to Agadir harbour and a new crisis was at hand. For the Germans to withdraw the gunboat and finally recognise French sovereignty in Morocco, Berlin demanded a huge portion of the French Congo. France and Britain stood firm in the face of this threat, and Germany signed, with France, the Franco-German Accord of 1911 (qv). This accord allowed France to move against Morocco and occupy the area, and Germany received a small section of the French Congo. France was able to take immediate steps to occupy Morocco, and this was recognised in 1912 by the Franco-Moroccan Treaty of Fez (qv). The Anglo-French Accords had again held firm. The Second Moroccan crisis of 1911 was another step toward World War I, and it created an air of absolute distrust in Europe.

Morocco   See: Abd el Aziz; Abdel Kader; Algeciras, Conference of; Comité du Maroc; Fez, Treaty of; Franco-Moroccan Accords of 1956; Franco-Spanish Moroccan Accords (1900; 1902; 1904; 1912); Madrid, Conference of; Moroccan Crisis of 1905, First; Moroccan Crisis of 1911, Second.

Mounier, Emmanuel (1905–1950)   Born in Grenoble in 1905, Mounier took a degree in philosophy in 1928. A follower of Charles Péguy (qv), Mounier tried to give Christian socialism a philosophical foundation. He formulated a position known as 'personalism' which stressed the social duties of the human being toward others. In 1932 he founded the journal *Esprit*, which he continued to run until he died at Chatenay-Malabry in 1950.

Mounier, Jean Joseph (1758–1806)   Born in Grenoble on 12 November 1758, Mounier studied for the law and became a lawyer in 1779. In 1783 he became a judge at Grenoble. Known for his extensive learning and liberal tendencies, Mounier was sought after as a leader. Because of his position as an intellectual and as a reformer, he was elected to deputy of the Third Estate in 1789. It was Jean Mounier who proposed the Tennis Court Oaths (qv) of 20 June 1789. Elected to the constitutional committee, he advocated a bicameral legislature for France. He presided over the Constituent Assembly, but, disgusted with the turn toward radicalism and violence in France, retired to Switzerland. In 1805 Mounier returned to France to serve Napoléon (qv) as a counsellor of state.

Mouvement pour le Triomphe des Libertés Démocratiques (MTLD)   The MTLD ran candidates for the outlawed *Parti Populaire Algérien* (PPA) (qv) in the Algerian elections on 1 November 1946 and obtained five seats in the Algerian Assembly. This open move by Algerians distressed French imperialists who saw the MTLD as a concrete example of independence sentiment among Algerian Muslims. In 1948 the MTLD lost its seats in the Assembly and in the same year it was also outlawed. By 1950 the movement was considered by police in Algeria to be a dangerous, subversive organisation.

Mouvement Républicain Populaire (MRP) A Christian democratic party, the MRP was formed in Lyons in 1944 by young progressive Catholics. Its primary goal was to reconcile industrial workers and staunch Catholics. With the support of the clergy and liberal Catholic youth, the MRP grew into a major party with 5 million votes in 1945. However, party fortunes dropped from 1946 to 1949. Several times during the Fourth Republic, the MRP formed ministries, but these were short-lived due to party factionalism and the fragmented state of French parliamentary politics. In May 1958 the MRP survived the crisis surrounding the return to power by General Charles de Gaulle (qv). Basically the MRP supported de Gaulle's policies vis-à-vis Algeria, which alienated some leaders like George Bidault (qv). However, in 1962 the MRP broke with the Pompidou government over President de Gaulle's position on European supra-nationalism. The party remained, after 1962, a strong party with young, dynamic Catholic leaders.

Mun, Albert de (1841–1914) A staunch Catholic born at Lumiguy (Sambre et Meuse) on 28 February 1841, de Mun was elected deputy in 1876 from the Marbehan, and sat with the right. He supported the Ralliement (qv) and after 1899 devoted his energies to the republican cause. He led the Catholic vote to support the Three Year Law (qv) of 1913. He died at Bordeaux on 6 October 1914.

Murat, Joachim (1767–1815) Murat, a marshal of France, was born to a family of innkeepers on 25 March 1767 in the Lot. He began his studies in a seminary but left to enter the army in 1787, and from February to March 1792 Murat served in the guard for Louis XVI (qv). He was promoted to junior lieutenant in October 1792 but lost his rank during Thermidor. However, Murat gained the support of Napoléon Bonaparte (qv), and in 1796 he fought in Italy where he was elevated to brigadier general. He served with distinction in Egypt and was promoted to division general. During the coup d'état of 18 Brumaire (qv), Murat sided with Napoléon and rose to command the Consul's guard. In 1800 he married Caroline Bonaparte (qv) and on 14 June 1800 he distinguished himself at the battle of Marengo in Italy. In May 1804 Napoléon made him a marshal of France, and in 1805 he added the title of Admiral and Prince. A year later Murat became the grand duke of Berg and of Cleves. In July 1808 he became the king of Naples where he followed an independent policy. During the retreat from Russia, Murat commanded the armies after Napoléon returned to western Europe. After Russia, Murat, trying to save his throne, secretly negotiated with the Austrians and English against the French. However, during the Hundred Days (qv) Murat rallied to Napoléon and fought at Waterloo. Returning to Italy, he tried without success to save his kingdom but was arrested and shot by a firing squad at Pizzo, Italy, on 13 October 1815.

Muscadins   The Muscadins were basically anti-Jacobin youth drawn from middle-class families. They were politically active and quite vocal in their opposition to Jacobin and Terrorist tactics. After Thermidor they broke busts of Jean Paul Marat (qv) and attacked former supporters of executed Maximilien de Robespierre (qv). Known for their exaggerated, foppish dress, the Muscadins were used by the Thermidorians as strong-arm squads to terrorise former radicals, and were finally repressed when they had served their purpose.

Nancy, Congress of   The Radical Socialist Party met at Nancy in 1907 to put forth a solid political programme. Since the collapse of the *Délégation des Gauches* (qv) in 1905 the radicals and socialists were in conflict. The Nancy Congress produced a coherent radical programme which was reformist, democratic, secularist and social. This platform was aimed at the labourers, rural population and progressive middle class.

Nancy Programme   In 1898 Maurice Barrès (qv) ran for a seat in the Chamber for Nancy. During his campaign he outlined his concepts of 'integral nationalism'. Anti-Jewish, extremely nationalistic and protectionist, Barrès's programme was a coherent statement of emerging rightist thought. He was anti-Dreyfus and openly opposed to the importation of foreign workers into France. France, according to Barrès, was to remain French, free from foreign thoughts and concepts.

Napoléon III (1808–1873)   Louis Napoléon Bonaparte, born at the Tuileries on 20 April 1808 to Louis Bonaparte (qv) and Hortense de Beauharnais (qv), experienced an uprooted life, being separated from both mother and father at a young age. He fought as a soldier in 1831 for the Italian nationalists, and in 1832 assumed, on his own, the title of pretender when Napoléon II, the Duc de Reichstadt (qv), died. In 1836 and 1840, with the Duc de Persigny (qv), Louis Napoléon tried to overthrow the government of Louis Philippe (qv). After the second attempt, Napoléon was incarcerated in the fortress of Ham where he wrote his Saint-Simonian book, *L'Extinction du Paupérisme* (1844). In it he called for republicans and socialists to rally to the Bonapartist cause, to effect vast social and economic changes in French life. In 1846 he fled to Britain, but returned in 1848 as deputy. He ran for election to the presidency in 1848 and won with $5\frac{1}{2}$ million votes. Aided by de Morny (qv) and Persigny, Napoléon III overthrew the government by a coup d'état in 1851. In December 1852 he established the empire. To ensure hereditary rule he married Eugénie de Montijo (qv), who bore him a son in 1856. Following an agressive foreign and imperial policy Napoléon III involved France in Mexico, Tonkin and Africa. In 1856 he engaged France in the Crimean War, and after the Plombières Conference (qv) with the Piedmontese Comte Cavour, he intervened in Italy in 1859 against Austria. From 1860 to 1870 Napoléon III tried to institute the liberal empire which he preferred to totally authoritarian rule. The results of this attempt at liberalisation failed to materialise because of the Franco-Prussian War of 1870 which swept Napoléon from the throne. Suffering from long-term kidney ailments, he fled to

England and died in exile at Chislehurst on 9 January 1873.

Napoleonic Codes   On 12 August 1800 Napoléon appointed a committee of great French scholars to begin working on a uniform civil code for France. Discussed in the Council of State, each article of the draft was carefully prepared. The Civil Code was issued on 21 March 1804. Revolutionary, yet in many respects authoritarian and traditional, this code reflected a trend toward centralisation and uniformity. It was brief yet very coherent and complete. In 1806 a Code of Civil Procedure was promulgated, and in 1810 the Code of Penal Procedure was completed. A Commercial Code established in 1807 helped standardise business law and practices. These new codes imposed a basic legal unity on France which broke down old provincial barriers, but was accomplished without the destruction of the French character. This was one of Bonaparte's greatest contributions to the modern era.

National Council of French Women   The National Council was founded in 1901 by delegates from over sixty women's groups in France representing all shades of political and social opinion. They were united, however, on the issue of integrating women into the mainstream of French political and social life without breaking down the traditional French family framework. The council proclaimed as goals the elimination of discrimination against women in salaries and hiring and the teaching of civic duties to women.

Necker, Albertine, née **de Saussure** (1766–1841)   The wife of the nephew of the famous French finance minister Jacques Necker (qv), she was born in Geneva in 1766. Very early in life she displayed a great ability in literature and education. Her principal contribution was *Education progressive, ou étude de la vie,* published in Paris in three volumes in 1828. In her work she argues for progressive education for women. Her work had an impact on such educators as Victor Duruy (qv). She died on 13 April 1841 at Mornay, France.

Necker, Jacques (1732–1804)   Born on 30 September 1732 in Geneva, Jacques Necker came to Paris as a youth with a flair for finance and banking. In 1762 he helped found his first bank, which brought him to the attention of the royal court and he was appointed director of the French treasury in 1776. In 1777 Louis XVI (qv) elevated him to director-general of finance. He served in that capacity from 1777 until May 1781 when he was ousted because of his advocacy of far-reaching financial reforms. He was recalled in 1788 because of a popular outcry over the bankrupt condition of the French state. In 1789 he tried to persuade the *Etats généraux* to adopt his reforms, which included an abolition of feudal rights and dues. In May 1789 Necker proposed his reforms, but they were opposed by the court. On 11 July he was dismissed from his post, which caused an immediate outcry. In Paris mobs marched through the streets to protest against Necker's ouster, and his bust was carried by the crowds as a symbol of their disagreement with Necker's dismissal. This manifestation to support Necker led ultimately to the storming of the Bastille (qv) on 14 July 1789. Recalled to the finance ministry, Necker tried to follow a moderate policy in respect to finance, but in 1790 he resigned to protest at the issuing of assignats (qv). After 1790 he devoted his time to his many business investments. Jacques Necker died at his estate at Coppet on 9 April 1804 as a man who had become embittered by his experiences of 1789–1790.

Nefftzer, Auguste (1820–1876)   A journalist of liberal persuasion, Nefftzer was born at Colmar, to staunchly Protestant parents, on 3 February 1820. He studied theology at Strasbourg but left to take a post on the *Courrier du Bas-Rhin*. His political articles attracted the attention of the Paris journalists, and in 1844 he joined *La Presse*. In 1856 he became political director of the journal. In 1861 he founded *Le Temps*, which became an outlet for liberal, middle-class views. In its pages, Nefftzer opposed Napoléon III (qv) and his imperial and internal policies. Nefftzer retired in 1871 and died at Bâle on 20 August 1876.

Ney, Michel (1769–1815)   A marshal of France, Ney was born in Saarlouis on 10 January 1769 to a respected, middle-class family. In 1787 he enlisted in the army and served from 1792 to 1797 in the army of the North. He became an officer in 1792 and a brigade general in 1796. After an excellent campaign in Switzerland in 1799, Napoléon (qv) appointed him to conduct negotiations for the 1803 Act of Mediation (qv). On 19 May 1804 Napoléon Bonaparte elevated Ney to the rank of marshal of France, and in the same year he took part in the campaigns against the Austrians. In 1806 to 1807 he fought against the Prussians, and for his service Napoléon made him the Duc d'Elchingen on 6 June 1808. From 1808 to 1811 Ney fought in Spain and Portugal. He again distinguished himself at Moscow, and in March 1813 Napoléon named him Prince de Moskow. In 1813 he fought in Germany, participating in the battle of Leipzig in October. Ney tried to rally to the Bourbons but disapproved of their military policies, and he joined Napoléon in March 1815 during the Hundred Days (qv). After Waterloo, he went into hiding but was captured, sent before a court in Paris, condemned to death, and executed on 7 December 1815.

Niel, Adolphe (1802–1869)   Marshal of finance and minister of state, Niel was born at Muret on 4 October 1802. A brilliant student, he joined the army and fought at the siege of Rome in 1849 where he was promoted to general. He became chief of engineers at the ministry of war and in 1853 was promoted to division general. During the Crimean War he served with distinction at Sébastopol in 1855 and in 1857 was made a senator. He became minister of war in 1867 and, without much success, tried to reform and reorganise the French armies. Niel died in Paris on 3 August 1869.

Noailles, Louis de (1756–1804)   A deputy in 1789, Noailles joined with the Duc d'Aiguillon (qv) to urge the Assembly to do away with all feudal dues, rents and rights. The proposals led to the decrees and actions of 5–11 August 1789.

Oeuvres des Cercles   This Catholic organisation was founded by Albert de Mun (qv) and other committed Roman Catholics to aid in the reconciliation of management and labour and to come to grips with the growing industrialisation of France. The workers' circles, founded in the 1870s, had a dramatic impact on Catholic opinion vis-à-vis industrialism.

Ollivier, Emile (1825–1913)   Born into a well-to-do commercial family in Marseilles on 2 July 1825, Ollivier was elected a deputy in 1848, and was named commissary general of the Republic. In 1867 he was elected to the *Corps Législatif* and became one of the five deputies who opposed the empire. Hoping to turn the empire toward a more liberal position, Ollivier served Napoléon III, but his efforts failed and he was not re-elected in 1869. In 1870 he became minister of justice and helped to prepare the 1870 constitution of the parliamentary empire. After the downfall of France in 1870, Ollivier exiled himself to Italy and returned to France in 1874. He died at Saint Gervais les Bains on 20 August 1913.

Ordinance of 21 April 1944   This ordinance, passed by the *Comité Français de la Libération Nationale* (CFLN) (qv) in Algiers marked a milestone in the fight for women's rights in France. In 1918, 1922, 1925, 1931 and 1932 the Senate defeated bills aimed at women's suffrage. However, during the war years (1940–4) many French women rallied to the cause of General Charles de Gaulle (qv) and the Free French. In recognition of their service and in awareness of the changing times the CFLN passed this historic ordinance which recognised women's right in voting and holding elective office. The theme of the ordinance was upheld in practice in the critical municipal elections of 1945. In 1946, when a new constitution was adopted, women's rights were incorporated as an integral part of French political life. In 1946, thirty-three women were elected to the first Constituent Assembly. From 1947 to 1948 Madame Poinsot-Chapuis held a cabinet post as minister of public health, the first woman to do so.

Ordinance of 4 October 1945   One of the key ordinances which made up the ordinances of 1945 (qv) was the law passed on 4 October 1945 which reorganised the social security system (see: Law of 5 April 1928). This law forced employers in

France to maintain basically equal funds which would be used to help defray the social security costs. These funds were handled by district rather than local organisations. Contributions were therefore standardised. All people who had a responsibility for a child were made eligible for the *allocations familiales* (qv). The amount paid by the allocations was raised. Maternity and post-natal allowances were created. This ordinance was later supplemented by the Act of 22 August 1946 which equalised benefits to all Frenchmen regardless of their situation in life. These benefits were paid by a number of agencies, but the financing was solely the province of the employer. These two pieces of social legislation set the tone for the encompassing security system which developed under the Fourth and Fifth Republics.

Ordinance of 7 January 1959 (military reorganisation) President Charles de Gaulle (qv) felt the necessity for a single direction for the military forces of France, and, under his guidance, the ordinance of 7 January 1959 was issued. The ordinance reorganised the three branches of the military service under one cabinet official, the minister of the armed forces, who is directly responsible for the organisation, administration, training and mobilisation of the French army, navy and air force. The president of the Republic still maintained the traditional role as commander in chief, but as a result of this ordinance the military was centralised in control and administration. By the reforms of 5 April 1961 a ministerial delegate for armaments assists the minister of the armed forces in matters relating to technological development. The ordinance of 7 January 1959 also created the national service of the draft which enrolled men between the ages of twenty and thirty-seven for a period of two years. A reserve pool of men aged thirty-seven to sixty formed the second stage of national service.

Ordinance of 8 January 1959 (labour relations) Following the acceptance of the constitution of 4 October 1958 which brought the Fifth Republic into being, there was a concerted effort by the government to end the labour-management strife which had marked the defunct Fourth Republic. The ordinance of 8 January 1959 provided for certain tax exemptions for management if they signed partnership agreements with labour unions. It was hoped that such agreements would end labour-management hostility. Management was also encouraged to set up profit-sharing programmes, stock share-buying options and benefits linked to higher production rates. While this ordinance had limited effect, it was a major effort, via social legislation, to lessen worker-management hostility.

Ordinances of 25 July 1830 In July 1830 elections for the Assembly ran against Charles X (qv) and his ultra-conservative government. On 24 July 1830 Charles held a meeting with his cabinet and with Prince Polignac (qv), his prime minister, who advocated extreme measures to silence all liberal opposition. Polignac drew up the ordinances of 25 July 1830 to counter the rise of liberal thought in France. The first ordinances suspended the liberty of the press and prescribed certain regulations for the publication of newspapers and political tracts. The second ordinance dissolved the newly elected Assembly with no guarantees for new elections. Another ordinance restricted the franchise to about one-quarter of the existing qualified electors, basing the right to vote on wealth and on position. This had the effect of taking away any semblance of political participation from the bulk of the rich middle class. A fourth ordinance convoked the conservative electoral colleges to elect a new, and for Charles X, hopefully a more Bourbon, more conservative Chamber. When it became clear that the ordinances of 25 July were going to lead to disturbances, Charles X decided to use the army to suppress the opposition, but most of the French army was in Algeria and he had no military force to rely upon. On 26 July 1830 the journalists of Paris protested bitterly against the ordinances, and the next day rebellion broke out in Paris. By 29 July a provisional government (qv) was installed and Charles X was forced to abdicate.

Ordinances of 1945 (comprehensive social insurance)
After World War II there was a definite trend within the provisional government of General Charles de Gaulle (qv) to extend the social insurance laws of the 1930s. The ordinances of 1945 were a series of laws which brought together all existing pieces of social legislation and broadened their application. All Frenchmen, regardless of their station in life, were guaranteed a minimum of social benefits. This concept was named simply *solidarité*. All persons, regardless of income, could apply for the *allocations familiales* (qv), and social security protection (see: Law of 5 April 1928; Ordinance of 4 October 1945) was broadened to encompass almost all wage and salary earners. The rates of payment for sickness and hospitalisation were increased, and in some cases up to 100 per cent of hospital costs were paid by the system. The ordinances of 1945 proclaimed the right of all Frenchmen to be healthy and to obtain proper medical care. The series of ordinances passed in 1945 set the general tone for the future of social legislation in France during the Fourth and Fifth Republics.

Orléans, Ferdinand-Philippe d' (1810–1842)   A brother of King Louis Philippe (qv), Ferdinand-Philippe faithfully served the cause of the Orléanist monarchy. In 1831 he put down the silk workers' revolt in Lyon, and from 1834 to 1837 he served in Africa. He died of an accident in 1842.

Orsini Bomb Plot   Orsini was an Italian patriot who attempted to murder Napoléon III (qv) by a bomb in January 1858. Orsini mainly wanted to dramatise Italy's plight. His defence was conducted by Jules Favre (qv), but he was condemned to death. However, the bomb plot had an affect on Napoléon III, who turned his attention toward the Italian question and met with Piedmont's Comte Cavour at Plombières (qv) to discuss French intervention in Italy.

Ozanam, Frédéric (1813–1858)   A student of law and a Saint-Simonian, Ozanam, a staunch Catholic, founded the Society of Saint Vincent de Paul to help the urban working poor. A Catholic liberal, he felt the need for a religious response to urbanisation. In 1848 he tried for a political career but failed to win election to the Assembly. His health broken, the bitter Ozanam retired to Italy.

Painlevé, Paul (1863–1933) A brilliant mathematician with many academic degrees and honours, Painlevé advocated aviation as an important form of transport for the future. He made numerous contributions to the science of aviation and aviation mechanics, and for his efforts he was elected deputy in 1910. He became minister of war in 1917, and thereafter he served as premier several times during the 1920s.

Paléologue, Maurice (1859–1944) Paléologue, diplomat and author, served as French ambassador to Russia from 1914 to 1917. Having an important post, Ambassador Paléologue seemed to pursue an independent policy during the critical month of July 1914. A personal friend of Raymond Poincaré (qv), the president of the republic, Paléologue was determined to convince Russia of France's faithful maintenance of the Franco-Russian alliances. However, the ambassador failed to keep Paris fully informed of Russian mobilisation plans in 1914. After World War I he maintained an interest in eastern Europe, and he advocated a system of French alliances with the emerging eastern European states. Paléologue retired from public life in the 1930s to write a series of books and articles on French policy vis à vis Russia during World War I.

Panachage This device, originated by a law in 1951, was aimed at giving the French voter a greater voice in picking candidates for the Chamber. Under the system voters could change official lists of candidates (by parties) by simply scratching out names and adding names of other party candidates to the list. This principle of *panachage* was never applied in a great number of elections, but the effect could have been devastating to an already confused political structure during the Fourth Republic. Basically, *panachage* was a device for voters to recognise a brilliant personality or striking political philosophy without actually deserting their own party. It ran counter to the party-dominated system of proportional representation.

Panama Affair   A French company, represented by Ferdinand de Lesseps (qv), secured large loans from the Chamber to dig a canal through the Isthmus of Panama. De Lesseps, a hero for his work on the Suez Canal, and other Panama backers were over-enthusiastic about the project, which simply did not materialise. The Chamber authorised a public lottery to raise funds, but this failed and with it the company. In 1892 many members of the Chamber, even Clemenceau (qv), were accused of accepting bribes to help the company. The Boulangists, though their movement was rapidly dying out owing to the suicide of their leader Boulanger (qv), violently attacked the decay of the Republic, as did the socialists. Both groups hoped to win the French voters to their particular political philosophies by showing that republicanism was unfit for France. There were two men, Jacques de Reinach and Cornelius Herz, who were responsible for popularising the Panama project and were given the task of raising money for it. Herz and Reinach kept the financial situation of the company from the press and public until 1889. In 1892, after the revelations of scandal were aired, Reinach committed suicide and Herz fled to England. Both Herz and Reinach were Jewish, and professional anti-Semites in the Chamber and in the press pointed to the illegal acts of those two disgraced financiers as proof of Jewish duplicity and criminal tendencies. The Panama Affair and the criminal acts committed by Herz and Reinach contributed to the rise of virulent anti-Semitism in France.

Paris, Capitulation of   On 31 March 1814 the coalition allies entered Paris while Napoléon Bonaparte (qv) was on the Marne River. The capitulation was signed by Talleyrand (qv) and the provisional government and allied representatives on that day. French troops which garrisoned Paris were moved from the city to Fontainebleau, and allied troops occupied the city. Talleyrand's provisional government remained in force until Louis XVIII (qv) could take up his duties as the restored king. During these discussions, Talleyrand assured his own political future and opened the way for the re-establishment, on the principle of legitimacy, of the Bourbon monarchy.

Paris, 1806 Treaty of After the failure of Prussia to accept the Preliminaries of Schönbrunn (qv), Napoléon imposed the Treaty of Paris of 1806 on the German state. On 15 February 1806 the treaty was signed. It called for the annexation of Hanover, and coastal areas in north Germany were closed to British shipping, which directly endangered British commerce with northern Europe. Prussia was forced to agree to Bonaparte's changes in regard to the Kingdom of Naples, which drew an unwilling Prussia into a scheme against Britain and, in the long run, Russia. Prussia decided to move against Napoléon and to abrogate the Treaty of Paris of 1806. This was ultimately an error because Prussian troops were soundly defeated at Jena and Auerstadt in October 1806. By late October French troops occupied Berlin.

Paris, First Peace of Signed on 30 May 1814 by the allies and France, this peace forced France to give up all rights to Germany, Italy, Belgium, Holland, Switzerland and Malta. Many colonies, including Tobago, were given to Britain. France's borders were reduced to those she held on 1 November 1792. However, by the inclusion of Avignon, Montbeliard and other areas, France gained territory and an additional population of almost half a million people. Secret clauses provided for a German union into some sort of vague confederation. The secret article aimed at helping to create a balance of power in Europe in the post-war period.

Paris, Pact of (Kellogg-Briand Pact) On 27 August 1928, Frank B. Kellogg, secretary of state of the United States, and Aristide Briand (qv), foreign minister of France, signed a pact which outlawed war as an instrument of national policy. The banning of war was adhered to by a vast number of states including Great Britain, the USSR, Germany and Italy, but the Pact of Paris did not provide for any mechanism whereby a nation which pursued an aggressive policy would be punished.

Paris Protocols of May 1941 These protocols were signed in Paris on 27 and 28 May 1941 between Admiral François Darlan (qv) and German representatives. They covered three major areas: Syria and Iraq; North Africa; French sub-Sahara Africa. The Middle East was opened to German aircraft. The Vichy government promised to defend this area and to ship war materials back to France. North African ports, especially Bizerta in Tunisia, were opened to Italian warships. There were definite clauses pertaining to French troops loyal to Vichy which allowed a certain freedom of movement within North Africa. In sub-Sahara Africa, the port of Dakar was open to German ships. There were troop levels assigned to French Africa to oust Gaullist forces and to re-establish Vichy control. These concessions mark the high point of collaborationist German-Vichy relations and represent the greatest of Vichy's concessions to Nazi Germany.

Paris, Second Peace of   After the 1815 restoration of Louis XVIII (qv) a second Peace of Paris was concluded on 20 November 1815. Basically shaped by England's Viscount Robert Castlereagh, this treaty was an attempt to impose some moderation on the reconstruction of post-Napoleonic Europe. By its provisions France lost some territory in Belgium and on the Swiss frontier, was restricted mainly to the frontiers of 1789 and was forced to pay an indemnity of 700 million francs. Also, France was obliged, for five years, to support an allied occupation army. While the major powers, at Castlereagh's insistence, guaranteed the Peace of Paris, it was only a temporary measure. France benefited from the tendencies of the allies to be lenient with the newly restored Bourbon monarchy. The French state lost little territory gained in the first Peace of Paris (qv) and her honour was preserved.

Parthénopean Republic   In January 1799 a popular revolt ousted the king of Naples. Naples was reorganised as the Parthénopean Republic, an ally of France. Joseph Bonaparte (qv) was made king of Naples and Sicily in 1806, and in 1808 Bonaparte conferred the title of king of Naples on Joachim Murat (qv), his brother-in-law.

Parti Colonial Français   The French Colonial Party,

formed in 1892 by Eugène Etienne (qv) and a group of colonial deputies, was not a political party in the strict sense of the word. It was a loose coalition of deputies and senators from all political parties who advocated the imperialist cause. The main function of the Colonial Party was the marshalling of votes in support of colonial questions. Its influence in French politics was greatest from 1894 to 1905.

Parti Communiste Français (PCF)   The PCF was formed in December 1920 as a result of a split in French socialism which became evident at the Congress of Tours (qv). The question of adherence to the platform of the Third International caused a majority to form the French Communist Party which accepted Lenin's Twenty-one Conditions for joining the Third International. In the 1930s the PCF was an open opponent of Fascism and Nazism until the signing of the Nazi-Soviet Pact of August 1939. Led by Maurice Thorez (qv), the communists played a prominent role in the resistance after Germany invaded the Soviet Union in the spring of 1941. The PCF opposed General Charles de Gaulle (qv), whom it saw as an ultra-conservative nationalist, and after his resignation in 1946 it tried to win power legally, but failed in 1947. From 1947 to 1956 the party played a strong role in French politics until the Soviet Union invaded Hungary in 1956. The brutal Soviet actions there disgusted even many party regulars, and they attempted in vain to dissociate the French Communist Party from the Russian action in central Europe. During the crisis of May 1958 the PCF found that many of the proletariat had lost faith in it and followed General de Gaulle. After the foundation of the Fifth Republic the PCF found itself a weakened party, but since 1958 it has tried to appear as a strong anti-Gaullist force, and has shown definite signs of political revitalisation.

Parti Ouvrier   The Workers' Party was founded by Jules Guesde (qv) in 1879 as a response to the industrial revolution and demands for reform. Guesde wanted a party which was revolutionary and not reformist. Doctrinaire in its approach, the *Parti Ouvrier* refused to associate itself with problems such as the Dreyfus affair or the Boulanger crisis which were seen as particularly bourgeois confrontations. The party under Guesde did reject anarchism and the coup d'état, which he saw as futile. Guesde led the *Parti Ouvrier* into the *Section Française de l'Internationale Ouvrière* (SFIO) (qv) in 1905, making the SFIO into a revolutionary party.

Parti Populaire Algérien (PPA)   The Popular Party of Algeria was founded in 1936 by Messali Hadj, a vocal exponent of alterations in Algeria's colonial status. The PPA replaced the *Etoile Nord Africaine* (ENA) (qv), which had become associated with communist elements in France. In 1939 the government forced the PPA to dissolve, but it went underground and survived World War II. By 1946 the PPA was still not allowed to operate openly, but it attracted some students and intellectuals into its ranks. The PPA ran candidates in Algeria under the banner of the *Mouvement pour le Triomphe des Libertés Démocratiques* (MTLD) (qv).

Parti Populaire Français   This pro-fascist political party was founded by Jacques Doriot (qv), who was known for his admiration of Mussolini and the Italian governmental system. Militant in its opposition to parliamentary government, the PPF was determined to overthrow it and establish a strong centralised state modelled after the Italian fascist system. Doriot and his followers opposed any action to alienate Hitler in 1939. This organisation supported Marshal Pétain (qv) and the Vichy government. Eventually supporters of Doriot served German interests as collaborators with the Nazis.

Parti Social Français   After 1936 the *Croix de Feu* (qv), damaged by its participation in the 1936 riots, changed its name to the French Social Party. It still remained anti-parliamentary and violently anti-communist, demanding that France reconstitute its governmental system along the lines of Fascist Italy.

Pavie, Auguste Jean Marie (1847–1925)   An officer of the colonial marines, Pavie was sent to Indo-China in 1868, where he studied the customs and the languages of Cambodia. In 1887 he was named viceconsul in Luang Prabang. He then studied in Laos and explored various areas of Indo-China. From 1892 to 1893 he was French consul in Siam and was then transferred to Laos. It was Pavie who determined the Laotian borders and, by his forceful actions, made Laos a French protectorate. From 1895 to 1905 he served as minister to Bangkok, and retired after 1905 to write.

Péguy, Charles (1873–1914) Born to a very poor family in Orléans on 7 January 1873, Péguy proved himself to be a brilliant student at the *Ecole normale supérieure*. However, dissatisfied with higher education, Péguy left school to devote himself to political action and to literature. In 1897 he published a tract, *De la cité socialiste*. The next year he published a dramatic poem *Jeanne d'Arc*. Filled with disgust for materialism and corruption in government, Péguy was at first attracted by Jean Jaurès (qv) and French socialism, but soon came to distrust Jaurès's dedication to socialist causes. In 1900 he founded the *Cahiers de la quinzaine,* for which he wrote up to the outbreak of war in 1914. After 1905 and the First Moroccan Crisis (qv) he started to drift towards nationalism. In *Notre Jeunesse*, published in 1910, he defended his now vehement nationalist feelings. By 1914 he had violently attacked Jaurès in his articles in *Cahiers de la quinzaine*. When war broke out in 1914, Péguy, true to his ideals, enlisted in the army and was killed at Villeroy on 5 September 1914 during the battle of the Marne.

Pelletan, Camille (1846–1915) A deputy and minister of the marine from 1902 to 1905 under Emile Combes (qv), Pelletan was a jingoist during the First Moroccan Crisis (qv). He served the Bouches de Rhône as a deputy from 1881 to 1912, and in 1912 he held the post of senator from that area. In 1906 the political right in the Chamber accused Pelletan of allowing the French navy to fall to a second-rate status. Their complaints seemed justified, and Pelletan was the target of bitter official criticism in the Chamber of Deputies. After 1906 Pelletan, his career ruined, slipped into political oblivion.

Père Lachaise, Cemetery of During the assault on the Paris Commune of 1871 (qv) the Versailles army executed a large number of Communards (qv) at the cemetery of Père Lachaise on 28 May 1871. Since that date the cemetery has served as a shrine for French leftists who continue to honour the memory of the slain Communards.

Pereire, Isaac (1806–1880) Born to a Jewish family in Bordeaux on 25 November 1806, Pereire and his older brother, Jacob Emile (3 December 1800–6 January 1875), affiliated with the Saint Simonians. Isaac wrote for various journals after the revolution of 1830, advocating railroad construction. From 1833 to 1835 he, along with financiers like the Rothschilds, built railways. In 1852, after he was granted a concession for the Midi railway, he, along with his brother, created the *Crédit Mobilier* (qv) to finance railways. From 1848, both Isaac and Jacob supported Louis Napoléon (qv) because of his adherence to Saint Simonian economics. The Pereire brothers became known as the financiers of the Second Empire until the *Crédit Mobilier* went bankrupt in 1867. During the peak of *Crédit* popularity the Pereire brothers broke with the Rothschilds, who sided with the traditional bankers in France. With the financial backing of the Rothschilds, anti-Bonapartist deputies singled out the Pereire brothers for attack. Both men served as deputies in 1863 and in 1869, but after 1869 they retired from public and political life. Isaac Pereire died in Armanvilliers on 12 July 1880.

Périer, Auguste Casimir (1821–1876) Born in Paris on 20 August 1821, Auguste Casimir Périer, son of Casimir Périer (qv) decided early in his life on a career in diplomacy and politics. Elected deputy in 1846 and in 1848, he was imprisoned after Napoléon III's coup d'état of 1851. After a period of political inactivity, he was elected deputy in 1871. From 1871 to 1872 and in 1873 he served as minister of the interior. Basically a conservative and a supporter of Adolphe Thiers (qv), Périer was elected senator in 1876. However, he did not serve in that position very long—he died in Paris on 6 July 1876.

Périer, Casimir (1777–1832)   Born in Grenoble on 11 October 1777, Périer proved to be a brilliant student. He served in the Italian army but left the military to open a bank. Of moderate persuasion, he survived the Bourbon restoration in 1815 and was elected deputy in 1817. He served as president of the Chamber during the revolution of 1830 and was premier in 1832. He drifted more toward political and economic conservatism and supported Louis Philippe's (qv) policies. During the early years of the Orléanist monarchy, Périer emerged as the leader of the Party of Resistance. In 1832, as president of the Council, Périer formed a block against reforms, resisting all efforts to change. He even imposed his tremendous authoritarian will on Louis Philippe. Casimir Périer died during a cholera outbreak in Paris on 16 May 1832.

Périer, Jean Casimir (1847–1907)   Born in Paris on 8 November 1847 to a famous political family, Périer first began his career with his father, Auguste Périer (qv), at the interior ministry. Elected deputy in 1876, he sat with the republican left. From 1877 to 1879 he served as undersecretary for public instruction and in 1885 was elected as vicepresident of the Chamber. He formed a ministry in 1893 and struggled against the rising threat of anarchism in France. He became a staunch defender of public order. After the murder of President Sadi Carnot (qv) in 1894, Périer was elected president of France, but retired in 1895. The remainder of his life was devoted to his extensive business interests. He died in Paris on 11 March 1907.

Persigny, Jean Gilbert Fialin de (1808–1872)   Born in the Department of the Loire on 11 January 1808, known as Napoléon III's faithful servant, de Persigny first met Louis Napoléon (qv) in 1835 in Germany. In 1836 de Persigny tried to prepare the ground for Napoléon's first coup d'état. The attempt was a failure, but from 1836 on de Persigny and Louis Napoléon were inseparable. During the month of March 1848 de Persigny returned to Paris to pave the way for Napoléon's return. It was Persigny who began the campaign to elect Napoléon president of France in late 1848. His advice to

Napoléon to champion a quick return to law and order was a key factor in the amazing electoral victory in December 1848 when Louis Napoléon, the heir of the Bonapartist tradition, polled over 5 million votes. Persigny's role in the December victory earned for him a place in Napoléon III's immediate entourage. From 1851 to 1852 Persigny urged Napoléon to turn the Republic into the Second Empire, and as minister of the interior, he played a decisive role in the coup d'état of 1851. From 1855 to 1859 he served as ambassador to Britain, and began to manifest anti-Catholic tendencies. He also opposed the concept of a liberal empire. Given the responsibility of managing the elections of 1863, he failed to deliver a total Bonapartist victory. From 1863 until 1872 de Persigny and Napoléon III were out of contact, but they were reconciled in 1872. Persigny died at Chamaraude in the Seine et Oise on 12 January 1872.

Pétain, Henri Philippe (1856–1951)   A professional soldier born at Cauchy la Tour on 24 April 1856, Pétain won fame as the defender of Verdun in 1916. In 1917 he rose to commander of the armies of the north-east. During his period as army commander, he had to deal with the mutinies of 1917 which threatened to undermine the war effort and his experiences with the mutinies and pacifist agitation soured him on democracy and freedom of speech. For his service he was promoted to marshal of France in 1918. From 1925 to 1926 he served in Morocco, and in 1934 he held the portfolio of war minister. Named ambassador to Spain in 1939, Pétain was recalled in France in 1940 to form a government which he called the *Etat français*. The *Etat français* was an open rejection of the republican, democratic traditions of France. (Pétain sought and got an armistice with the Germans.) Reflecting his conservatism, Pétain governed France from Vichy, replacing 'Liberty, Equality, Fraternity', with 'Family, Work, and Fatherland'. He believed firmly that France had suffered from an overdose of democracy which brought on moral decay and the death of basic national values. To accomplish a moral and patriotic revitalisation of France, however, Pétain felt that relations with Germany had first to be normalised. In 1940 he met with Adolf Hitler at Montoire (qv) and accepted the principles of collaboration. He used Pierre Laval (qv) and Admiral François Darlan (qv) as premiers, but despite his efforts to the contrary Vichy fell more and more under German control. In 1944 Pétain, along with Laval, was deported to Germany and in April 1945 returned to France to stand trial. He was found guilty of treason and sentenced to death, but General Charles de Gaulle (qv) commuted his sentence to life imprisonment because of his advanced age. Marshal Pétain died at Port Joinville (île d'Yeu) on 23 July 1951.

Pflimlin, Pierre (1907–   ) A member of the *Mouvement Républicain Populaire* (MRP) (qv), Pflimlin became a deputy in 1945. The ex-mayor of Strasbourg also became the leader of the MRP from 1956 to 1959. He formed a government in May 1958 which was destined to failure because of the Algerian revolution. There had been a revolt of the military in Algeria, and in May 1958 France appeared to have three basic choices: civil war, a military coup d'état or Charles de Gaulle (qv). It was Pflimlin who called on General de Gaulle to come to Paris to save France from terrible bloodshed. While Pflimlin received a vote of confidence from the Chamber on 27 May 1958 he still resigned in deference to de Gaulle.

Philippe-Egalité, Louis-Philippe d'Orléans (1747–1793) Born at Saint Cloud on 13 April 1747, Louis Philippe manifested a liberal nature as a young man. Known for his work in changing the gardens of the *Palais Royal* into a business centre, Louis became very popular among the middle class. Even before 1789 he defended the rights of the Third Estate. A popular liberal cousin of Louis XVI, Philippe d'Orléans was elected to the *Etats généraux* in 1789 and aligned with Mirabeau (qv). Generally, however, he sat with the Montagnards (qv). To show his support for the revolutionary cause, he changed his name to Philippe-Egalité, and he voted for the death of Louis XVI, which earned him the undying hatred of the

Bourbon royalists. Compromised by the defection of his son Louis Philippe (qv) and of General Dumouriez (qv), Philippe-Egalité was arrested in 1793 and was sentenced to death by the revolutionary tribunal. He died on the guillotine in Paris on 6 November 1793.

Pichegru, Jean Charles (1761–1804) Pichegru was born to a humble family at Arbois on 16 February 1761. He served in the American revolution as a non-commissioned officer and received his commission in 1792. After brilliant service in the army of the Rhine, he was elevated to general in 1793. A revolutionary officer, he first attracted attention by forcefully suppressing the revolt of Germinal (1 April 1795). For his quick actions, the Convention entitled him 'Saviour of the Fatherland'. An excellent officer with many brilliant victories, such as the capture of Brussels in 1794, Pichegru became ambitious; he conspired with the Austrians in late 1795 and lost his command. He was ordered to go to Sweden as the French Ambassador but refused to take up his new post. After he had been restored to favour, he entered into secret negotiations with British agents in Switzerland. A member of the Five Hundred (qv), he used his position to betray France. Arrested as a conspirator with English agents in Switzerland during the coup d'état of 18 Fructidor (4 September 1797) (qv), he was deported to the colony of Guyane. He continued to work with anti-revolutionary, anti-Bonapartist elements, and in 1804 returned to France to take part in a royalist coup d'état. Arrested at the same time as the Duc d'Enghien (qv) was kidnapped, Pichegru was incarcerated and was found hanged in his cell on 5 April 1804. It was rumoured that his death was not suicide.

Pillnitz, Declaration of This declaration, issued on 27 August 1791 by Prussia and Austria, concerned revolutionary France and the fate of King Louis XVI (qv). By the statement, those powers warned that they were prepared to intervene 'to set up a monarchical government in conformity with (the king's) rights and the welfare of the nation'. Pillnitz on the surface appeared to serve a very clear warning on France that the autocratic powers would use force to crush the revolution and restore the Bourbon monarchy. On closer examination, it would seem that the declaration was actually far less than a clear-cut threat to France. The declaration stated that Austria and Prussia would move against France when all other powers decided to take action. It was certain that Britain would not enter into action against France, and the declaration lost a good deal of its force. This also damaged the position of Louis XVI within France. The Girondins (qv), however, took the declaration to mean what it said, and war hawks within the Girondist ranks demanded war against Austria and Prussia. Because of this Girondist position war with Prussia and Austria was almost a certainty.

Pinay, Antoine (1891–   )   First elected deputy in 1936, Pinay after World War II represented the Republican Independents. From March to December 1952 he held the premiership. Basically, Pinay, who was fairly conservative, succeeded in halting rising inflation at the cost of limiting industrial expansion.

Piou, Jacques (1838–1932)   A liberal Catholic, Piou was given the task of organising a political Catholic action group to support a reconciliation of the church and republic. He formed the *Droite constitutionnelle* (qv). Piou opposed Emile Combes's (qv) efforts to separate church and state totally.

Plain, The   Known as the Plain, or the Marsh, they were the deputies of the centre who were in a numerical majority in the Assembly. At first, the Plain leaders like Abbé Sieyès (qv) and Barère (qv) supported the Girondins (qv), because they openly distrusted the radical views of the Montagnards (qv). Slowly the Plain switched their support to the Mountain. As demands for war against the autocratic powers of Europe grew in intensity in 1791–2 the Plain cast its lot with the Montagnards, and followed the radicals in casting many votes for the death of Louis XVI (qv) in January 1793. Overshadowed by the great Girondin and Montagnard personalities, the Plain was courted openly by both sides, and the success or failure of measures depended on its support.

Plan Seventeen   In the three years prior to World War I the French general staff was convinced that the best strategy against the German army was an aggressive offensive on the battlefield. This was expressed in the adoption of Plan Seventeen by the general staff in May 1913. The Chamber at the same time was grappling with the proposed Three Year Law (qv) to increase the size and effectiveness of the French armies. The plan, originated by Ferdinand Foch (qv), called for the deployment of five French armies in eastern France in the event of war. The majority of forces would strike into Alsace-Lorraine and then across the Rhine into Germany. However, the northern sector, along the Franco-Belgian border, was left relatively weakly defended, and this was Plan Seventeen's fatal flaw. In August 1914 German armies used that weakly held area as their main avenue of march in France. The plan failed to do what the general staff had hoped, since in late August 1914 French troops had to be hurried back to the Marne River to defend Paris from the oncoming German armies. Based on the concepts of *élan* and aggressive offensive, Plan Seventeen was weak because of its concentration of troops in Alsace-Lorraine and its disregard of the defence of the Franco-Belgian border.

Plaswitz, Armistice of   Napoléon Bonaparte (qv) called this armistice, signed on 4 June 1813, the worst error of his life. Austria and France agreed to a general armistice which would eventually lead to a peace congress. However, Austria took advantage of the armistice to prepare for war with France. The peace congress at Prague accomplished nothing, and on 14 August war began again between the two states.

Pleven, René (1901–   )   René Pleven served as a deputy and president of the *Union Démocratique et Socialiste de la Résistance* (UDSR) which grew out of the five major non-communist resistance groups in 1945. A conservative finance minister under General Charles de Gaulle (qv), Pleven helped found the

UDSR, which tried to cooperate with the Radicals and the Gaullists. From July 1950 to February 1951 and from August 1951 to January 1952 Pleven was premier. Accused of having no party ideology or discipline, the UDSR finally collapsed by 1956, and with its demise so fell the political fortunes of René Pleven.

Plombières, Conference of This secret conference took place between Napoléon III (qv) and Comte Cavour of Piedmont on 21 July 1858. Napoléon III had a long association with the cause of Italian nationalism, and at Plombières Cavour tried to commit him to a specific course of action. Napoléon came to the conference already convinced about intervention in Italy against Austria, and, contrary to popular opinion, he forced Cavour to make far-reaching concessions. For French aid Nice and Savoy would be ceded to France, the cousin of Napoléon III would marry Clotilde, daughter of King Victor Emmanuel, and a formal treaty would ensure these agreements. Cavour, on the other hand, refused to accept Napoléon III's concept of a confederated Italy. On 26 January 1859 a formal treaty was indeed concluded, and on 30 January the royal wedding took place. On 12 May 1859 French troops entered Italy to aid the Piedmontese.

Poincaré, Raymond (1860–1934)   The son of an engineer, Poincaré was born at Bar le Duc on 20 August 1860. He manifested a desire to pursue a career in law, and in 1880 he became a lawyer. He became *chef de cabinet* for the republican politician Jules Develle and was first elected deputy in 1887 for the Meuse. He became known as a staunch enemy of General Georges Boulanger (qv), and for his defence of the republican tradition, Poincaré won the respect of his colleagues. He vehemently attacked the government over the Panama affair (qv). In 1893 he became minister of public instruction, and three years later he was again minister of public instruction under Alexandre Ribot (qv). During the Dreyfus affair (qv), Poincaré remained aloof from the entire conflict. Elected senator in 1903 for the Meuse, he served as minister of finance in 1906.

Rising in popularity, he formed his own ministry in 1912, when he also took the portfolio of the foreign ministry. In 1913 he was elected president of the Republic and sought to reinforce the alliances with Britain and Russia. As president, Poincaré was determined to see the war to a successful conclusion and to avenge the humiliation of 1870. In 1920 he stepped down from the presidency and returned to the Senate. He headed the French reparation committee, and in the Senate he demanded that Germany pay the full amount levied against it. Two years later Poincaré became premier and followed a harsh policy in regard to Germany. The victory of the *Cartel des Gauches* (qv) in 1924 toppled him from power. After 1924 Poincaré spoke out continuously on financial matters, and in 1928 he formed the government of National Union, which contained Aristide Briand (qv) as foreign minister, Louis Barthou (qv) as justice minister, André Tardieu (qv) as interior minister and Paul Painlevé (qv) as minister of war. It was basically a conservative union of all important, anti-leftist politicians. Poincaré retired from public life in 1929 because of ill health. He devoted the remainder of his life to writing his *Mémoires* and to giving advice to fellow republicans. He died in Paris on 15 October 1934.

Polignac, Auguste, Duc de (1780–1847)　Prince de Polignac was born at Versailles on 14 May 1780 to a family of noble blood. Allied with the royalist cause, the Polignac family became the intimate followers of the deposed Bourbon family. Imprisoned for his uncompromising royalism, Polignac was freed and made a peer in 1815. In 1820 he was elevated to prince. He served Charles X (qv) in 1830, and his repressive press laws sparked off the July 1830 revolt. He was arrested and imprisoned until 1836, and after his release he retired from public life. He died in Paris on 2 March 1847.

Pompidou, Georges (1911–1974)　An excellent student of Latin, Greek and philosophy, Pompidou accumulated a record of brilliance in school. He began a career in teaching, but was called to military service in 1939. After fighting from May to

August 1940, he was released from the army and returned to Paris to teach. Deeply affected by the German occupation of France, he joined the resistance and served on General Charles de Gaulle's political staff. In 1953 Pompidou advised de Gaulle to disown the *Rassemblement du Peuple Français* (RPF) (qv) and to remain aloof from the politics of the Fourth Republic. From 1946 to 1953 he consistently refused a governmental position because of his close relationship with de Gaulle. After 1958 he continued to serve de Gaulle as an advisor, and in 1961, at the request of the general, he opened contacts with the Algerian rebels in Switzerland. In 1962 Pompidou became premier, and in 1967 he was elected deputy. After a period away from the premiership, Pompidou decided that upon de Gaulle's retirement he would seek the office of president. On 15 June 1969 he was elected president of the Republic. After a series of illnesses he died on 2 April 1974.

Popular Front   After the severe February 1934 riots (qv) the parties of the left tended towards unification. On 14 July 1934 the Socialist and Communist Parties signed a pact of unity to fight against anti-democratic tendencies within France. In May 1936 Léon Blum (qv) became the first socialist premier of France, after the victory at the polls in April and May as a result of the *Section française de l'Internationale Ouvrière* (SFIO) (qv) and communist alliance. By 4 June 1936 Blum had constituted his government, which included no communists. Blum called for drastic reforms, but his calls inflamed the workers, who began a series of strikes which abated with the *Matignon Accords* (qv). The accords, a compromise between labour and capital in France, turned the capitalists against Blum. Popular Front legislation amounted to great gains in the way of substantive reforms for labour. Paid vacations, a forty-four-hour working week and compulsory arbitration were the sum total of the legislation. The Spanish Civil War caused great distress, as Blum would have liked to intervene but chose to remain neutral, thereby alienating some of his leftist allies. In 1937 Blum was ousted because of his failure to maintain a working majority in support of the programmes. He had attempted to deal with the Bank of France and other financial institutions but failed. The labour reforms, especially the reduced working week, were great gains for the French workers. While management viewed Blum's reforms with distaste, labour saw them as definite improvements. Many members of the middle class in France gave grudging approval to Popular Front legislation simply because they feared a possible communist surge at the polls and a possible victory for the extreme left. The devaluation of the franc in October 1936 and the March 1937 decision to slow down the pace of reform, all the responsibility of Léon Blum, led to defections from the ranks of those supporting the Front. Attacked by the left for the pause in reformism and verbally assaulted by Joseph Caillaux (qv), who championed financial orthodoxy, he resigned in June 1937.

Poujade, Pierre (1920–) A member of Jacques Doriot's (qv) fascists, Pierre Poujade escaped to Algeria during the Vichy period. After World War II his ultra-conservative political philosophy appealed to the small shopkeeper, the farmer and other members of the lower-middle class. The *Union de Défense des Commerçants et des Artisans* (UDCA) was formed in 1953, but was not extremely right-wing. By 1955 Poujadism was a force in republican politics. The Poujadists advocated a tax strike by the middle class as a way to protest at the policies of the government of the Fourth Republic. But by 1957 the Poujadist movement had fragmented over internal questions and the relationship of France to Europe. Basically, it was an outburst of anger by an alienated class against colonial losses, a weakened France, modernity, urban super-sophistication and what they saw as moral and national decay.

Prairial, Coup of 30 On 18 June 1799 the directors under Abbé Sieyès (qv) purged their own ranks, adding new men who were loyal to Sieyès. This coup d'état of 30 Prairial Year VII was in the upper echelons of the Directory (qv) government. The elections of 1799 were serious setbacks for the government, and the Directors were afraid to take any action to shore up the power of the government. On 16 June (28 Prairial) one director was removed because his election was declared illegal. The Council of Five Hundred and the Council of Ancients announced that they would convince a special commission to examine the deteriorating military situation. This was a move of very doubtful legality. Sieyès, seeing the opportunity, quickly replaced three directors with men loyal to himself. The real victor appeared to be Sieyès as he controlled the Directory and the Councils. It was followed by an immediate reorganisation of the executive machinery, which strengthened the five directors. With the Abbé Sieyès in control, the power of the Assemblies was weakened and the authority of the executive directorship was definitely strengthened.

Pressburg, Treaty of   Signed on 26 December 1805 between France and Austria, this treaty humiliated Austria. The Austrians recognised all changes made in Italy, while Venetia, Istria and Dalmatia (but not Trieste) were ceded to the king of Italy. The crowns of France and Italy would be separated only upon the conclusion of a general peace. The Tirol and Trent went to Bavaria, while Bavaria lost her Swabian possessions to Baden and to Württemberg. These German territories were freed from Austrian influence. This treaty also struck a death blow at the Holy Roman Empire, since a new German confederation was formed, by Bonaparte, at the Austrian empire's expense.

Prieur, Pierre-Louis (1756–1827)   A lawyer of middle-class persuasion, Prieur was known as Prieur of the Marne. A member of the Committee of Public Safety, he was dispatched to Brittany where he attempted to settle a mutiny of the Atlantic fleet. Acting with Jeanbon Saint-André (qv), Prieur of the Marne settled the situation. He survived the reaction of Thermidor, and gradually slipped from public view.

Prieur-Duvernois, Claude Antoine (1763–1832)   Prieur-Duvernois, known as Prieur de la Côte d'Or, was born at Auxonne on 22 December 1763. He became an officer in the engineers after making an excellent record at the *Ecole de Mézières*, where he studied science and mathematics. A member of the Legislative Assembly in 1791 and Convention in 1792, he voted for the death of Louis XVI (qv). In 1793 he became a member of the committee of public safety, where he concerned himself with arms production, and under his guidance France produced massive numbers of arms. Prieur survived Thermidor and worked to build up the *Ecole Polytechnique*. Later he served with the committee of public instruction. Prieur-Duvernois argued for the establishment of the metric system in France, which was brought into force before he retired from public service. After a period of service within the Five Hundred (qv), he retired in 1801. He survived the restoration and continued to work on scientific projects. He died in Dijon on 11 August 1832.

Proudhon, Pierre Joseph (1809–1865) Proudhon was born into a working-class family at Besançon on 15 January 1809. His father was a labourer and his mother was a domestic servant. At the age of eight Proudhon worked as a cowherd. His parents made sacrifices to send him to school, but Proudhon gave up his educational pursuits to earn a living in journalism. By 1837 he was publishing works, and in 1839 he won a prize for his research on French grammar. After 1840, with his *Qu'est-ce que la Propriété?*, the main concept of which was that property, as acquired by the bourgeoisie, was theft and that the working classes were the victims of bourgeois avarice, he turned toward social questions. Following this in 1841 with *Lettre à Blanqui*, in 1843 with *Création de l'Ordre dans l'Humanité* and in 1846 with *Système des Contradictions Economiques*, he established himself as a social thinker. Proudhon disliked Louis Blanc (qv) and the social workshops of the revolution of 1848 because it was governmental direction from the top down. To Proudhon this stood counter to his belief that government was best when it governed least and that control should come from the bottom to the top. As a member of the left in the Assembly of 1848, Proudhon voted against Blanc's proposals. During the June insurrection Proudhon aided the rebels and their families, which earned him a prison term. In 1849 he wrote *Les Confessions d'un Révolutionnaire*. Exiled in 1858, he remained in Belgium until 1863. Proudhon proclaimed a socialist doctrine, and in many ways his ideas were preludes to marxist thought. His intellectual contributions to the left in France were great. He detested government and once remarked to Napoléon that he wanted to see a society where he (Proudhon) would be beheaded for being a conservative. His concepts of government by the people, the working classes, had a direct impact on French leftist and marxist thought.

Provence, Count of See: Louis XVIII.

Provisional Government of 1830 From 29 to 31 July 1830 France was ruled by a provisional government of six men. Officially named the Municipal Commission, the government filled the void created by the fall of Charles X (qv) on 29 July 1830. There was no Assembly in session, and the provisional government led by Laffitte (qv), Casimir Périer (qv), Lafayette (qv), the old liberal and conventional, Guizot (qv), and Thiers (qv) met to repeal the 25 July Ordinances (qv) and restore certain basic liberties. General Lafayette (qv) also re-established the liberal-oriented National Guard. Most of the members of the provisional government, including Laffitte and Casimir Périer, favoured a restoration of the monarchy under the Orléanist Louis Philippe (qv). Backed also by Lafayette, Louis Philippe appeared to have the full support of the deputies who were reassembling in Paris on 30 July. On the next day Louis Philippe assumed the duties of constitutional monarch as king of the French.

Provisional Government of 1848 From 24 February 1848 to 9 May 1848 France's Second Republic existed under the guidance of a provisional government. The list of the provisional government was proclaimed at the *Palais Bourbon* by Ledru-Rollin (qv). The members of the government then marched to the *Hôtel de Ville*, where they were presented to the people who acclaimed them by their cheers and applause. The president of this new government was the eighty-year-old Jacques Dupont de l'Eure (qv), who was supported by Alphonse de Lamartine (qv), Adolphe Crémieux (qv), François Arago (qv), Alexandre Ledru-Rollin, Louis Blanc (qv), Louis Antoine Garnier-Pagès (qv) and Alexandre Thomas Marie (qv). A provisional ministry was instituted with Dupont as president of the Council. On 27 February 1848 they proclaimed France to be a republic and set in motion elections for a National Assembly which convened on 4 May. On 10 May 1848 the Assembly created the Executive Commission (qv) to replace the provisional government.

Provisional Government of 1944–1947   France, after the liberation in 1944, was a confused nation. The demise of the Third Republic in 1940, the loss of a war, and the Vichy interlude had thrown French politics into disorder. Despite the fact that the allies opposed him, General Charles de Gaulle (qv) had seized the reins of government, and in August 1944 declared a provisional government in France. De Gaulle made every attempt to settle the confused political scene by bringing various parties into government, including the communists. The general believed that France needed a strong central government, but failed in his efforts in that direction. He served as premier from September 1944 to January 1946, giving up the premiership (known as president of the provisional government) to Félix Gouin in early 1946. Georges Bidault (qv) held the premiership from June to November 1946 and Léon Blum (qv) served in that capacity from December 1946 to January 1947. Blum relinquished the position in January 1947 when the first cabinet under the constitution of the Fourth Republic took effect. In April 1947 de Gaulle founded the *Rassemblement du Peuple Français* (RPF) (qv) as an opposition to the decentralised Fourth Republic. Overall, the provisional government of 1944–7 brought stability to France when stability was greatly needed, but it failed to provide for long-term strong and effective executive leadership, primarily because the French were unwilling to accept it.

Pyramids, Battle of   On 21 July 1798 Napoléon Bonaparte (qv) and a French army defeated the Mameluke masters of Egypt at the Battle of the Pyramids. The Directory (qv) had decided in early 1797 against peace with England, and an expedition to Egypt was planned which would cut Britain's overland route to India. Napoléon was placed at the head of an army which set sail from Toulon on 28 May 1798 and arrived at Alexandria on 1 July 1798. The great victory, in sight of the ancient Egyptian monuments, opened the way to Cairo, but on 1 August 1798 the English fleet under Lord Nelson nearly annihilated the French fleet at Abouku Bay. Bonaparte's army was in reality, despite the victory of the pyramids, a trapped army.

Queuille, Henri (1884–   )   Queuille was first elected deputy in 1914 and rose to the leadership of the Radical Party. During the Fourth Republic he opposed Pierre Mendès-France's (qv) policies. Forming three unspectacular and often brief governments, Queuille was premier from September 1948 to October 1949, in July 1950, and from March to July 1951.

Ralliement   Pope Leo XIII was very much interested in a reconciliation between the church and the Third Republic. Afraid of extreme anti-clericalism, the pope in 1890 urged Catholics to accept the Republic, and Cardinal Lavigerie (qv) began in November 1890 to make very friendly gestures toward the French republicans. In February 1892 Leo XIII again stated the official position in an encyclical, *Au Milieu des Sollicitudes*, that Catholics should work within the framework of constitutional, republican government. Royalists and extreme Catholics disregarded the pope, while Catholic liberals like Albert du Mun (qv), in the Chamber, attempted to reconcile the church and the Third Republic. In 1892 and again in 1893 the Ralliement sparked bitter debates in the Chamber, and in 1892 it toppled one government. The reconciliation hoped for by Leo XIII, de Mun and Lavigerie, was further hurt by the Dreyfus affair and later by the extreme anti-clerical position taken by Premier Emile Combes (qv).

Ramadier, Paul (1888–1961)   Ramadier began his political career as a deputy from Aveyron, a post which he held from 1924 to 1942. Under Léon Blum (qv) in 1936 Ramadier served in the public works ministry as undersecretary for mines, electricity and combustible liquids. He held a post under Camille Chautemps (qv) in 1937 and was minister of works in the Chautemps cabinet of 1938. He held the same post under Edouard Daladier (qv) from 1938 to 1940 and emerged from World War II with an untarnished reputation. Ramadier, a long-time socialist party member, emerged as one of the leaders of that party after 1946. He represented Aveyron as a socialist and as a socialist republican. A staunch republican, he served as premier of France from January to November 1947. He broke with socialist tradition and invited communists into the cabinet. Receiving the support of Vincent Auriol (qv) Ramadier later fought with the communists in the government. This brought about one of the first severe governmental crises in France. In 1956 he briefly held the portfolio of the finance ministry under Guy Mollet (qv).

Ranc, Arthur (1831–1908)   A journalist and opponent of the empire, Ranc served with Léon Gambetta (qv) at Tours, but returned to Paris after being elected a member of the Commune. He was exiled, but allowed to return to France in 1879. He supported Gambetta, Ferry (qv) and the republicans, and through his journalism bitterly opposed General Georges Boulanger (qv).

Raspail, François Vincent (1794–1878)   Born to a very modest family at Carpentras on 29 January 1794, Raspail first attended school at the seminary at Avignon but departed in 1813 and then taught for a period at the local school in Carpentras. After 1815 he found himself in difficulties with the Bourbon authorities and lost his teaching position. He went to Paris, and after 1822 he associated with the *Charbonnerie*. Pursuing studies in natural science and law, Raspail took part in the revolution of 1830. After the fall of the Bourbons, Raspail began to write for republican journals such as the *Bulletin de la* *société des Amis du Peuple* in 1833 and the *Réformateur* in 1835. In 1846 Raspail was accused of illegally practising medicine. In 1848 Raspail was one of the leaders of the revolution but was arrested in May for leading demonstrations in favour of Polish independence. In December 1848 Raspail stood for the office of presidency, but garnered only 30,000 votes. In 1855 he was imprisoned then banished from France for four years. In 1869 Raspail was elected deputy, but in 1870–1 he refused to participate in the Commune. He was arrested again in 1874 but was elected deputy in 1876 and 1877. Raspail died on 7 January 1878 at Arcueil.

Rassemblement du Peuple Français (RPF)　This party, founded in 1947, was a Gaullist organisation. Founded on 7 April 1947 by General Charles de Gaulle (qv) after his fall from power in 1946, the RPF was a loose coalition of factions in France. The RPF was noted for its vehement opposition to communism as a factor in French politics or as an element in French life. The party, reflecting de Gaulle's attitudes, fought bitterly with members of the French communist party in the Chamber. The primary aim of RPF was to gain power for the Gaullists through parliamentary means. However, by 1951 it was clear that this goal was unobtainable. In 1953 the RPF was replaced by the *Républicains Sociaux* (RS). Charles de Gaulle had decided that the RPF was no longer a viable party within the political structure of the Fourth Republic, and in 1953 he withdrew his support from the party. By 1955 the RS had ceased to be a force in French parliamentary politics.

Reichstadt, François Charles, Duc de (1811–1832)　The Duc de Reichstadt was born in Paris on 20 March 1811. The son of Napoléon I (qv) and Marie Louise (qv), the Duc de Reichstadt received the title of King of Rome. In 1814 and 1815 Napoléon abdicated in his favour, but the allies refused to allow Napoléon's son to remain on the throne. He was taken by his mother to Austria and then to Italy, and during this period he became known as the 'little eagle'. In 1818 he received the title of Duc de Reichstadt. He died of tuberculosis at Schoenbrünn on 22 July 1832.

Reinach, Joseph (1856–1921)   A historian, Reinach served as a deputy and was a follower of Léon Gambetta (qv). From 1889 to 1898 he held the post of deputy from the Basses-Alps, and from 1906 until 1914 he represented the same region in the Assembly. Interested in colonialism, he served as an advocate of assimilation (qv).

Renan, Ernest (1823–1892)   Ernest Renan was born at Tréguier on 27 February 1823 and spent his early life with his mother and sister. He entered school at Tréguier, and in 1838 his sister Henriette placed him in the small seminary of Saint-Nicholas du Chardonnet. Renan quickly displayed a brilliance for theology and literature but soon became restive. A brilliant and sensitive thinker, he was one of the prophets of nationalism after 1870. In 1841 he entered Saint Sulpice in Paris, but his interest in theology waned, and in 1845 he gave up his ideas of a clerical career. He worked as a tutor at *Collège Stanislas* and at the *Pension Crouzet* until 1849. In 1847 he won his first literary prize. After his marriage, he travelled in Italy and in Syria. His *La Vie de Jésus* appeared in 1863, and he began to write for many major French periodicals. It was his *La Vie de Jésus* which brought his fame or infamy. Renan, the once devout Breton, used scientific research to portray Jesus as a human being. Arguing for the introduction of scientific German research methods into French education, Renan used the controversial book to popularise the concept. After the fall of France in 1870, Renan published *La Réforme Intellectuelle et Morale de la France* (1871). In 1866 the empire had deprived him of a teaching position at the Collège de France, but in 1871 the republic restored him to his chair. Not a revanchist in the most virulent sense of the word, Renan called for a moral and intellectual revival of France. However, he conceived of a France governed by a moral and intellectual élite. After the appearance of *Les Souvenirs d'Enfance et de*

Jeunesse in 1883, Renan went through a series of illnesses and died in Paris on 2 October 1892.

Républicains de Gauche   A right-wing political party in the Chamber of Deputies, this group opposed the policies of the *Cartel des Gauches* (qv) and united at elections to keep moderate and conservative governments in power during the 1920s.

République des Camarades   This was a group of communist deputies in the Chamber and Senate during the Fourth Republic. Under the Fourth Republic it became a leftist legislative fraternity of sorts.

Revolutionary Tribunal   Instituted by a law and organised on 10 March 1793, the revolutionary tribunal was a criminal-type court with immense powers. While it had a judge and jury, it did not function like other courts. Its members were chosen strictly on political grounds first by the Convention and later by the Committee of Public Safety (qv). The revolutionary tribunal was given sweeping powers under the Law of Suspects which was passed on 17 September 1793. This law decreed that all 'suspect persons' were to be arrested and tried by the tribunal. Vague and brutal, the law defined suspects as those who by thought, word or deed had opposed the revolution and those who showed themselves to be 'the enemies of liberty'. The law also called for the arrest of those who could not prove that they were doing their civic duty. All relatives of *émigrés* were to be arrested. This draconian law opened the door for widespread arrests and trials before the revolutionary tribunal. The sentences, usually death, were carried out without benefit or appeal. The tribunal's most famed member was the methodical, cold-blooded Fouquier-Tinville (qv).

Reynaud, Paul (1878–1966)   Known as a moderate in in French politics, Reynaud was named finance minister in 1938. After a brief period he was ousted, but in March 1940 he became premier. Reynaud had to face the German invasion of 1940, and he advocated a continuation of the struggle from the North African colonies. His ministers deserted him and he fell on 16 June 1940. Arrested by the Germans, he was deported to Germany, but survived the war. Reynaud was never able to erase the fact that he was premier in the spring of 1940 when France was crushed by Germany.

Rhine, Confederation of the On 13 July 1806 Talleyrand-Périgord (qv) presented to an assembly of German delegates a plan for a German confederation which Napoléon Bonaparte (qv) wanted implemented. Fifteen German states were ordered to sign the protocol. Prussia and Austria were not consulted and were not asked even to venture an opinion on the confederation. Napoléon wanted a union free of Austrian or Prussian influence. Allied to France, the confederation did bring some order to a confused Germany, but at the price of a Bonapartist hegemony. In August Francis II of Austria was forced to recognise the *fait accompli* and to abolish the Holy Roman Empire.

Ribot, Alexandre (1842–1923) Alexandre Ribot entered the Chamber in 1878 and served until 1885. Re-elected in 1885, he was a deputy until 1909. From 1909 to 1923 he served as a senator from Pas-de-Calais. In 1890 he was foreign minister under Charles de Freycinet (qv), and held the post in 1892 under Emile Loubet (qv). During his term as foreign minister, Ribot began to negotiate a treaty with Russia which became the Franco-Russian Alliance of 1894 (qv). Premier in 1892 and 1893, Ribot made every effort to strengthen the new ties between France and Russia and to break France's diplomatic isolation. In 1895 he served again as premier, and again for a very short period in 1913. In the *Union Sacrée* (qv), Ribot was minister of finance, a post which he held in the Briand (qv) cabinet. His health failing, he left active cabinet service in 1917 and returned to the Senate.

Richelieu, Armand du Plessis Louis, Duc de (1766–1822) Born in Paris on 25 September 1766, Richelieu was a noble who fled from France in 1789 and served in Russia as governor of Odessa in 1803. He attached himself to Louis XVIII and in 1815 became minister of foreign affairs. Chosen by Louis XVIII to be a leader in the Chamber because of his moderation, he advocated even-handed policies which would heal the wounds caused by the revolutionary and Napoléonic eras. From 1815 to 1816 he fought against the ultra-conservative, vindictive *Chambre Introuvable* (qv). Because of his liberal, conciliatory leanings, he was toppled from power in 1821 as a result of the bitter feeling caused by the murder of the Duc de Berry (qv) in 1820. Richelieu, an embittered man, died in Paris on 17 May 1822.

Riom Trials   During the late summer and autumn of 1941, the Vichy government (qv) prepared to proceed against certain figures of the Third Republic who held power in the 1930s. Léon Blum (qv), Edouard Daladier (qv) and several other key politicians and soldiers were tried by a civilian court at Riom in France. The major charge against these men was a failure to maintain the nation's preparedness and to safeguard France's morale prior to 1940. The Riom Trials opened on 19 February 1942, and the judge was picked by Marshal Pétain (qv), the Vichy head of state. However, Blum and his fellow defendants became very aggressive in their defence, and they turned the Riom trials to their benefit. In April the Vichy government, under pressure from Nazi Germany, indefinitely adjourned the trials. While Blum, Daladier and the others remained in prison until liberated, the Vichy government had failed to place the blame for the disaster of 1940 on their shoulders.

Riots of 6 February 1934   The government of France during the first four years of the 1930s had fallen into disrepute. In 1933 the famous Stavisky scandal (qv) struck France, as it was revealed that many highly placed officials were involved in graft and corruption. Right-wing groups such as the *Action Française* (qv) seized the opportunity to attack the government and also to take to the streets in violent protest. In early February 1934 there were vicious street fights in Paris with the rightists calling for the downfall of Edouard Daladier (qv), the president of the Council of Ministers. During the rioting the police fired on the mobs, killing 14 and injuring over 200. The bloodshed increased, but by the morning of 7 February it appeared that the authorities had the situation in hand. Daladier resigned from his post, giving way to a more conservative cabinet. The effect of riot was immediate as the republic was seriously weakened and there was much more political disaffection. The left and the right, from that point on, faced each other as antagonists.

Rivet Law   On 31 August 1871 the Chamber passed this law which defined the position of chief executive as president, under the authority of the Assembly. It reconfirmed powers and duties delegated to him by the Decree of 17 February 1871. The executive enforced laws as passed by the Assembly. He could appoint and dismiss ministers, but every act and decree of the president had to be co-signed by a cabinet minister.

Robespierre, Maximilien de (1758–1794)   Robespierre was born to a noted lawyer of the Council of Artois on 6 May 1758 at Arras. He began his studies at Arras and worked at the Louis le Grand school in Paris. After his sojourn in Paris, where he studied law, Robespierre returned to Arras and began a career at law. Known as a member of local literary societies, Robespierre won some fame as a liberal. Elected to the Third Estate in 1789, Robespierre still had some monarchist feelings, but he sat with the left. Within three years, however, he had become more democratic and eventually allied himself with the Jacobin Club (qv), moving constantly to the extreme left. In 1791 he stood as a Jacobin against the Girondins, and on 10 August 1792 he supported the violent attack against the king. Elected again as a deputy in 1792, he allied himself with the Montagnards (qv) and argued for the condemnation of Louis XVI (qv). But he opposed France's war policies and made his opposition known through his brilliant oratory. His power rising, he was elected to the Committee of Public Safety (qv) in 1793. By using factionalism with the Montagnards and by stirring popular indignation against the Girondins, he was able to institute, by the law of 22 Prairial Year II, the Law of Suspects, which accelerated the unfair procedures within the Revolutionary Tribunal (qv). Robespierre advocated a Terror to purge France of undesirable elements and undemocratic thoughts. He envisioned a France which would be ruled by civic virtue and where all citizens would be free and equal. To him, the Terror was simply a means to exterminate those who would oppose such a republic. He purged the Girondins (qv) after the murder of Jean Paul Marat (qv) and also eliminated his chief rivals, Danton (qv) and Hébert (qv), in 1793. As the Terror grew in intensity, the general populace and the Convention feared that Robespierre was mad with power. On 9 Thermidor, Robespierre fell and was executed on 10 Thermidor (28 July) in Paris.

Rochefort, Henri (1830–1913) Scion of a noble family, Rochefort, known as the Marquis de Rochefort-Lurcay, was born on 31 January 1830 in Paris. He worked from 1851 to 1861 as an official of the Préfecture of the Seine. He began his career as a liberal opponent of the Second Empire. In 1861 he turned to journalism, fighting the empire through the pages of *La Lanterne*. Arrested in 1868, he was freed in 1870 by the republicans. He sided with the Commune and was deported to New Caledonia in 1873. Pardoned in 1880, he founded *L'Intransigeant*, which supported radicalism and also defended General Boulanger (qv). He fled to Belgium with Boulanger but was later pardoned. After his return to France in 1895, he wrote against Dreyfus (qv) and supported ultra-nationalist causes. Rochefort died at Aix-les-Bains on 3 July 1913.

Rocque, François de la (1886–1946) A career army officer from Lorient, de la Rocque served in Poland from 1922 to 1924 and spent four years (1924–8) in Morocco. After his retirement he founded the *Croix de Feu* (qv) in 1931 and the *Volontaires Nationaux* in 1933. These rightist groups participated in the February 1934 riots. After 1934 he founded the *Parti Social Français* (PSF) (qv), a petty fascist, anti-parliamentarian group. De la Rocque served the Vichy government, and was deported to Germany in 1945. After 1946 he was officially disgraced and was forced to retire from politics. He died in Paris on 28 April 1946.

Rohan, Louis Prince de (1734–1803)   Rohan, a member of an old and noted noble family, was born in Paris on 25 September 1734. He entered the service of the Bourbons by serving as ambassador to Vienna from 1771 to 1774. Elevated to cardinal in 1778, Rohan became Bishop of Strasbourg in 1779. In 1785 he was accused of giving a very expensive necklace to Marie Antoinette for which he expected, but did not receive, special favours. Opposing the revolution of 1789, he remained a staunch enemy of reformism. Rohan fled France and exiled himself in Italy, refusing to return even after the signing of the Concordat. He died at Ettenheim on 17 February 1803.

Roland de la Platière, Jean-Marie (1734–1793)   Born at Thizy on 18 February 1734, Roland became the inspector of manufacturing in Picardie. After service in Lyon, Roland moved to Paris. A man of wealth and education, Roland was one of the Girondist leaders. Madame Roland's salon was a rallying point for the intellectuals of the revolution, especially the Girondins (qv). In 1792 Roland became minister of the interior but was removed a few months later. He grew more antagonistic to the radical Jacobins and was arrested during the Terror. His wife, Marie Phlipon (1754–93), was also accused of corresponding with the British, and she was executed during the Terror. Roland escaped from Paris before his wife's execution and hid in Normandy. After hearing of his wife's death and to save family property from confiscation, he committed suicide on 10 November 1793.

Roman Republic   By the Treaty of Tolentino (qv), Pope Pius VI retained the city of Rome at a high price. In February 1798 French troops occupied Rome, drove out the pope, and established the Roman Republic. It was part of Napoléon Bonaparte's (qv) religious policy to allow the pontiff to use Rome as his capital, since he desired the pope's goodwill during the hectic 1801 negotiations concerning the Concordat (qv). The Roman Republic was short-lived because of Bonapartist policy. Once the Concordat was signed Napoléon allowed the Republic to wither away.

Roucher, Jean Antoine (1745–1794)   Born in Montpellier in 1745, Roucher attracted the attention of the royal court
of Louis XV when he composed a poem in honour of the wedding
of the Dauphin, the future Louis XVI (qv), to Marie Antoinette
(qv). Roucher attached himself to the court and became a loyal
follower of the Bourbons. A poet who staunchly defended Bourbon royalism, Roucher was supported by Marie Antoinette. He
published from 1790 to 1791 the *Journal de Paris*, which criticised
leftist revolutionary policies. He was executed in Paris during
the Terror on 25 July 1794.

Rothschild, Alphonse (1827–1905)   A regent for the Bank
of France and a manager for the Paris branch of the House of
Rothschild, Alphonse de Rothschild silently supported republican and colonial causes. Staying in the background because of
anti-semitism caused by the Dreyfus (qv) affair, he contributed
to organisations such as the *Comité de l'Afrique française* (qv).

Rothschild, Jacob (1792–1868)   Jacob Rothschild created
the Paris branch of the House of Rothschild in 1812. He played
a key role in the downfall of Charles X (qv) in 1830, and supported the policies of Louis Philippe (qv).

Rouvier, Maurice Pierre (1842–1911)   Rouvier began his
career as a deputy from Marseilles who defended industrial
and commercial interests in France. He rose to the forefront of
moderate politics after the Wilson affair (qv). The imperialists
knew him as a staunch supporter of expansion since he had
extensive interests in the Marseilles shipping industry. In 1905
he formed a ministry during the confusion caused by the First
Moroccan Crisis. Unlike Emile Combes (qv), his predecessor,
Rouvier did not take forceful action against the church, since
he firmly believed in a definite policy of moderation in respect
to church-state relations. In 1906 Rouvier strengthened the
Anglo-French Entente Cordiale of 1904 (qv). He retired in
1906, but maintained his links with the business community.

Roux, Jacques (?–1794)   A fanatical priest who supported
the revolution, Roux renounced his clerical status and joined
in the violence of 10 August 1792 (qv). As a chief leader of the

enragés (qv), he demanded violent measures to revitalise the revolutionary ardour of the Paris mobs. His radicalism growing more extreme, Roux tried to continue *L'Ami du Peuple* after the death of Marat (qv) in 1793. This paper, already noted for its violent editorials and articles, moved even further toward the extreme. Arrested and scheduled to be tried by the Terror which he himself helped to create, Roux killed himself at Bicêtre on 20 January 1794.

Saint-André, André Jeanbon (1749–1813) A Protestant minister and ship's captain, Saint-André felt deeply about Bourbon anti-Protestant measures. Not a doctrinaire Calvinist, he adopted the ideals of the Enlightenment and espoused the concept of strong central government. After 1789 he joined the Jacobins (qv) and was elected to the Convention, where he was named to the Committee of Public Safety (qv). He spent most of his time out of Paris during the Terror, and he survived Thermidor. Saint-André served the state by undertaking various diplomatic and political missions for France. He was captured by the Turks and put into prison. After three years' captivity he returned to France in 1801 and accepted a post in the diplomatic service offered by Bonaparte. Saint-André died of pneumonia which he contracted during the retreat from Moscow.

Saint-Arnaud, Armand Leroy de (1801–1854) Saint-Arnaud, the son of an imperial prefect, was born in Paris on 20 August 1801. He entered the army in 1817, and after a life filled with adventure, he joined the Foreign Legion in 1836. Saint-Arnaud was now a dedicated career soldier who served in Algeria and helped preserve order in Paris during the revolution of 1848. In 1851 he became minister of war and helped prepare the coup d'état of 2 December 1851. For his service Napoléon III (qv) named him marshal, but preferring a direct command, Saint-Arnaud took a demotion to serve as a combat officer. However, he died on 29 September 1854 aboard ship before reaching his post.

Saint-Just, Antoine Louis Léon de (1767–1794) Born

at Decize on 25 August 1767, the son of a cavalry officer, Saint-Just threw himself into the revolution and was elected deputy from Aisne in 1792. He became a follower of Robespierre (qv) and became a member of the Committee of Public Safety (qv) in 1793. He supported the Terror, since he believed in the purging of society so that the French state could find a virtue based on Spartan discipline and Roman republican dedication. With fanatical zeal he purged the Girondins (qv) and Hébertists (qv). He decided to change allegiances and planned to denounce Robespierre on 9 Thermidor. However, Saint-Just was unable to speak in the Chamber, and he was violently attacked there. His will to survive crumbled, and he was taken prisoner. He died on the guillotine with Robespierre on 28 July 1794.

Saint Mandé Programme   In 1896 Alexander Millerand (qv), a socialist leader, addressed a meeting in the suburb Saint Mandé near Paris. During the speech he outlined his approach to evolutionary socialism. In line with the basic socialist goals of Jean Jaurès (qv) and Jules Guesde (qv), Millerand called for the transformation of capitalist society and values through peaceful, parliamentary means. He differed from Jaurès on the points of working with other parties within the Chamber, and cooperating with governments in any way. Millerand argued that socialists had to cast their lot with other socially progressive parties. He also maintained that it would be acceptable for socialists to accept cabinet posts because they would be in a position to effect the course of reformist legislation. Most socialists in the Chamber disagreed with the Saint Mandé programme and sided with Jaurès's concept of non-cooperation with any government. Millerand's programme was greeted with great distrust by some French socialists who demanded that he be purged from the party, but others hailed it as a major step toward socialist control of the legislative process.

Saint-Simon, Claude-Henry de (1760–1825)   The Comte de Saint-Simon began his career as a soldier, but lost his fortune by unwise speculations. He turned to a scientific study of man and proposed to develop a comprehensive social reform programme. In 1802 he published *Les Lettres d'un Habitant de Genève à ses Contemporains*, and in 1814 he wrote *La Réorganisation de la Société Européene*. Discouraged with the course of French politics, Saint-Simon founded *L'Organisateur*. Moving more toward socialist thought, from 1820 to 1825 he collaborated with Auguste Comte (qv). He wrote *Système Industriel* and *Catéchisme des Industriels*. While Saint-Simon preferred to see government control production by the submission of the means of production to the government, he staunchly maintained the dignity of labour. The benefits of production would be used to benefit labour in general. Proclaiming the glories of 1789, Saint-Simon was also concerned with the morality of industrialism, expounded in *Le Nouveau Christianisme* which appeared before his death. In this work he wrote that religion was obliged to direct society toward the goal of helping the poorest classes.

San Ildefonso, Treaty of The Directory (qv) government set itself the task of making peace in Europe and within France and also to win friends and allies. In early 1796 France moved to sign a number of peace treaties, for example, one with the Sardinians was signed on 15 May 1796. Naples and Tuscany also signed treaties aimed at peace with France and action against the British. Spain and France signed the Treaty of San Ildefonso on 19 August 1796, which allied the two states against Britain. On 1 October 1800 France and Spain again signed a treaty at San Ildefonso which restored the large territory of Louisiana in America to France in return for the establishment of a Spanish family on the throne of Etruria. France took over the colony on 21 March 1801.

Sand, George (Amadine-Aurore Lucie Dupin) (1804–1876) Born in Paris on 1 July 1804, George Sand was the daughter of a very prominent social and political family. Her childhood was not happy, and she received her education in various schools. She inherited a fortune after the death of her grandmother in 1821, and married François-Casimir Baron Dudevant, but their marriage was a stormy one ending in separation. Valuing her independence above all else, she decided on a career in literature. Author and social critic, George Sand was a well-educated, well-travelled woman. In 1831 she published a co-authored novel, *Rose et Blanche*. After this she wrote on her own using the name George Sand. Her novels *Indiana* in 1832, *Valentine* in 1832, *Lélia* in 1833, and *Jacques* in 1834 won her instant acclaim as a social critic and commentator. Her novels, attacking society and Orléanist social values, were well received in France. Basically Sand had a feeling for the emerging working class, although she had a large personal fortune. In 1848 she rallied to the revolution, using her pen to popularise the republican cause. A friend of Louis Blanc (qv) and Ledru Rollin (qv), she fought against the election of Louis Napoléon (qv) in December 1848. Deeply affected by the fall of France in 1870 and the destruction of the Commune, she wrote little after 1871. Before her death on 8 June 1876 she was recognised as one of the great authors of France.

Sangnier, Marc (1873–1950)   The son of a lawyer, Sangnier was born in Paris on 3 April 1873. After studying at the *Ecole Polytechnique* he served in the army. He believed strongly in the reconciliation of the state and church, and in 1898 he left the army to work for that cause. He wrote for the *Sillon*, but the Vatican looked with disfavour on his militant approach. In 1912 Sangnier turned to politics and founded the *Jeune République*. In 1919 he was elected deputy from Paris. During the 1930s Sangnier favoured pacifism and a Franco-German accord. Hating anti-Semitism and the fascist right in France, he helped to found the *Auberges des Jeunesse* in 1930. During the Vichy period he was arrested by the Nazi authorities. After the liberation, Sangnier was elected deputy and became the honorary president of the *Mouvement Républicain Populaire* (MRP) (qv) and tried to integrate the ideals of the *Jeune République* with the MRP. He died in Paris on 29 May 1950.

Sans-Culotte   The term *sans-culotte* referred to men who did not wear the short knee trousers and silk stockings of the middle and upper classes. The *sans-culottes* were the poorer, lower classes and the term was originally a derisive one applied to the impoverished. During the French revolution the *sans-culottes* were a volatile class in Paris which could be manipulated by popular leaders such as Marat (qv) and Robespierre (qv). The Jacobins (qv) used the *sans-culottes* to control the streets of Paris, thereby intimidating moderate leaders in the Assembly. The Committee of Public Safety (qv) under Robespierre understood how to use the discontented masses, and in September 1793 a decree established a revolutionary *sans-culotte* army. At Lyon, in October 1793, the *sans-culotte* army participated in great violence and brutality against so-called enemies of the republic. Much of the revolutionary spirit of the poor faded as bread prices stabilised, cheap land became available and wages were paid for serving in the army. In January 1794 the *sans-culotte* army, having served its purpose, was sent out of Paris, and in the spring of that year the army was disbanded by the Terror government. The *sans-culottes* had been a major factor in the support of Robespierre's policies, but having completed their task they were no longer important. After 9 Thermidor, the conservative governments were careful to watch the potentially violent masses of Paris.

Sarraut, Albert (1872–1962) Albert Sarraut served as a deputy from the Aude from 1902 to 1924. From 1924 to 1945 he held the post of senator from the same district. A leading socialist politician, he was minister of public instruction under René Viviani (qv) in 1914. In 1920 he was minister of colonies, and in 1924 he left cabinet politics to assume his duties as senator. In 1926, however, he became interior minister in the Poincaré (qv) government. Under Camille Chautemps (qv), he served as minister of the marine in 1930 and in the Paul-Boncour cabinet he held the portfolio of the colonial ministry. In October 1933 Sarraut formed a ministry which tried to deal with the rising tide of political fragmentation and violence in France. In 1936 he formed another government, but it quickly fell. After 1936 he remained active in French politics until the liberation, when he retired from public political life.

Say, Jean Baptiste (1767–1832)   Say was born in Lyon on 5 January 1767 and began his career as a secretary to a well-known Lyon banker. A financier and disciple of Adam Smith, he espoused scientific economics. He founded the journal *La Décade philosophique* which was published from 1794 to 1800. This was dedicated to the philosophy of Adam Smith. He fell out of favour with Bonaparte and was ruined financially during the restoration. Say began a teaching career in 1815 and influenced his son Horace Say (1794–1860), who became president of the Paris Chamber of Commerce and founder of the Society for Political Economy. Say died in Paris on 15 November 1832.

Say, Léon (1826–1896)   Grandson of Jean Baptiste Say (qv), Léon Say was a famed economist who opposed the Second Empire. He served in the National Assembly from 1871 to 1876. Elected senator in 1876 from the Seine et Oise, he held that post until 1889 when he resigned to seek a post in the Chamber from the Basses-Pyrénées. He won his election and served in the Chamber until his death. From 1872 to 1873 he held his first post as minister of finance. He held the same portfolio from 1875 until 1876 and again under Jules Dufaure until 1879. Recognised as a financial genius, he was asked to head the same ministry by Charles de Freycinet (qv) in 1882. He advocated massive public works after 1883, and he turned his brilliant mind to the opposition of socialism. Léon Say died in Paris on 22 April 1896.

Schnaebelé Incident   Guillaume Schnaebelé, a French espionage agent, was arrested on German soil in April 1887. He had been lured across the border by German agents, and once this was known in France there was an indignant outcry. General Georges Boulanger (qv) demanded immediate mobilisation of the French armies, causing a war scare in Europe. When Otto von Bismarck, the German chancellor, learned that in fact Schnaebelé had a safe-conduct letter to confer with

German officials, he ordered that the captured agent be released from prison and returned to France. The actual beneficiary of the incident was General Boulanger, who claimed credit for obtaining the spy's freedom. French rightists saw the general as the true hero of the hour, and Boulanger's fame as a staunch revanchist soared.

Schneider, Joseph Eugène (1805–1875)   Born in the Meurthe at Bidestroff on 29 March 1805 to a noted family, Joseph Schneider was orphaned while still young. He was the founder of the Schneider Creusot Works in 1836 and was elected a deputy in 1845. He supported Guizot's (qv) conservative policies, and, after 1852, Napoléon III's economic plans. He served as vicepresident and president of the *Corps Législatif*, where he was a strong advocate of the liberal empire. After September 1870, he retired from active public service to look after his large financial empire. He died in Paris on 27 November 1875, but his sons Henri (1840–98) and Eugène (1868–1942) continued to direct the Schneider Creusot Works. Both men were deputies and were very influential in industrial and imperial affairs.

Schoelcher, Victor (1804–1893)   Schoelcher was born into a wealthy manufacturing family in Paris on 22 July 1804. His father manufactured porcelains of a high quality. Victor, however, was not inclined toward a career in commerce and trade, and after a trip to the United States in 1829 he became a vocal partisan of the anti-slavery cause. From 1829 to 1848 he became known as France's greatest advocate for the ending of slavery in the empire. As a vocal abolitionist, Schoelcher held the post of undersecretary of state for the navy in 1848, and he prepared the decrees abolishing slavery in the colonies. In 1848 he was elected deputy from Martinique, and from Guadaloupe in 1850. He was exiled for opposing Napoléon III's (qv) coup d'état of December 1851. Allowed to return to France in 1870, he was elected deputy in 1871 and senator in 1875. Until his death at Houilles on 26 December 1893, Schoelcher campaigned for the end of capital punishment in France.

Schönbrunn, Peace of   See: Vienna, Treaty of.

Schönbrunn, Preliminaries of   Following the brilliant victory of Austerlitz (qv) and prior to the Treaty of Pressburg (qv), Napoléon induced the Prussians to sign the Preliminaries of Schönbrunn on 15 December 1805. Prussia gained Hanover, but agreed to recognise changes in Italy and to give up Cleves to the French. Prussia allied herself to France and gave full recognition to Bavaria as an equal. The Prussian king unwisely attempted to change the agreement. Napoléon was outraged at his actions and altered the Schönbrunn agreement, forcing the Prussians to accept the Treaty of Paris of 1806 (qv).

Schuman, Robert (1886–1963)   Elected a deputy in 1919, the well-known economist served as chairman of the French financial committee from 1945 to 1946. A member of the *Mouvement Républicain Populaire*, he sat as a deputy from that party from 1945 to 1962. Known as the father of the European Coal and Steel Authority, Schuman served as premier from November 1947 to July 1948 and in September 1948. Riding to power on a conservative trend in 1947, as premier he announced a policy dedicated to strengthening French finances. Crisis after crisis was precipitated by the left, and he fell from power. From 1948 to 1952 he served as foreign minister in several cabinets.

Scrutin d'Arrondissement   The republicans of the early Third Republic searched for a more direct method of electing a deputy to the Chamber. From 1871 to 1875 deputies were elected by *scrutin de liste* (qv), which meant that a party presented a list of candidates and the voters picked one list for each department. Those in favour of the list method argued that the deputy was free from constituent pressures and could devote all of his time to national rather than local matters. Those who opposed it stated that the voters lost the chance to really pick a representative and that local issues and needs would be disregarded in Paris. By the Organic Law of 30 November 1875 the *liste* method was replaced by *scrutin d'arrondissement*, also known as *scrutin uninomal*. This method divided the department into a number of *arrondissements* with one deputy for each 100,000 voter units. Candidates ran for the seat appealing directly to voters on the basis of national and local interests. A candidate had to receive a clear majority, and if he failed to garner enough votes on the first ballot, a run-off, or second election known as the *deuxième tour*, was held one week later between the top vote-getter and other major candidates. The selection of the other contestants was done by party selection, deals, and sometimes bribes. Until the elections of 1877 this method favoured monarchist candidates, but after 1877 it shifted to republicans who stressed local issues as well as general national trends. Republicans felt more at home with the single-member districts. There were definite drawbacks to the *scrutins d'arrondissement*, however, since local issues dominated elections and in the long run controlled the Chamber. In a system of legislative dominance, such as practised in the Third Republic, it became difficult to formulate effective national policy due to local needs and constituent pressures.

Scrutin de Liste   The method of electing a member of the Chamber of Deputies became a critical issue in the first five years of the Third Republic. A deputy was elected for four years and had to be at least twenty-one years old. The basis for election was universal manhood suffrage, restricted to males. In 1871 deputies were elected by a device known as *scrutin de liste*, which meant that a political party or a pressure group drew up a list of candidates for each department. The voters voted for one list from among many lists. The seats were then, in reality, controlled by party bosses or leaders of successful pressure groups. The basic argument in favour of this method was that a deputy would be free from local pressures and could concentrate his efforts on national matters. This method was replaced by the *scrutin d'arrondissement* (qv), which was part of the Organic Law of 30 November 1875. Even Léon Gambetta (qv), in his Grand Ministry of 1881–2, wanted to return to the *scrutin de liste* because the new single-member districts produced, as he saw it, *mares stagnantes* or districts mired in local concerns. The *scrutin de liste* was used only sparingly in the Third Republic during the elections of 1885, 1889 and in 1919. As Gambetta had hoped, the *liste* method could produce parties with some semblance of order and discipline, but, despite this obvious advantage, the *scrutin d'arrondissement* remained in force during the Third Republic.

Section Française de l'Internationale Ouvrière (SFIO) In 1905 the socialists of France organised the SFIO as an official party. Striving for unity, the socialists were split over cooperation with bourgeois parties in the Chamber, and from 1905 to 1914 the leftist party remained divided on critical international questions. Jean Jaurès (qv), who opposed cooperation with any party, urged the SFIO to take a definite stand for peace and pacifism, but others rejected this. By 1914 the French socialists were the second largest party in the Chamber. During World War I socialists cooperated with the various governments in order to present a united front against the Germans. After World War I the SFIO split over doctrinal issues in 1920 when a majority of socialists attending the Congress of Tours (qv) in December 1920 voted to join the Third International and called themselves communists, adhering to Lenin's Twenty-one Conditions for joining the international. Even the newspaper *L'Humanité* became a part of the new communist bloc. It fell to Léon Blum (qv), a brilliant Jewish intellectual, to hold the minority together and to reforge the socialist party in France. After the war the SFIO restated its refusal to participate in cabinets until 1936, when it united with other leftist and communist parties to bring Léon Blum's Popular Front (qv) to power. In 1940 the SFIO split on the question of support for Marshal Pétain (qv) and the Vichy government. After World War II the SFIO was again divided on the issue of cooperation with the government, but in 1951 returned to the status of an opposition party. In 1958 many members of the SFIO leadership supported Charles de Gaulle (qv) as an alternative to the extreme right. By the 1960s socialism showed definite signs of revitalisation as a political factor in French parliamentary life.

Seize Mai, Le The crisis of 16 May 1876 was an opportunity for the republicans to assume control of the Chamber of Deputies. On that date President MacMahon (qv) forced Prime Minister Jules Simon, a leader of the moderate republicans, to give up his office. The president replaced Simon with a conservative. The republicans in the Chamber argued that ministers were responsible to the legislative branch of government rather than to the executive branch. To prove their point the deputies simply refused to recognise the new prime minister, and MacMahon, certain of victory at the polls, dismissed the Chamber and called for new elections. The struggle between royalist and republicans for control of the Chamber became a decisive victory for the new republicans. Adolphe Thiers (qv) and Léon Gambetta (qv) led in the bitter electoral campaign to turn back the royalist tide. Thiers died during the hard-fought campaign. MacMahon remained staunchly conservative, convinced that he had pursued the correct course in 1876. However, the crisis had the ultimate effect of weakening the powers of the French president, since he was never again powerful enough to dismiss the Chamber. The electoral results of 14 October 1877 were conclusive, as the republicans in the Chamber received 54 per cent of the popular vote. This appeared to settle two points of conflict. The ministers were indeed responsible to the legislative branch of government and the legislature held the power to decide its own existence.

Septennate, Law of This law was a conservative response to the Republic. Passed on 23 November 1873, the law called for a presidential term of seven years. The conservatives and monarchists who devised the law hoped that before 1880 the question of restoration would be settled. That question was impossible owing to the attitudes of the Bourbon pretender as expressed in Chambord's Manifesto (qv). The law also confirmed the powers of the president only until modified by constitutional laws.

Siegfried, André (1875–1959)   André Siegfried, a Protestant, was a constant observer of French political and social life. Journalist and historian, he was one of France's first true political scientists.

Sieyès, Emmanuel, Abbé (1748–1836)   Sieyès, sometimes spelled Sieys, was born in Fréjus on 3 May 1748. Deciding on a clerical career, he studied at Saint Sulpice. Rising rapidly, he became vicar at Chartres in 1784. A liberal cleric, he published his famous tract *Qu'est-ce que le Tiers Etat* in 1789. Elected deputy in that year, he played a great role in the early actions of the Third Estate, especially the Tennis Court Oaths (qv). In 1792 he served in the Convention and acted as a moderating force. Turning to diplomacy, Sieyès negotiated the Treaty of La Haye in 1795. One of the Five Hundred, he served as ambassador to Berlin in 1798 and for his service was named a director. Fearing for the political future of France because of the weak Directory, Sieyès began to plan a coup d'état but needed a military figure to assist him. He gained the support of Napoléon Bonaparte (qv) and Lucien Bonaparte (qv). Persuading the Directory to move from Paris to Saint Cloud, Sieyès set in motion the coup of 18 Brumaire (qv). Part of the Consulate, he was slowly eased from power by Bonaparte but became a senator and count and served the empire. Remaining loyal to Bonaparte, he was deported from France as a regicide after the Hundred Days (qv). He was allowed to return only after the downfall of Charles X in 1830. For six years Sieyès resided in Paris, and on 20 June 1836 he died there.

Sismondi, Simon de (1773–1842)   A historian of note, Sismondi became known as one of the fathers of French socialism. With a historian's critical eye he analysed the industrial revolution and its impending moral crisis in France. In 1819 he published his *Nouveaux principes*, which appeared in a second edition in 1826. He believed that the state tended to accumulate riches, and since this was the case it was important for the state to provide the means whereby all citizens would enjoy the good life which those riches could provide. Karl Marx rendered homage to Sismondi's scientific, critical investigation into capital, the state and the citizen. In 1834 de Sismondi began to speculate on a Christian economic policy for France, but his main interest remained the working classes. His impact was felt in the works of Karl Marx and Joseph Proudhon (qv).

Social Legislation   See: Allocations Familiales; Code de la Famille; Great Act of 1892 (working conditions); Law of 5 April 1928 (social security); Law of 11 February 1950 (labour-management contracts); Law of 14 July 1913 (family assistance); Law of 15 July 1893 (medical care); Ordinance of 8 January 1959 (labour relations); Ordinance of 4 October 1945; Ordinances of 1945 (comprehensive social insurance); Statuts du Fermage.

Society of the Friends of the Constitution   See: Jacobins.

Solferino, Battle of   Fought on 24 June 1859, this battle was a decisive French victory over the Austrians. The army was commanded by Emperor Napoléon III, and like Magenta (qv) the battle was a part of his Italian policy. Despite the fact that the French were outnumbered they were able to rout the Austrians. Napoléon wanted to attack the retreating forces, but was unable to because of the heavy losses. A little later he concluded the armistice of Villafranca (qv) with the Austrians, which took France out of the war.

Solidarité Française   Founded by François Coty (qv) in 1933, the *Solidarité Française* was a rightist organisation with an active interest in politics. Anti-parliamentary and violently anti-communist, this group participated in the riots of 6 February 1934 (qv).

Sorel, Georges (1847–1922)   Born in Cherbourg on 2 November 1847, Sorel was educated at the *Ecole Polytechnique*. He began his career as an engineer. After 1892 Sorel turned to a study of marxism, socialism and violence. In 1906 he published his famous *Réflexions sur la Violence*, which advocated direct forceful action. Sorel believed that the French proletariat had to remain basically suspicious of being deeply involved in politics. He advocated the concept of the general strike as the basis of labour-trade union actions. Revolutionary syndicalism also remained a basic foundation of his philosophy. Sorel, who once flirted with the *Action Française* in the 1890s, preferred action to theory, and, seeing the republic as a decadent institution, he advocated violence as a method to purify France. Parliamentary socialism to Sorel was a myth, since only violent action could help the working masses. He was hailed by both left and right as a philosophical father. He died at Boulogne-sur-Seine on 30 August 1922.

Soult, Nicolas-Jean de Dieu (1769–1851)   Born at Saint-Amans-la-Bastide in the Tarn on 29 March 1769, Soult entered the army as a private of the Royal Infantry in 1785. He received his commission in 1792. After service in the army of the Moselle, he was promoted to general in October 1794. In April 1799 he was elevated to general of division and fought in Switzerland in 1799 and in Italy from 1800 to 1802. Napoléon Bonaparte (qv) made him a marshal of France and a colonel general of the Guard in May 1804. During the battle of Austerlitz in 1805 he distinguished himself, and in 1807 Napoléon made him governor of Prussia. Created Duc de Dalmatia in 1808, Soult fought in Spain until 1812. Recalled to France in 1813, he saw service in Germany. He rallied to the Bourbons and from December 1814 to March 1815 he served as minister of war. During the Hundred Days (qv) he rallied to Napoléon, and after Waterloo he was banished. Recalled to service by Louis Philippe (qv), Soult held the war ministry from 1830 to 1834 and from 1840 to 1845. Soult was also minister of foreign affairs from 1839 to 1840. For two years, 1845 to 1847, he served as president of the Council of Ministers. Louis Philippe restored his title of marshal on 26 September 1847. Ageing, Soult retired to his estate in the Tarn and died at Château Soultberg on 26 November 1851.

Spuller, Eugène (1835–1896)   From 1876 to 1885 Eugène Spuller represented the Seine as a Gambettist republican. From 1885 to 1892 he held the position of deputy from the Côte d'Or, and in 1892 he was elected senator from the same district. A lawyer and staunch republican, Spuller served with Léon Gambetta (qv) in the Government of National Defence and held the post of undersecretary of state for foreign affairs during Gambetta's 'grand ministry'. Under Maurice Rouvier (qv), in 1887, he was minister of public instruction, and he was foreign minister under Pierre Tirard in 1889. His last cabinet post was minister of public instruction in the Jean Casimir Périer cabinet in 1893.

Staël-Holstein, Anna Louis de (1766–1817)   Born in Paris on 22 April 1766, Anna de Staël was the brilliant and cultured daughter of Jacques Necker (qv), the Paris financier and famous finance minister under Louis XVI (qv). In 1786 she married the Swedish ambassador to Paris, and in the same year published *Sophie ou les Sentiments Secrets*, which was basically a tragic story of a young girl. Her salon on the Rue du Bac, which she inherited from her mother, became an intellectual centre. While there she wrote, in 1788, *Lettre sur les écrits et le caractère du J. J. Rousseau*. She left Paris in 1792, and in 1795 she wrote *Réflexions sur la Paix, Addressées à M. Pitt et aux Français*. Madame de Staël believed that she had the personality and force of will to alter the course of the revolution, and she returned to Paris. She failed to exert any influence on the course of events and fled from France. She lived in Lausanne where she wrote *De l'influence des passions sur le bonheur des individus et des nations*. In 1797 she returned again to France and attached herself to Talleyrand (qv). She refused to rally to Napoléon Bonaparte (qv) and again left Paris for a few years. When she returned in 1802, her salon became a centre for anti-Bonapartist agitation. Also in 1802 she published *Delphine*. Napoléon ordered her to reside at least forty leagues from the capital city. Choosing exile in 1803, she went to Germany and Italy. In 1812 she travelled in Russia and Sweden and the following year she published her classic work *De l'Allemagne*. Returning to Paris with the allies, she tried to reinstitute her salon, but her efforts were cut short by the Hundred Days (qv). She lived in Italy until

1816 when, an ailing woman, she returned to Paris and died there on 14 July 1817. After her death, the work *Dix Ans d'Exil* was published in 1821. Madame de Staël is best remembered for her clear and coherent comments on the society of her era.

Statuts du Fermage The *statuts du fermage* were a major piece of social legislation passed after World War II to preserve the social structure of France, and at the same time weave a progressive thread into the fabric of that life. The laws stated that a small non-landholding *fermier* (tenant farmer) had the first option to purchase land should the owner decide to sell it. A court was given the responsibility of seeing that the *fermier* was charged a fair price. The *fermier* was protected from arbitrary eviction, and the landowner was obliged to pay for improvements if the tenant left after the expiration of a nine-year legal contract. The democratising effect of this statute was great in that it gave equal political status to the *fermier* and the large landowner. However, the architects of the *statuts du fermage* had hoped to bring about the modernisation of agriculture, and this did not work as they had hoped.

Stavisky Affair Serge Alexander Stavisky was a corrupt businessman in France in the 1930s, and being a Russian Jew he was the target of right-wing anti-semitic agitators. His criminal activities appeared to have been aided by a number of cabinet members and highly placed civil servants. The revelations of dealing in faked municipal bonds for the city of Bayonne were first aired in late 1933, but finally became public in January 1934. A parliamentary investigation headed by Georges Mandel (qv) began to scrutinise Stavisky's dealings, and when Stavisky died under strange circumstances more riots occurred. As names of Stavisky's protectors became known rightist gangs took to the streets, and on 6 February 1934 (qv) a full-scale battle took place in Paris leaving fifteen people dead. Edouard Daladier (qv) resigned as president of the Council of Ministers, but the situation continued to get worse. This affair, like the Wilson affair (qv) and the Panama affair (qv) in the late nineteenth century, weakened the powers of the Third Republic, because it gave a chance for political factions to attack violently the democratic parliamentary system.

Stendhal   See: Beyle, Marie Henri.

Stofflet, Jean-Nicholas (1751–1796)   Born at Lunéville in 1751, son of an old soldier, Stofflet joined the royalist army in the Vendée in 1793. Promoted to major general, Stofflet kept the royal army intact. In 1794 Stofflet organised guerrilla bands in the Vendée. After great confusion in the royalist ranks, he left the army until 1796 when he returned to the Vendée to lead the troops. He was taken prisoner and tried by a military court. Known for his rule with an iron hand and brutality to revolutionaries, Stofflet was shot at Angers on 15 February 1796.

Suchet, Louis-Gabriel (1772–1826)   Born in the industrial town of Lyon on 2 March 1772, Suchet joined the national guard of the Rhône in 1792. A brilliant soldier, he rose to command a battalion in 1793, and after service in Italy, was promoted to general in 1798. His distinguished record of battles included Jena (qv) and Austerlitz (qv), and Napoléon Bonaparte (qv) made him a count in 1808. Sent to Spain, he again displayed a natural military genius, and Napoléon elevated him to the rank of Duc d'Albuféra. Suchet rallied to the Bourbons and defended Lyon during the Hundred Days (qv). In 1819 he entered the Chamber of Deputies and served until his death. He died at Saint-Joseph-Montredon near Marseille on 3 January 1826.

Surcouf, Robert (1773–1827)   Surcouf, born at Saint Malo on 12 December 1773, served as a corsair for the French revolutionary cause, and he captured or sank many British ships. He was offered an independent navy command by Bonaparte, but turned down any connection with the regular navy. Bonaparte made him a baron in 1814. Surcouf retired from the sea, survived the Bourbon restoration, and died in Saint Malo on 8 July 1827.

Syndicalism, Revolutionary   The concept of syndicalism

is associated mainly with the rise of the *Confédération Générale du Travail* (CGT) (qv) and labour's response to the state. Revolutionary syndicalism should not be confused with the *syndicats* (qv). By the Charter of Amiens in 1906 syndicalism was defined as a desire to confront the capitalist state by every means possible, the general strike being one of the preferred methods. An undercurrent of violent class struggle was evident in the movement. While many French socialists preferred to work within the political system, the revolutionary syndicalists placed emphasis on direct and often violent action, such as strikes and even sabotage. This movement was associated with the CGT after the Congress of Amiens (qv), but by 1913 the revolutionary zeal of the CGT had weakened and they adopted the more evolutionary tactics of the socialists. Between 1906 and 1912 France experienced violent strikes, but the government responded vigorously to crush them with force, but by 1913, with the war clouds gathering, syndicalism's impact was definitely lessened.

Syndicats The law allowing occupational *syndicats* or associations was passed on 21 March 1884, and repealed Article 291 of the 1810 penal code which forbade gatherings of over twenty people, for most puposes, without a permit. The occupational syndicat was the forerunner of the labour union. By section 2, related occupations could combine into a syndicat and management was also permitted to syndicalise. The final blow to Article 291 came in the Law of Associations of 1901 (qv), which, for all purposes, legalised labour unions in France. The occupational *syndicats* played a vital role in the support of the 1901 law, and they were one of the chief beneficiaries of the legislation.

Taine, Hippolyte (1828–1895) Born at Vouziers on 21 April 1828, at the age of twelve Taine lost his father, which deeply affected the young boy. He studied first at home, then at the *Collège Bourbon* in Paris. From 1848 to 1851, as a student, he was involved with the politics of Paris, and in 1853 he published his first major work *Essai sur les fables de la Fontaine*, which served as his doctoral thesis. Soon he became known as a major literary figure. *Tite-Live,* published in 1856, brought him more fame. In 1855 Taine began to write for the *Revue de l'Instruction publique,* the *Revue des deux mondes* and *Journal des débats.* His books included *Philosophes françaises en XIXe siècle* (1857) and *Histoire de la littérature anglaise* (1864). Deeply moved by France's downfall in 1870, he began to write *Origines de la France contemporaine,* which was finished in 1893. He issued a call for national revitalisation of France after the humiliation of the defeat during the Franco-Prussian War. Elected to the *Academie Française* in 1880, Taine continued to write about reforging France's glory. He died in Paris on 5 March 1895.

Talleyrand-Périgord, Charles Maurice de (1754–1838) Talleyrand, born in Paris on 2 February 1754, was a sickly child who decided on a career in the church. His studies at the Saint Sulpice and at the Sorbonne were brilliant. From 1780 to 1785 he served as the general agent of the French clergy. Talleyrand, a now noted liberal, became bishop of Autun in 1788 and was elected deputy in 1789. In February 1790 he served as president of the Constituent Assembly, and on 14 July of that year he celebrated the Mass of the Festival of the Federation. He accepted the Civil Constitution of the Clergy (qv) and consecrated the first elected bishop. Talleyrand gave up the clerical life in 1791 to devote his time to politics and diplomacy, and in 1792 he served as ambassador to Britain and in 1794 toured the United States. He returned to France after Thermidor and briefly held the post of minister of foreign affairs. He played a key role in the coup d'état of 18 Brumaire (qv). Until 1807 he held a position as advisor to Napoléon Bonaparte (qv) in foreign affairs, but in 1809 he opposed the war with Britain and the creation of the Continental System. After openly clashing with Napoléon over Spain, he retired in semi-disgrace but was recalled to public life during the first Bourbon restoration in 1814. Talleyrand received Tsar Alexander I in Paris and became president of the Provisional Government. Made a peer, he negotiated the Treaty of Paris in May 1814. He participated in the Congress of Vienna, winning many concessions for France before he was replaced in 1815 by the Duc de Richelieu (qv). From 1815 to 1830 he grew disenchanted with the Bourbons and sat with the left opposition in the Chamber. After the fall of Charles X (qv) in 1830, he became ambassador to Britain, where he worked successfully for Franco-British friendship. He returned to Paris shortly before his death and was reconciled to the church. Talleyrand died in Paris on 17 May 1838.

Tallien, Jean Lambert (1767–1820)   A journalist, Tallien, born in Paris on 23 January 1767 to a modest but respected family, founded the republican *L'Ami des Citoyens* in 1792. In August 1792 he cast his lot briefly with the revolutionary Paris Commune, and he supported the violence of 10 August 1792 (qv). He served as a Montagnard deputy but distrusted Robespierre (qv) and played a key role in Thermidor (qv). Tallien advocated a policy of clemency toward many participants in the Terror. He followed Bonaparte to Egypt and returned to France with him. After 1802 Tallien retired from public life and survived the restoration by taking on a false name. Deserted by his wife, embittered, Tallien served for a while as a consul to Alcante. He died in poverty in Paris on 16 November 1820.

Tardieu, André (1876–1945)   Born in Paris on 22 September 1876, André Tardieu, one of the most brilliant presidents of the Council of Ministers of the late Third Republic, began his career as a deputy in 1914 and held that post until 1936. He wrote for the *Figaro* and the *Temps,* and in 1909 served for a time as professor of political science. After 1936 he retired from politics. From 1914 to 1918 he served in the French army, and in 1926 he held his first cabinet post as minister of public works. In Briand's (qv) eleventh cabinet he held the portfolio of the interior ministry. On 3 November 1929 Tardieu formed his first cabinet, and he took for himself the portfolio of the interior ministry. In 1930 he formed his second ministry, which had to grapple with the effects of the worldwide depression.

Pierre Laval (qv) picked him to serve as minister of war in 1932, and on 20 February 1932 Tardieu formed his third cabinet, taking this time the portfolio of the foreign ministry. In 1934 he was minister of state in the second Doumergue (qv) cabinet, where he had to deal with the violent riots of 6 February 1934 (qv). It was rumoured that Tardieu secretly gave funds to rightist groups in France. In 1939 he was struck with a sudden illness and retired from public life. He died at Menton on 15 September 1945.

Tennis Court Oaths After stormy sessions at Versailles on 17 June 1789 the Third Estate and a handful of priests and nobles declared themselves to be the National Assembly of France. This action, which had been promoted by Abbé Sieyès (qv), caused great distress among the royalist supporters of the king, and they persuaded the king to take action against the Third Estate and its adherents. The deputies of the Third Estate found the throne room locked on 20 June 1789. They were told that the hall was closed for repairs. Not believing this, the infuriated representatives adjourned to a nearby indoor tennis court. The actions of the king had solidified their opposition, and Jean Mounier (qv) kept them from moving their deliberations to Paris. Mounier took the lead in urging an oath that they would never adjourn until France had a workable, liberal, enlightened constitution. After the oath was read to the deputies, each one swore to it. Only one deputy, a certain Martin Dauch, refused to take the oath of 20 June. This deputy from Castlenaudary argued that he could not vote for any measure which Louis XVI (qv) did not know or approve of. The deputies left the tennis court with new confidence and with a stronger resolve to carry the revolution forward.

Têtes de Liste This term refers to the device, popular during the Fourth Republic, of placing a well-known and popular politician at the top of an election list. Those lower on the lists were picked for balance or for compromise. This implied a multi-member district and constituency. The device was opposed by those who argued that it worked against the democratic process.

Thermidor, The Ninth   For a year Robespierre (qv) and the Terror had complete sway over France. From 1793 to the summer of 1794, the Robespierrists purged anyone who opposed their concepts of social and political government. However, as French military victories in the spring of 1794 brought security to France, members of the Convention were convinced that they must act to rectify the internal situation. When Robespierre began to purge such men as Danton (qv), the Convention became certain that Robespierre had either gone insane or had become power-mad. In June and July Paris was alive with rumours of plots against Robespierre. Saint-Just (qv) secretly plotted against the leader of the Terror. On 9 Thermidor (27 July 1794) Robespierre, Saint-Just and Cauthon (qv) were arrested, and executed on the next day. The Thermidorian coup d'état was basically a reaction against the excesses of the Terror and against the over-concentration of power in the hands of one man. From 9 Thermidor to Napoléon's (qv) coup of 18 Brumaire (qv), France would maintain a weakened, decentralised executive branch.

Thierry, Augustin (1795–1856)   A schoolteacher by profession, Thierry left education in 1815 to become a follower of Saint-Simon (qv). With Saint-Simon he wrote *De la réorganisation de la société européene*, which appeared a year before Thierry left his post. In 1817 he broke from Saint-Simon and devoted himself to the writing of history. In 1825 he published *Histoire de la conquête de l'Angleterre par les Normands*. Although he was afflicted by paralysis, he published works on the Merovingians, and in 1853 he wrote *Essai sur l'histoire de la formation et du progrès du Tiers-Etat*. He died in Paris on 22 May 1856.

Thiers, Adolphe (1797–1877)   Born in Marseille on 14 April 1797 and from an impoverished but good family, Thiers manifested an aptitude for the law. He studied law first in Marseille and then in Aix. In 1820 he began his career as a lawyer and in 1823 started his famous *Histoire de la Révolution*, which was finished in 1827. In 1830 he founded *Le National* with the help of Talleyrand (qv); this was an Orléanist newspaper which opposed the policies of Polignac (qv) and Charles X (qv). During the revolution of 1830 Thiers openly supported Louis Philippe (qv), and for this he was given a post in the finance ministry. In 1830 he was also elected deputy. From 1832 to 1836 Thiers served as minister of the interior, leaving this in 1836 for the post of foreign minister. After losing his post in late 1836, he began to work on his famous *Histoire du Consulat et de l'Empire*. The actual writing began in 1843 and was finished in 1862. In 1848 Thiers briefly rallied to Louis Napoléon (qv), but by 1851 the two men were enemies. For a short time in 1851 Thiers was banished from France. In 1863 he was elected deputy and sat with the opposition. After France's defeat in 1870 he was given the unpleasant task of negotiating an armistice with Germany. He was then made the chief executive of the Provisional Government and used force to crush the Commune of 1871 (qv). In August 1871, with the support of the royalists, he became president of the republic but was ousted in 1873. Disgusted with the politics of the royalists and extreme conservatives, Thiers threw his support to the republicans in 1873, and this support would prove to be vital in any electoral contest. Thiers was elected senator from Belfort in 1876 and made peace with Léon Gambetta (qv) and the republicans in the same year. In 1877 he participated with Gambetta in a massive effort to oust the royalists. Elected deputy from Paris in 1876, Thiers, with his new republican allies, fought the bitter electoral campaign of 1877. He died suddenly at Saint-Germain-en-Laye on 3 September 1877 and was buried at the cemetery of Père Lachaise.

Thomas, Albert (1878–1932) A historian and socialist intellectual, Thomas was elected deputy in 1905. In 1915 he served with Jules Guesde (qv) at the armament ministry, and from 1915 to 1917 held ministerial rank. However, he resigned his position and in late 1919 was named director of the International Labour Bureau in Geneva in Switzerland.

Thomson, Gaston (1848–1932)   Elected deputy from Constantine in Algeria in 1877, Thomson served in that position until 1932. After 1890 he was one of the major leaders of the *Parti colonial* (qv) and a co-founder of the *Comité de l'Afrique française* (qv). Thomson advocated sea-power as a vehicle for colonial expansion, and in 1905 he became minister of the marine in the cabinet of Maurice Rouvier (qv). He continued in that post under Jean Sarrien in 1906 and under Georges Clemenceau (qv) from 1906 to 1909. In the *Union Sacrée* (qv) in 1914 he held the post of minister of commerce. Ageing, Thomson devoted the remainder of his life to his duties in the Chamber and to leading the colonial group.

Thorez, Maurice (1900–1964)   Thorez, the son of a miner, emerged as the leader of the French Communist Party in the 1930s. Claiming to be in the Jacobin tradition, he displayed an aggressive nationalism which distressed some old-line French communists. In 1932 Thorez was elected to the Chamber and was the leader of the extreme left. As war grew near, he maintained the party line toward Germany and Russia, and, like many communist leaders, he was disturbed over the Russian-German Pact of August 1939. Called to colours in 1939, Thorez deserted and fled to Russia. General Charles de Gaulle's (qv) trip to Russia in 1944 resulted in an agreement to allow Thorez to return to France. Thorez believed that Russia's participation in the war against Nazi Germany and de Gaulle's grudging acceptance of two communists on the 1944 cabinet opened the way for a possible communist-led cabinet. In 1946 he tried for the premiership but failed, and later he broke with André Marty (qv) over Thorez's advocacy of communist participation in governments. Hostile to General Charles de Gaulle in 1958, Thorez tried to mount strikes to keep the general from coming to power. By the time of his death Thorez had made the Communist Party an independent but somewhat staid political institution in France.

Thouvenel, Edouard (1818–1866)   Diplomat and minister of foreign affairs, Thouvenel served under Napoléon III as foreign minister and advocated France's neutral attitude toward Italy. In 1862 he was dropped from the cabinet because of his neutrality toward some sort of French intervention in respect to Italy.

Three Year Law Passed on 7 August 1913, after bitter debate in the Chamber, this law extended the tour of service in the French army from two to three years. It built the French army to 750,000 men. Supported by the right and centre, the Three Year Law was vehemently opposed by the left led by Jean Jaurès (qv).

Tilsit, Treaty of A series of treaties signed on 7–9 July 1807 between France and Russia allied the two states. The two emperors, Alexander of the east and Napoléon of the west, met in a raft in the middle of the Nieman river near the town of Tilsit. Tsar Alexander I was highly impressed with Bonaparte, and the two men quickly reached an agreement on the main points. Prussia lost her western and Polish provinces. The new kingdom of Westphalia (qv) was recognised, as was the Grand Duchy of Warsaw. The French evacuation of Prussia was made contingent upon the payment of heavy war indemnities. Russia gave up her claims to the Ionian isles and recognised Joseph Bonaparte as the King of Sicily. Tsar Alexander secretly promised to declare war on England and join the continental system if Britain refused mediation. Denmark, Portugal and Sweden would be obliged to do likewise. If Turkey refused mediation, the allies would drive her from Europe, and the only exception to this would be Turkish retention of Constantinople and the province of Rumelia. Basically the Tilsit treaties were aimed at Britain, and the signing of the agreements marked the zenith in Bonaparte's career as emperor.

Tocqueville, Alexis Clerel de (1805–1859) Born in Verneuil on 29 July 1805 to a family related to the famed author Châteaubriand (qv), de Tocqueville enjoyed the position of a member of a family favoured by the Bourbon restoration. A professional judge in 1827 at Versailles, de Tocqueville travelled to the United States to study the American penal and governmental system. His *La Démocratie en Amérique* was written from 1835 to 1840. Elected deputy in 1839, de Tocqueville became a member of the liberal opposition. Re-elected in 1848 he sat with the moderate right and accepted the republic. However, he supported republican General Cavaignac (qv) for president in 1848, and for this he earned many enemies among the followers of Napoléon III (qv). De Tocqueville, because of his immense prestige, became foreign minister in 1849 but was imprisoned briefly after the coup d'état of December 1851 as it was known that he strongly opposed Louis Napoléon's bid for total power. In 1852 he retired from public life to write and in 1856 he published his study on the French revolution *L'Ancien régime et la Révolution*. He died in Cannes on 16 April 1859.

Tolain, Henri-Louis (1828–1897) Tolain, the son of a dancing master, was born in Paris on 18 June 1828. He pursued a career in art. He served Napoléon III (qv), and after an official trip to Britain from 1861 to 1862 became dedicated to the cause of trade unionism. Later he attended the First International, and there he defended traditional property against state collectivism. In 1871 Tolain was elected deputy and fought against the Commune. Elected senator from the Seine in 1876, he allied himself with the left but cooperated with the Opportunists. While serving in the Assembly in 1884 he tried to introduce laws to help the trade unions, and in 1885 he was one of the founders of the *Alliance Républicaine*. In 1890 he was named delegate to the Workers' Conference in Berlin, and in 1893 he was re-elected senator. Until his death in Paris on 3 May 1897 he worked for trade union causes.

Tolentino, Treaty of Signed on 17 February 1797 between Napoléon Bonaparte (qv) and the pope, this treaty ceded Avignon, Comtat Venaissin, Bologna, Ferrara, Romagna and Ancona to France. Most of these areas were included in the Cisalpine Republic (qv). A huge indemnity, payable to France, was also agreed upon.

Tours, Congress of In 1920 the French socialists met at

Tours to debate issues affecting the workers and socialism in general. At this congress the communists split off from the *Section Française de l'Internationale Ouvrière* (SFIO) (qv), forming their own party. Actually in the majority at the congress, they wanted to adhere to the Twenty-one Conditions, laid down by Lenin at the 1920 Moscow Conference for joining the Third Internationale. Léon Blum (qv), the brilliant Jewish intellectual, distrusted Leninism, and after the Congress voted three to one to adhere to the Third International, Blum led the orthodox socialists from the hall. Blum's socialists even lost control of the old SFIO newspaper *L'Humanité* to the new communists. This division eventually worked against the extreme left because the French socialists were able to isolate the communists in elections for the Chamber and defeat them. After the Congress of Tours the leadership of the socialist movement, including politicians like Léon Blum, collaborated with various parliamentary factions like the Radicals within the Chamber. However, the Tours Congress permanently divided the socialists from the communists except for special occasions. The Congress had the effect of dividing and weakening the left in French politics for several decades.

Trafalgar, Battle of   On 21 October 1805 a decisive naval battle took place between the French and British navies off Cape Trafalgar. The battle, lasting for six hours, was an indisputable triumph for the British navy which lost not a single ship in wrecking the French fleet. While Lord Nelson was killed in battle, the British navy emerged as the master of the seas, and France was forced to give up any invasion plans for Great Britain. It must be noted, however, that by August 1805 Napoléon Bonaparte (qv) had changed his mind about the English invasion project and turned his attention toward eastern Europe.

Turgot, Anne Robert Jacques (1727–1781)   Turgot was born in Paris on 10 May 1727, and his father pushed him toward a career in the church. In 1751 he left the church and began to ally himself with the French physiocrats, men who believed in natural economic laws. In 1761 he became an Intendant in Limoges. Like many men of the enlightenment, Turgot delved into science, philosophy and economics. Under his enlightened guidance Limoges was transformed into an economically viable region. Louis XVI (qv) first called Turgot to the ministry of marine, but his talents finally in 1774 brought him to the position of controller general of finances. His reforms were not radical. He demanded an end to the *corvée* (qv), and tried to maintain free trade in grains. Opposed to privilege, Turgot argued against the rising deficit in French finances. In May 1776 he was removed from his post. Retiring from public service, he continued to maintain his links with the reformers. He died in Paris on 20 March 1781.

Union Coloniale   Founded in 1893 by imperialists in the business and banking community, the union's main goal was the popularisation of colonial ventures. Joseph Chailley-Bert (qv) was the editor of the union's journal, *La Quinzaine Coloniale*, and became one of France's leading expansionist theoreticians. Like the *Comité de l'Afrique française* (qv), after 1904 the union devoted its efforts to the acquisition of Morocco.

Union des Droites   The union of the right was formed in 1885 by monarchists and rightists. The conservatives called for an end to religious persecution and for drastic reduction in public spending. However, the rightists were not actually able to decide which monarchist pretender they would support. After the death of the Comte de Chambord (qv) in 1883, most Bourbons rallied to the Orléanist Comte de Paris. The Bonapartists refused to recognise Orléanist leadership and caused great disunity in the royalist conservative ranks. During the elections of 1885 the right made advances, but without unity of the Bourbons, Orléanists, Bonapartists and others they stood little chance of taking the government. Most rightists vehemently attacked the government during the Wilson affair (qv) and supported General Georges Boulanger (qv) whom they wrongly saw as a champion of ultra-conservatism.

Union Nationale   The *Union Nationale* replaced the *Bloc*

National (qv) as the main conservative political force in French political life. Raymond Poincaré (qv), premier in 1926, called for the national union which would also include the moderate left, such as the radicals, in the cabinet. He divided cabinet posts into two groups, political and economic, and shared them among the right and the left. Poincaré retained the ministry of finance, and Aristide Briand (qv) was brought to the foreign ministry. The union, through the rather conservative economic policies of Poincaré, maintained a balance in French political life but began to dissolve quickly when Poincaré retired and André Tardieu (qv), more committed to the right, became president of the Council of Ministers. The patchwork of political alliances began to disintegrate under Tardieu's less compromising attitudes towards the left.

Union pour la Nouvelle République (UNR)   The UNR, as a political party, was founded after the crisis of May 1958 which brought Charles de Gaulle (qv) to power as the last premier of the Fourth Republic and the first president of the Fifth Republic. The Union for the New Republic was basically a Gaullist party with its roots in the defunct *Rassemblement du Peuple Français* (RPF) (qv). Its basic thrust aimed at the establishment of a strong president who would not be under the sway of parliament, but would guide the actions of the legislature. During the elections of 1958 over 200 UNR deputies went to the Chamber, giving de Gaulle and his premier a working majority. Led by Michel Debré (qv) from 1958 to 1962, and after by Georges Pompidou (qv), the UNR continued to deliver a unified front for Gaullist programmes. While not a truly conservative party, the UNR did not attract leftist Gaullists, who formed themselves into the *Union Démocratique du Travail* (UDT) which has continued to participate in Gaullist cabinets until 1962 when the UNR and UDT merged. The principles of Gaullism and the UNR were questioned as to their lasting value. Many political observers in France believed that the principles of Gaullism would not survive the retirement or death of General Charles de Gaulle, but after his resignation in 1968 it appeared that the basic ideals would probably be long lasting.

Union Républicaine Démocratique (URD) The URD, a right-wing political party, was opposed to the policies of the political left in the Chamber of Deputies. Founded in 1903 to oppose such groups as the socialists under Jean Jaurès (qv), and headed by Louis Marin (qv), the party relied heavily on traditionalist, landholding, conservative families for funds and for its basic membership. Dedicated to confronting the growing left wing in France, the URD also opposed Emile Combes' (qv) anti-clerical fanaticism. Unlike many rightist groups, the URD did not want to overthrow the parliamentary government of France, nor did its leadership have any sympathy for the *Action Française* (qv) in the 1930s. As World War II drew close, Marin and his supporters urged France to strengthen her ties with fascist Italy and to halt Nazi Germany's aggressive tendencies in eastern Europe.

Union Sacrée This Sacred Union, formed in 1914, had the purpose of uniting all political parties in common cause to prosecute the war against Germany. The government was able to get even the socialists to join, and they were given seats in the union cabinet. Théophile Delcassé (qv) was brought to the foreign ministry. Alexandre Millerand (qv), once a socialist, went to the war ministry. Aristide Briand (qv) took control of the ministry of justice, and Jules Guesde (qv), a firm member of the socialist party, became a minister of state. Louis Malvy (qv), a radical and friend of Joseph Caillaux (qv), held the interior portfolio. Denys Cochin (qv), one of the leaders of the Catholics in France, and Emile Combes (qv), anti-clerical ex-president of the Council of Ministers, held positions as ministers of state. Alexandre Ribot (qv), confidant of Georges Clemenceau (qv), held the portfolio of finance. However, the *Sacrée* government saw fit to curb individual liberties and allowed military courts to try civilian offenders in cases directly involving the war effort. By 1915 the government had collapsed, and by 1916 it was only a memory of sorts. Possibly the Sacred

Union overlooked the fact that the longer war dragged on the greater would be the tendency for political fragmentation.

Valmy, Battle of Not a great battle in the sense of size of armies or number of men killed, Valmy was a moral victory for the French revolutionary armies. On 20 September 1792 French forces under General Kellermann (qv) held off a Prussian army and in the long run forced a combined Austrian-Prussian army to withdraw from France. Valmy, therefore, was a definite boost for the morale of revolutionary France and a moral disaster for the autocratic powers. Valmy was seen by the French as a miracle which saved the revolution.

Van Vollenhoven, Joost (1877–1918) A Dutchman, born in Rotterdam on 21 July 1877, who settled in Algeria, Van Vollenhoven became one of France's leading imperialists. In 1899 he took French citizenship, and the same year he finished a course of study at the *école coloniale* in Paris. After a brief period of service in the colonial army he began a career in the colonial administration. However, in 1905 he returned to Paris and became a professor of colonial studies. In 1906 he was sent to Senegal as secretary general of the colony, and in 1908 he served in the same capacity in French Equatorial Africa. Sent to Indo-China in 1912, Van Vollenhoven reformed the administrative apparatus there. In 1917 he went to West Africa to raise troops for France's war effort. On 18 July 1918 Van Vollenhoven, a genius in administration, died because of complications after surgery.

Varennes On 22 June 1791 Louis XVI (qv), Queen Marie Antoinette (qv) and the royal children were arrested at the small town of Varennes in Lorraine. Louis XVI had attempted to flee Paris in disguise and reach the waiting Prussian and Austrian allies. The king was detected on 21 June and soldiers arrived the next day to escort him back to a hostile Paris, which they reached on 24 June 1791.

Vendémiaire, Rebellion of On 5 October 1795 over 20,000 rebels marched against the Convention. Led by royalist agents and malcontents the insurgents tried to overthrow the

Assembly, but 4,000 regular troops, commanded by Napoléon Bonaparte (qv), easily dispersed the mobs with 'a whiff of grapeshot'. Napoléon emerged as the hero of the day, and the Assembly was more than willing to impose a rule of law and order on France. Napoléon's actions led to his being given command of the army of Italy.

Vergniaud, Pierre (1753–1793)   The son of a military outfitter, Vergniaud was born in Limoges on 31 May 1753. He studied law and opened a practice in Bordeaux in 1781. In 1791 Vergniaud went to Paris as a deputy and a staunch defender of constitutionalism and advocate of a strictly controlled monarchy. He demanded stern measures against the *émigrés*. However, he secretly negotiated with Louis XVI (qv) for a position of power but was rebuffed. Closely allied with the Girondins, Vergniaud earned the enmity of the rising Jacobins (qv). He then sought the position of president of the Assembly, proclaiming his adherence to democratic ideals. He became president of the Assembly and after the violence of 10 August 1792 (qv) proclaimed that the monarchy was suspended. Fearing radicalism, which he himself had helped in some measure to create, Vergniaud, as a member of the Commission of Surveillance, tried to suppress ultra-democratic movements. Because of his connections with the Girondins, he was marked for arrest, and during the purge of the Girondins during the Terror was arrested and died on the guillotine on 31 October 1793.

Versailles, Treaty of   On 28 June 1919 Germany, a defeated state, signed the massive Treaty of Versailles, which comprised fifteen sections and 440 separate articles. The victorious allies—England, France, Italy and the United States —had for months argued over the basic sections of the treaty, including the controversial section creating the League of Nations. The main provisions dealt with the disarmament of Germany, the placing of responsibility for the outbreak of war in August 1914 on Germany, reparations and territorial readjustments. For example, Alsace and Lorraine, taken from

France by the 1871 Treaty of Frankfurt, were returned to France. Clemenceau (qv), premier of France, demanded the creation of states, strong and vital, on Germany's eastern border. In respect to Poland, Clemenceau demanded a Poland which was 'forte, forte et très forte', a Poland created with the famous corridor which took German territory and people and placed them under Polish political control. All in all the territorial concessions, excepting Alsace and Lorraine, proved to be quite unsatisfactory, as many states in eastern Europe had definite minority population problems. These problem areas, such as the Sudetenland in Czechoslovakia, would be the cause of later bitter controversies and would help bring on World War II. Most historians agree that German resentment over the placing of blame on her for the war and the loss of territory was deep and, in the long run, would cause great inter-European difficulties. Germany's loss of eastern territories to Poland for the creation of the Polish Corridor to the sea, and the division of her colonies among Britain, France and Japan added truth to the German complaint that she was being dismembered. Most of her western German industrial heartland was neutralised. In the final analysis the Treaty of Versailles proved to be unworkable; it contributed to a continued air of hatred and distrust between European nations, and it helped to create propaganda for extremist German political groups such as the Nazis.

Veuillot, Louis François (1813–1883)   Born at Boynes on 11 October 1813 to a very modest family, Veuillot became one of France's leading defenders of the conservative Catholic faith. At the age of seventeen he wrote for *L'Echo de la Seine-Inférieure*, published in Rouen. He displayed a remarkable talent for polemics. In 1839, after a visit to Rome, Veuillot became a vehement partisan of *Ultramontain* Catholicism. Writing for the journal *L'Univers religieux*, Veuillot advocated conservative causes, and after Napoléon III's coup d'état of 2 December 1851 he re-allied to the Bonapartist cause. Veuillot became known as the most bitter enemy of liberal Catholics, and he defended any French attempt to assist the pope. Veuillot, almost a fanatic, hated any Christian liberal or socialist movement. He demanded total control of education in France by the church, and he even found the 1830 Falloux Law (qv) to be too moderate. In 1869 he went to Rome to attend the council which upheld the doctrine of papal infallibility. After 1871 Veuillot continued to write, defending ultra-conservative Catholic policies. He died in Paris on 7 March 1883.

Vienna, Treaty of   After the defeat of Austria at the battle of Wagram (qv), Austria asked, on 12 July 1809, for an armistice. While by no means crushed, Francis I of Austria signed the draconian treaty, as dictated by Napoléon I (qv) on 14 October 1809. Austria lost vast territory and population. Bavaria received Austria's western provinces; Trieste was ceded, with other Adriatic areas, to France; Galacia went to the Grand Duchy of Warsaw. Austria agreed to break relations with England and join the Continental System (qv). She was reduced militarily, and Bonaparte agreed to guarantee the existence of the Austrian state. The Austrian state lost over $3\frac{1}{2}$ million inhabitants and some very valuable territory. Francis was also forced to agree to alterations on the Iberian peninsula. The Peace of Vienna of 1809 disgusted Francis, who felt that fanatical Austrian patriots had dragged him into a war which he lost. To silence the zealots, he appointed Prince Metternich as his major advisor. After Vienna, Napoléon had to recognise that a new nationalistic feeling was abroad in the German states.

Villafranca, Armistice of   On 9 July 1859 Napoléon III and Emperor Francis Joseph of Austria met at Villafranca to discuss the French intervention in Italy. Napoléon III had promised Piedmont's brilliant premier Comte Cavour that France would intervene in North Italy and help drive the Austrians from there. Despite Napoléon III's well-meaning desire to help Italians, he came under attack from influential French Catholics such as Louis Veuillot (qv), who argued that Italian nationalism would in the long run hurt the pope's control of Rome. French conservative Catholics threatened to withdraw support from the empire. The bloodshed of Solferino (qv) and Magenta (qv) angered some military leaders who feared a weakening of the French armies. With these pressures in mind, Napoléon III and Francis Joseph met to disengage French and Austrian forces. Austria would give Lombardy to France, and France in turn would give it later to Piedmont. On the other hand, Venetia was retained by Austria. A *status quo ante bellum* was imposed on Modena and Tuscany. Piedmont's Comte Cavour was outraged and resigned in protest, and Victor Emmanuel was bitterly disappointed. Napoléon III, however, felt that he had fulfilled his pledges to Piedmont and Italy, and he withdrew French forces from the war.

Villèle, Jean Baptiste de (1773–1854)   Born in Toulouse on 14 April 1773, a staunch anti-revolutionary monarchist from the Ile Bourbon, Comte de Villèle returned to France in 1807. In 1815 he became one of the leaders of the ultra-deputies, and in 1821 became minister of finance. In 1821 he formed his own ministry which lasted for seven years. From 1824 to 1830 Villèle was known as a faithful servant of King Charles X (qv). After the revolution of 1830, unable to accept the new king, Louis Philippe (qv), he retired from public life and died in Toulouse on 13 March 1854.

Vittoria, Battle of   This battle, fought in Spain on 21 June 1813, marks the end of the French presence in that state. The Duke of Wellington totally defeated the French and forced them to retreat in complete chaos to France.

Viviani, René (1863–1925)   Viviani began his career as a socialist deputy and a member of the *Délégation des Gauches* (qv). He disagreed with Jean Jaurès (qv) over non-cooperation with governments, and broke with the *Section Française de l'Internationale Ouvrière* (SFIO) (qv). In 1914 President Raymond Poincaré (qv) persuaded Viviani to serve as president of the Council of Ministers. After the outbreak of World War I Viviani formed the *Union Sacrée* (qv), which fell in 1915. He continued in politics until his death.

Vogüé, Eugène Melchior de (1848–1910)   A famous French novelist, de Vogüé was influential in the colonialist movement and was a member of the *Comité de l'Afrique Française* (qv). He had a great impact on Marshal Lyautey (qv) by reinforcing Lyautey's conservative catholicism and persuading him to write.

Waddington, William Henry (1826–1894)   A firm republican, follower of Léon Gambetta (qv) and opponent of the Second Empire, Waddington served from 1871 to 1876 as a member of the National Assembly. In 1876 he was elected senator from Aisne and served in that post until his death in 1894. In 1873 he held his first portfolio as minister of public instruction under Jules Dufaure. In the Dufaure cabinet of 1876 he held the post of minister of public instruction. He became foreign minister in 1877, and in 1879 he formed his own ministry, which was short lived. After 1879 Waddington devoted his time to his senatorial duties.

Wagram, Battle of   From 5 to 6 July 1809 Napoléon Bonaparte (qv) engaged the forces of Austria at Wagram. After the bloody engagement, the Austrians signed an armistice on 12 July 1809 as a preliminary to a peace settlement which was finalised as the Treaty of Vienna (qv) on 14 October 1809.

Waldeck-Rousseau, René (1846–1904)   Born in Nantes, Waldeck-Rousseau became a lawyer in his home town. Elected as a republican deputy in 1879, he held the portfolio of the interior ministry under both Jules Ferry (qv) and Léon Gambetta (qv). This marked him as a staunch supporter of the republican opportunists. In 1894 he became a senator, and by 1898 he had emerged as an eloquent defender of Dreyfus (qv). In 1902 he suffered a severe stroke and retired to write against Premier Emile Combes's (qv) anti-church policies which Waldeck-Rousseau saw as seriously divisive for the French nation.

Walewska, Marie Lacznska (1789–1817)   Mistress of Bonaparte, she bore him an illegitimate son, Léon Walewski (qv). She influenced Napoléon's policy toward Poland and eastern Europe. In fact, one of the motives of their affair was to influence him and to create the Grand Duchy of Warsaw. Countess Walewska married General d'Ornano in 1815.

Walewski, Léon (1810–1868)   Born in Walewica, Poland, on 4 May 1810, the illegitimate son of Napoléon Bonaparte (qv) and Marie Walewska (qv), Walewski became a French citizen in 1830 and enlisted in the French army. In 1837 he became a journalist, and three years later he left journalism for the diplomatic service. By 1851 he had risen to ambassadorial level. Napoléon III picked Walewski to serve as minister of foreign affairs from 1855 to 1860. In 1860 he became a minister of state, and in 1865 he became a deputy. For three years, 1865–1868, he served as president of the *Corps Législatif*. After an illness and his decline in political power, Walewski retired from public life and died in Strasbourg on 27 September 1868.

Waterloo, Battle of   Napoléon Bonaparte had been exiled on the island of Elba, but events in France convinced him that he could make a successful return to the mainland. During the period known as the Hundred Days (qv) he ruled again over France. After raising an army he marched against the allies, and engaged the allied forces on 18 June 1815 at Waterloo, a Belgian village only a few kilometres from Brussels. There he was defeated by the Duke of Wellington, and with this defeat the hopes for a revitalised French empire under Napoléon died.

Westphalia, Kingdom of   In 1807 Napoléon Bonaparte (qv) created the Kingdom of Westphalia from the western provinces of Prussia, part of Hesse and a portion of Hanover. The small states of Brunswick, Hesse-Cassell, and Westphalia were also incorporated into the kingdom which was given to Jérôme Bonaparte (qv) in 1807. It was granted recognition by Tsar Alexander I in the Tilsit Treaties (qv). In August 1810 Westphalia was formally annexed by France. After the downfall of Napoléon Bonaparte, the powers convening at Vienna dealt with the question of the future of Westphalia. In 1815 the kingdom was broken up into its component parts as they existed prior to 1807.

Weygand, Maxime (1867–1965) A career officer, Weygand saw heroic and distinguished service in World War I, and during the inter-war period he advocated a policy of defence. He rejected the concept of *élan vital* which had so dominated French military thought prior to 1914. The ideas of the offensive and *élan*, to him, had caused much of the terrible slaughter of World War I. He did not understand nor approve of Charles de Gaulle's (qv) emphasis on mobile tank warfare. In May 1940 Weygand became supreme commander of the French military forces which were already bending under heavy German attacks. Weygand, like Marshal Pétain (qv), had little hope of saving France from defeat in 1940, but he made every attempt in late May to counterattack the Germans. This failed, and Weygand advocated an immediate armistice to save the French armies from total defeat. He opposed the transfer of troops to North Africa to continue the fight against the Germans. Throwing his support behind Pétain's Vichy effort, Weygand undertook various missions for the aged marshal. In February 1941 he negotiated the Weygand-Murphy Accord (qv). Because Weygand did not rally to General de Gaulle he was distrusted by the liberation forces. After World War II he remained as active in governmental and military affairs as his age would allow. He remained distrustful of de Gaulle and openly opposed de Gaulle's policies toward Algeria after 1958.

Weygand-Murphy Accord As a result of a conversation between General Maxime Weygand (qv) and Robert Murphy, an agreement was signed on 26 February 1941. This accord pertained to French North Africa and its place in the diplomatic relationship between the Vichy government and the United States. General Weygand promised to recommend to Vichy that there would be no excessive stockpiling of war material in North Africa, no material would leave North Africa and the American representatives had authority to watch over the ports of Algeria, Morocco and Tunisia. The United States promised to continue to trade with North Africa and to free certain frozen French governmental assets in the United States to help pay for enumerated essential non-military products. Negotiations would begin between France and the United States over the shipment of essential foodstuffs to North Africa. This accord was approved and confirmed by Admiral François Darlan (qv) on 10 March 1941.

Wilson Affair   Senator Daniel Wilson (qv) was the son-in-law of President Jules Grévy (qv) and occupied a position on the president's staff. In 1886 it was rumoured that Wilson, using his position, openly sold offices, military commissions and the Legion of Honour for his personal gain. Georges Clemenceau (qv) and other politicians attacked not only Grévy but the government in power. During 1886 and 1887 they succeeded in toppling ministries and even in ousting President Jules Grévy. During this period there was an upsurge of Boulangist feeling and revanchist sentiment against the republican form of government.

Wilson, Daniel (1840–1902)   Daniel Wilson was a senator and the son-in-law of Jules Grévy (qv), the president of the republic. Wilson used his position, presidential stationery and his influence with the presidential staff to sell offices and the Legion of Honour to the highest bidders. He held many cabinet posts of importance before his dishonesty was discovered. He entered the Senate in 1876 and remained in that body until 1902. In 1879 he was undersecretary in the finance ministry, and held that post until 1880. He was discovered as a thief and a fraud, and this caused a popular outcry in 1887. Grévy was toppled by the Republicans and Radicals, and Sadi Carnot (qv), a political moderate, became president, but the chief beneficiary of the entire scandal was General Georges Boulanger (qv), who also attacked what he called the corrupt political republic.

Women's Rights   See: French League for Women's

Rights; National Council of French Women; Ordinance of 21 April 1944.

Zola, Emile (1840–1902)   One of France's greatest authors, Zola championed social justice and rose to great fame as a staunch defender of the wrongly accused Captain Alfred Dreyfus (qv). Born in Paris on 2 April 1840, Zola's father, an Italian immigrant, died when Emile Zola was only seven years of age. Zola and his mother lived in Aix-en-Provence until 1857 when they returned to Paris where he was employed at the Hachette Publishing Company. In 1867 he wrote his first novel, *Thérèse Raquin*. *Madeleine Férat* appeared a year later. From 1871 to 1893 he published the bulk of his realistic novels, and during that period he became the foremost exponent of the naturalist school of French literature. *L'Assommoir*, published in 1877, was a depressing but highly accurate story of drunkenness. In 1880 *Nana*, a tale of prostitution, appeared, and in 1892 *La Débâcle*, the story of the crushing defeat of France by Germany in 1870. In 1898, Zola, at the pinnacle of his fame, began his classic defence of Captain Dreyfus, who was wrongly accused of treason because of his Jewish faith. On 13 January 1898 Zola addressed his famous letter *J'Accuse* to the president of France. In it he indicted those who had accused Dreyfus. Zola was maligned and persecuted for his defence of justice. Retiring to Britain, he continued to write but in 1899 returned to France. *Fécondité* was published while Zola lived in Britain in 1899. Once back in France, he published *Travail*, and a year after his death *Vérité* appeared. On 29 September 1902 he died, and in 1908 his remains were placed in the Panthéon.

Members of the Committee of Public Safety
1793–1794*

Bertrand Barère	1755–1841
Jean Billaud-Varenne	1756–1819
Lazare Carnot	1753–1823
Jean Marie Collot d'Hérbois	1750–1795
Georges Couthon	1756–1794
Marie Hérault de Séchelles	1759–1794
Robert Lindet	1743–1825
Claude Prieur-Duvernois	1763–1832
Pierre Prieur	1756–1827
Maximilien de Robespierre	1758–1794
André Jeanbon Saint-André	1749–1813
Louis Antoine Saint-Just	1767–1794

* The *Comité de Salut Public* and each of the twelve members have separate entries. This is merely a convenient reference. These are also the committee members during the period of the Terror. While there were other members before that time, only those who participated in the Terror are recorded.

The Revolutionary Calendar

The New Era and new year began on 22 September 1792. The revolutionaries altered the old calendar, and it was claimed that reason and the 'truth of nature' would replace religious superstition. The new calendar remained in force until 1 January 1806.

Autumn months:
Vendémiaire, Brumaire, Frimaire
Winter months:
Nivôse, Pluviôse, Ventôse
Spring months:
Germinal, Floréal, Prairial
Summer months:
Messidor, Thermidor, Fructidor

The Coalitions against Napoléon

First Coalition 1792–1797:
Austria and Prussia, later joined by Britain, Spain, Portugal, Naples, Tuscany and the Papal States.

Second Coalition 1799–1801:
Britain, Russia, Turkey, Austria, Naples and Portugal.

Third Coalition 1805–1806:
Russia, Austria, Sweden, Britain and Prussia.

Fourth Coalition 1812–1814:
Britain, Russia, the German states of Prussia, Württemberg, Baden, Hesse and Austria as well as Italian and Scandinavian states. (The Quadruple Alliance, a result of this coalition, was created by the Treaty of Chaumont on 9 March 1814.)

Fifth Coalition 1815:
This coalition contained all of the European powers—Britain, Austria, Russia, Prussia and other smaller states, excluding Naples.

Presidents of the Council under King Louis XVIII 1815–1824*

Prince de Talleyrand-Périgord	9 July 1815–24 September 1815
Duc de Richelieu	26 September 1815–29 December 1818
General Dessolle	29 December 1818–19 November 1819
Comte de Decazes	19 November 1819–20 February 1820
Duc de Richelieu	20 February 1820–14 December 1821
Comte de Villèle	14 December 1821–4 January 1828†

* King Louis XVIII ruled from 8 July 1815 to 16 September 1824.
† De Villèle's presidency spans the reigns of Louis XVIII and Charles X.

Presidents of the Council of Ministers under King Charles X
1824–1830*

Comte de Villèle	14 December 1821–4 January 1828†
Vicomte de Martignac	4 January 1828–8 August 1829
Prince de Polignac	8 August 1829–29 July 1830

* King Charles X ruled from 16 September 1824 to 29 July 1830.
† De Villèle's presidency spans the reigns of Louis XVIII and Charles X.

Presidents of the Council of Ministers under King Louis Philippe 1830–1848*

Jacques Dupont de l'Eure	11 August 1830–28 October 1830
Jacques Laffitte	2 November 1830–13 March 1831
Casimir-Pierre Périer	13 March 1831–11 October 1832†
Marshal Soult	11 October 1832–18 July 1834
Marshal Gerard	18 July 1834–10 November 1834
Duc de Brassano	10 November 1834–14 November 1834‡
Marshal Mortier	18 November 1834–12 March 1835
Duc de Broglie	12 March 1835–22 February 1836
Adolphe Thiers	22 February 1836–6 September 1836
Marshal Molé	6 September 1836–20 February 1839§
Adolphe Thiers	1 March 1839–29 October 1840
Marshal Soult	29 October 1840–19 September 1847
François Guizot	19 September 1847–23 February 1848

* King Louis Philippe ruled from 9 August 1830 to 24 February 1848. From the fall of Charles X until 11 August 1830 the government was controlled by a group of commissioners.

† On 16 May 1832 Casimir-Pierre Périer died, and Louis Philippe assumed the presidency of the Council until 11 October 1832.

‡ This ministry is also known as the 'Three Day Ministry'.

§ Molé resigned on 20 February 1839, and it took over a week to find the new president of the Council.

APPENDIX 7

Presidents of the Council of Ministers under the Second Republic 1848–1851*

General Louis Cavaignac	28 June 1848–20 December 1848
Odilon Barrot	20 December 1848–31 October 1849†

* The concept of the president of the Council of Ministers is introduced during the presidency of Cavaignac from 28 June 1848. From February to June France was ruled by the Provisional Government of 1848 (qv) and the Executive Commission of 1848 (qv).

† With the fall of the Barrot ministry on 31 October 1849 the title of president of the Council of Ministers was abolished and did not reappear until 9 March 1876.

Presidents of the French Republic

Adolphe Thiers
1870–1873
Marshal Marie MacMahon
1873–1879
Jules Grévy
1879–1887
Sadi Carnot
1887–1894
Jean Casimir Périer
1894–1895
Félix Faure
1895–1899
Emile Loubet
1899–1906
Armand Fallières
1906–1913
Raymond Poincaré
1913–1920

Paul Deschanel
1920
Alexandre Millerand
1920–1924
Gaston Doumergue
1924–1931
Paul Doumer
1931–1932
Albert Lebrun
1932–1940
Vincent Auriol
1947–1954
René Coty
1954–1959
Charles de Gaulle
1959–1969
Georges Pompidou
1969–1974

From 1940 to 1947 there is no president of the Republic. In the interim period France is controlled by the Vichy government under Marshal Pétain, and after 1944 France exists under a provisional government until 1947.

Presidents of the Council of Ministers of France under the Third Republic 1870–1940*

Jules Dufaure	2 September 1871–25 May 1873
Duc de Broglie	25 May 1873–22 May 1874
General de Cissey	22 May 1874–10 March 1875
Louis Buffet	10 March 1875–23 February 1876
Jules Dufaure	9 March 1876–12 December 1876
Jules Simon	12 December 1876–16 May 1877
Duc de Broglie	17 May 1877–23 November 1877
Grimaudet de Rochebouet	23 November 1877–13 December 1877
Jules Dufaure	13 December 1877–23 February 1879
William Waddington	24 February 1879–28 December 1879
Charles de Freycinet	28 December 1879–23 September 1880
Jules Ferry	23 September 1880–14 November 1881
Léon Gambetta	14 November 1881–30 January 1882
Charles de Freycinet	30 January 1882–7 August 1882
Eugène Duclerc	7 August 1882–29 January 1883
Armand Fallières	29 January 1883–21 February 1883
Jules Ferry	21 February 1883–6 April 1885
Henri Brisson	6 April 1885–7 January 1886
Charles de Freycinet	7 January 1886–11 December 1886
René Goblet	11 December 1886–30 May 1887
Maurice Rouvier	30 May 1887–12 December 1887
Pierre Tirard	12 December 1887–3 April 1888
Charles Floquet	3 April 1888–22 February 1889
Pierre Tirard	22 February 1889–17 March 1890

Charles de Freycinet	17 March 1890–18 February 1892
Emile Loubet	27 February 1892–28 November 1892
Alexandre Ribot	6 December 1892–4 April 1893
Charles Dupuy	4 April 1893–3 December 1893
Jean Casimir Périer	3 December 1893–30 May 1894
Charles Dupuy	30 May 1894–1 November 1895
Léon Bourgeois	1 November 1895–5 April 1896
Jules Méline	5 April 1896–28 June 1898
Henri Brisson	28 June 1898–1 November 1898
Charles Dupuy	1 November 1898–22 June 1899
René Waldeck-Rousseau	22 June 1899–7 June 1902
Emile Combes	7 June 1902–24 January 1905
Maurice Rouvier	24 January 1905–14 March 1906
Jean Sarrien	14 March 1906–25 October 1906
Georges Clemenceau	25 October 1906–24 July 1909
Aristide Briand	24 July 1909–2 March 1911
Ernest Monis	2 March 1911–27 June 1911
Joseph Caillaux	27 June 1911–14 January 1912
Raymond Poincaré	14 January 1912–21 January 1913
Aristide Briand	21 January 1913–22 March 1913
Louis Barthou	22 March 1913–9 December 1913
Gaston Doumergue	9 December 1913–9 June 1914
René Viviani	9 June 1914–29 October 1915
Aristide Briand	29 October 1915–20 March 1917
Alexandre Ribot	20 March 1917–12 September 1917
Paul Painlevé	12 September 1917–16 November 1917
Georges Clemenceau	16 November 1917–20 January 1920
Alexandre Millerand	20 January 1920–20 September 1920
Georges Leygues	24 September 1920–16 January 1921
Aristide Briand	16 January 1921–13 January 1922
Raymond Poincaré	13 January 1922–14 June 1924
Edouard Herriot	14 June 1924–16 April 1925
Paul Painlevé	16 April 1925–27 November 1925
Aristide Briand	27 November 1925–23 July 1926
Raymond Poincaré	23 July 1926–28 July 1929

Aristide Briand	29 July 1929–1 November 1929
André Tardieu	2 November 1929–12 December 1930
Theodore Stegg	12 December 1930–26 January 1931
Pierre Laval	26 January 1931–20 February 1932
André Tardieu	20 February 1932–3 June 1932
Edouard Herriot	3 June 1932–18 December 1932
Joseph Paul-Boncour	18 December 1932–31 January 1933
Edouard Daladier	31 January 1933–26 October 1933
Albert Sarraut	26 October 1933–27 November 1933
Camille Chautemps	27 November 1933–30 January 1934
Edouard Daladier	30 January 1934–9 February 1934
Gaston Doumergue	9 February 1934–13 October 1934
Pierre Laval	13 October 1934–8 November 1934
Pierre Etienne Flandin	8 November 1934–7 June 1935
Pierre Laval	7 June 1935–24 January 1936
Albert Sarraut	24 January 1936–4 June 1936
Léon Blum	4 June 1936–22 June 1937
Camille Chautemps	22 June 1937–12 March 1938
Léon Blum	12 March 1938–10 April 1938
Edouard Daladier	10 April 1938–18 May 1940

* The term 'premier' is somewhat misleading. Actually, the position occupied is that of president of the Council of Ministers which was instituted in 1848 by General Cavaignac. The term was not used again until 9 March 1876. Jules Dufaure used the term 'president of the Council of Ministers' to denote the expanded powers of the executive arm of the government.

Premiers of the Fourth Republic

Charles de Gaulle	August 1944–January 1946
Félix Gouin	January 1946–June 1946
Georges Bidault	June 1946–December 1946
Léon Blum	December 1946–January 1947
Paul Ramadier	January 1947–November 1947
Maurice Schuman	December 1947–June 1948
André Marie	June 1948–August 1948
Maurice Schuman	September 1948
Henri Queuille	September 1948–October 1949
Jules Mock	October 1949
Daniel Mayer	October 1949
Georges Bidault	October 1949–July 1950
Henri Queuille	July 1950
René Pleven	July 1950–March 1951
Henri Queuille	March 1951–September 1951
René Pleven	September 1951–January 1952
Edgar Faure	January 1952–March 1952
Antoine Pinay	March 1952–January 1953

(series of short ministries—Reynaud, Mendès-France, Bidault, Marie—from January 1953 to June 1953)

Joseph Laniel	June 1953–June 1954
Pierre Mendès-France	June 1954–February 1955
Edgar Faure	February 1955–February 1956

Guy Mollet   February 1956–June 1957
(series of short ministries—Bourgès-Maunoury, Pinay,
    Mollet—from June 1957 to November 1957)
Félix Gaillard   November 1957–May 1958
Pierre Pflimlin   May 1958
Charles de Gaulle   May 1958–June 1958